Development Finance

Springer
*Berlin
Heidelberg
New York
Hong Kong
London
Milan
Paris
Tokyo*

P.K. Rao

Development Finance

Springer

Professor P.K. Rao
Director, Global Development Institute
86 Sycamore Court
Lawrenceville, NJ 08648
USA
pkrao@att.net

ISBN 3-540-40153-9 Springer-Verlag Berlin Heidelberg New York

Cataloging-in-Publication Data applied for
A catalog record for this book is available from the Library of Congress.
Bibliographic information published by Die Deutsche Bibliothek
Die Deutsche Bibliothek lists this publication in the Deutsche Nationalbibliografie; detailed bibliographic data is available in the Internet at <http://dnb.ddb.de>.

This work is subject to copyright. All rights are reserved, whether the whole or part of the material is concerned, specifically the rights of translation, reprinting, reuse of illustrations, recitation, broadcasting, reproduction on microfilm or in any other way, and storage in data banks. Duplication of this publication or parts thereof is permitted only under the provisions of the German Copyright Law of September 9, 1965, in its current version, and permission for use must always be obtained from Springer-Verlag. Violations are liable for prosecution under the German Copyright Law.

Springer-Verlag Berlin Heidelberg New York
a member of BertelsmannSpringer Science+Business Media GmbH

http://www.springer.de

© Springer-Verlag Berlin · Heidelberg 2003
Printed in Germany

The use of general descriptive names, registered names, trademarks, etc. in this publication does not imply, even in the absence of a specific statement, that such names are exempt from the relevant protective laws and regulations and therefore free for general use.

Hardcover-Design: Erich Kirchner, Heidelberg

SPIN 10932124   43/3130-5 4 3 2 1 0 – Printed on acid-free paper

For my Family

Preface

The phenomenon of economic development is the result of the interplay of resources and institutions that govern economic, social and political processes. The critical roles of financial resources and financial institutions in economic growth and development deserve greater attention than under the broad subject 'Development Economics'. Improved understanding of the key role of financial aspects in the growth and development of economic systems is an operationally important aspect of economic analysis. The concern of much of development economics has been with the processes of economic development in relatively less developed regions, and amenable for development with the impetus of economic inputs. At the global level, the International Monetary Fund (IMF) and the World Bank (WB) were set up after World War II, designed primarily for providing underdeveloped regions of the world with financial resources. The role of market institutions in the mobilization of sources of development finance emerged as a new economic paradigm, complementary to the role of the global apex financial institutions. Thus, market-oriented reforms and globalization (including trade liberalization and financial liberalization) have become prominent phenomena since 1990s.

The study of development economics has lead to the advancement of relevant knowledge and policies in varied economic configurations. Considerable literature exists on these aspects, including several textbooks on development economics. In contrast, hardly any textbooks address the specific topic of the governance of financial resources from an economic development perspective. It is rather surprising that major collections of literature on development economics as well as related survey papers do not include finance as a significant theme. The operational significance of financial policies and decisions in the short and long term differs from several elements of traditional development economics. Problem solving approaches with actionable strategies or policies merit attention in the governance of an economic system. These stand in contrast to relatively non-actionable philosophical approaches for economic development, often covered in the traditional texts of development economics. It is useful to note that in an inequitable world with ever-increasing income and wealth inequalities, with about a third of the global population living in poverty, the multilevel role of development finance remains a critical topic requiring further attention.

Much of finance literature (including the subfield, financial economics) deals with private capital market transactions, profitability in corporate debt and equity markets, and risk management. Financial engineering and management for maximizing private returns with financial operations subject to known and unknown risks, remains the focus of the broad subject of finance. Some of these issues are of relevance in the context of methods and policies for development finance as well. Financial efficiency is a necessary but not sufficient ingredient for economic development. Although supportive of market functions and their efficiency, the role of non-market interventions in order to direct the flows of resources and returns in a socially desirable manner remains a key feature of development finance. Perfect capital markets, even if existent, do not lead to efficient economic development processes in the absence of institutional interventions at the national and other levels of financial governance. The design and governance of financial institutions is itself an important aspect of development finance, and is addressed in this book to some extent. Analytical and policy perspectives are incorporated in each of the chapters of this book. Detailed technical presentations are not included in order to economize on the size of the book. Various chapters attempt to bridge the gaps between the literature of economics and finance, with a review of the interdependencies of financial development and economic development. This book addresses various important concerns that include the design of relevant policies and institutions for effective development finance, bilateral and multilateral financial aid and capital transfers, sovereign debt management and sustainable development.

This first textbook on development finance addresses various issues of practical significance in financial and economic development processes. The emphasis is on concepts, approaches and issues of policy relevance rather than on techniques and mechanics. Analytical foundations, however, are explained here. These should enable further research, formulation of formal models and empirical analyses. The roles of public and private finance, domestic and external finance, short-term and long-term capital flows, sovereign debt management features, country risk and other determinants of foreign direct investments, multilateral official development assistance and development of financial institutions are some of the topics examined in this book.

At least one prior course in economics and/or finance is a useful prerequisite for the study of this text. This book is aimed primarily at graduate and senior undergraduate level courses in departments of economics and finance. Researchers in related fields, senior officials and policy makers in banking and financial institutions, international development institutions and other international economic institutions are likely to find here advanced resources and new insights on the theme of development finance.

The author gratefully acknowledges constant and enthusiastic support of Dr. Martina Bihn and colleagues at Springer-Verlag in the implementation of this book project.

P.K. Rao

New Jersey, USA
April 2003

Contents

Preface VII

CHAPTER 1:
Markets, Institutions and Transaction Costs 1

1.1 **Introduction** 1

1.2 **Contracts, Agency and Transaction Costs** 2
    Transaction Costs (TC) 2
        Box 1.1: Main Concepts and Definitions 3
    Transaction Costs and Financial Institutions 5
    Economics of Contracts 6
    Principal-Agent (PA) Theory 8

1.3 **Asymmetric Information (AI)** 9
        Box 1.2: Economics of Information: Concepts and Definitions ... 9
    Welfare Maximization 11
    Proposition 1.1 11
        Box 1.3: Mission Impossible: Social Welfare Maximization ... 12

1.4 **Capital Markets and Credit Rationing** 13
    Credit Rationing 13
        Box 1.4: Equilibrium Credit Rationing 15
    Proposition 1.2 16
    Proposition 1.3 16

1.5 **Risk Management** 17
    Value-at-risk (VAR) 18
    Capital Asset Pricing Model 19
    Financial Crises 20

1.6	**Domestic and International Capital Flows**	21
	Foreign Direct Investment (FDI)	21
	Developing Countries and Credit Markets	22
1.7	**Concluding Observations**	23
Review Exercises		25
References		26

CHAPTER 2:

Finance, Economic Growth, and Development   29

2.1	**Introduction**	29
2.2	**Capital Flows and Economic Growth**	30
	Financial Stability Forum	33
2.3	**Financial Institutions and Economic Growth**	34
	How is Economic Growth Influenced?	34
	Financial Intermediaries and Economic Growth	35
	Empirical Analyses	37
	Towards a Formal Model	38
2.4	**Financial Development and Economic Growth**	39
	Box 2.1: The Role of Expectations	40
	Empirical Studies	41
	Methodological Issues	41
	Endogenous Growth	42
2.5	**Financial Development and Economic Development**	44
	Box 2.2: Law and External Finance	45
	Macroeconomic Openness	46
2.5	**Concluding Observations**	47
Review Exercises		49
References		50

CHAPTER 3:

Microcredit and Inverted Banking   53

3.1 Introduction   53

3.2 **Social Collateral and Inverted Banking**   54
       Gender and Credit   56

3.3 **Credit Markets: Formal and Informal Systems**   56
       Credit Market Imperfections   57
       Proposition 3.1   58

3.4 **Rural Credit Markets**   59
       Rural Credit Environment   59
       Role of Information Economics   60

3.5 **The Design of Rural Credit Institutions**   61
       Institutional Credit and TC   62
       Group Lending   63
       The Design of Cooperative Institutions   64
       Role of Joint Liability   64
       A Heuristic Model   65

3.6 **Model Case: Grameen Bank of Bangladesh**   66

3.7 **Concluding Observations**   68

Review Exercises   70

References   71

CHAPTER 4:

Global Financial Architecture   73

4.1 Introduction   73

4.2 **Capital Adequacy and Financial Soundness**   74
       Financial Soundness Indicators (FSI)   74
       Credit Ratings and Financial Management   75
       Definition of Credit Ratings   76

	Capital Adequacy Guidelines	77
	Box 4.1: New Basel Capital Accord	78
4.3	**Financial Liberalization and Globalization**	**79**
	The Washington Consensus	79
	Financial Liberalization and Growth	80
	Banking Crises and Other Risks of Financial Liberalization	81
4.5	**International Financial Institutions**	**82**
	External Finance and Data Improvements	82
	Box 4.2: Data on External Financial Positions	83
	Legitimacy of Sovereign Debts	84
	Box 4.3: Are All External Debts Legitimate?	84
	The IMF	85
	Methods of Assessment	87
	Recommendations on Reform	87
4.4	**Financing for Development: The Monterrey Consensus**	**89**
	Limitations of the Consensus	90
4.6	**Concluding Observations**	**91**
Review Exercises		**93**
References		**94**

CHAPTER 5:

External Aid and Development 97

5.1	**Introduction**	**97**
5.2	**Official Development Assistance**	**98**
	Trends in ODA	99
	Rationale for ODA	99
5.3	**External Aid and Economic Growth**	**101**
	Two-Gap/Financing Gap Model	101
	Aid Fungibility	102
	Aid Experiences	103
	Performance-Based Aid and Conditionalities	104

5. 4	**The Effectiveness of Aid**	**106**
	The Role of International Factors	107
	Toward Relevant Theories	108
	Box 5.1: External Aid and Game Theory	110
5.5	**Concluding Observations**	**111**

Review Exercises   **112**

References   **113**

CHAPTER 6:

Sovereign Debt Management   117

6.1. Introduction		**117**
6.2	**Debt Management – A Historical Perspective**	**118**
	Debt Restructuring Experience of 1980s	118
6. 3	**External Debt and Economic Growth**	**119**
	Debt Levels and Economic Growth	119
	Empirical Study	121
6.4	**Debt Contracts and Renegotiation**	**121**
	Long Term and Short Term Contracts	122
	Analytical Aspects	123
	Optimal Debt Contracts	124
	Methodological Improvements	125
	Box 6.1: Improved Approaches and Analytical Methods	125
6. 5	**Debt Relief Policies**	**127**
	High Indebtedness	127
	Recent Developments	128
	Box 6.2: The HIPC Initiative	129
6. 6	**The Design of Incentives**	**130**
	Role of Sanctions	131
	Incentives	133

6. 7	**Sovereign Debt Management**	**134**
	Sovereign Debt Restructuring	135
	New Reforms	137
	Box 6.3: Sovereign Debt Reorganization and Global Chapter 9	138
6.8	**Concluding Observations**	**140**
	Review Exercises	**142**
	References	**143**

CHAPTER 7:

Project Appraisal – Improved Methods　　147

7. 1	Introduction	147
7. 2	Objectives and Commensurability	148
	Box 7.1: Main Definitions	148
7. 3	Standard Methods of Cost-Benefit Analysis	149
7. 4	Changing Preferences and Discounting	150
	Discount Factors and Discount Rates	153
	Box 7.2: Hyperbolic Discount Functions	154
	A Framework for Improved Methods	155
	Transient Costs and Equilibrium Costs	155
	Missing Markets, Uncertainty and SCBA	156
	Box 7.3: Uncertainty and Discount Rates	156
7.5	Concluding Observations	157
	Review Exercises	**158**
	References	**159**

CHAPTER 8:

Finance and Sustainable Development　　161

8.1	Introduction	161

8.2	**Sustainable Development**	**162**
	Classification of Environmental Dimensions	162
	Categories of Capital	162
	Sustainable Development	163
	Box 8.1: Protecting the Environment for Future Generations	164
	Millennium Development Goals (MDG)	165
	Box 8.2: Millennium Development Goals	165
	Financial Aspects	166
8.3	**Environmental Taxes**	**167**
	Environmental Taxes and Double Dividend	169
	The World Bank and IMF Role	171
	Debt Relief	172
	New Deal for Debt-For-Nature Swaps?	172
8.4	**Finance and the Global Environment**	**174**
	Zedillo Commission Report	174
	Box 8.3: Innovative Sources of Development Finance?	175
	FDI, Environmental Standards and Global Finance	175
	Box 8.4: Global Environmental Facility	176
8.5	**Environment and Lender Liability**	**177**
	Export Credit Agencies	177
	The World Bank	178
	Extended Lender Liability (ELL)	179
8.6	**Concluding Observations**	**179**
	Review Exercises	**181**
	References	**182**

CHAPTER 9:

Perspectives   185

9.1	**Broad Approaches**	**185**
	Maintaining Financial Stability	186
	Infrastructural Improvements	188

9.2	**Country Risk Analyses and Credit Ratings**	**189**
	Motives for Borrowing and Assessment of Risk	189
	Sovereign Debt	190
	Sovereign Risk	191
	Credit Risk	191
	Country Risk	191
	Box 9.1: Solvency Assessment	192
	Box 9.2: Country Risk Analysis and Managing Risk	193
	Sovereign Credit Ratings and Limitations	194
9.3	**Main Conclusions**	**195**
	Review Exercises	**198**
	References	**199**

Select Website Addresses   201

Index   203

CHAPTER 1:

Markets, Institutions and Transaction Costs

1.1 Introduction

The current economic paradigm promoting the role of market institutions in the financial and economic governance in various regions and sectors has several valid justifications and some meaningful objections as well. It is important to appreciate complex interdependencies of institutions and their activities, and the evolution of norms of governance over time. Globalization or economic and financial integration that emerged during the 1990s has made both positive and negative contributions (for a critical review of globalization policies and effects see Baker et al, 1998 and Stiglitz, 2002). The role and limitations of globalization or expansion of markets globally deserve careful scrutiny in the financial sector in relation to the role of this sector in the attainment of development objectives of less developed areas of the society. Some of the implications of financial liberalization and globalization are discussed in chapter 4. The widely debated roles of the government institutions (including regulatory regimes) in contrast to those of market institutions are an excessive simplification of the underlying processes. What is relevant is a judicious combination of government institutions and market as well as other private institutions built on a sound judicial system and the rule of law.

The complex interrelationship between financial resources, economic growth processes and economic development deserve greater focus in academic and policy studies. Until recently, many economists did not pay attention to the critical role of financial resources and institutional infrastructure in economic growth and development. One of the notable contributions is Hulme and Mosley (1996), which focused on the principles and applications of finance in relation to poverty alleviation. Some of the major collected volumes of development economics literature did not mention finance as a theme, and some survey papers did not mention finance for development even in their list of their omitted topics. Similarly, much of development economics literature is oblivious to the roles of environmental factors as well. This does not bode well for the sustainability of development economics as an important field of modern economics. Any comprehensive approach must accord high priority to the role of financial resources and institutions as well as the emerging problems of sustainable development. Accordingly, there is an increasing need for further advancement within development finance to address the critical role of financial factors, and the quantitative significance of financial systems in economic growth and development processes. With about a third of the population of the world living in poverty, and more than one billion people surviving on less than US$1 per day, the role of development finance deserves greater attention in the interests of the poor as well as the non-poor. Several multilateral financial and development institutions claim to have accorded high priority for poverty elimination but seem to fall short in the attainment of such goals.

In development finance, the nature and extent of interaction between various sources of finance, formally distinguished in terms of finance from formal institutions and from informal sources/institutions, is an important aspect. The roles of the economics of institutions and of the economics of contracts are important in the design of financial policies and their implementation. This chapter is primarily concerned with the features relating to the role of institutions and transaction costs (TC) in the formation and governance of financial institutions and formulation of relevant policies. After examining the salient features of the economics of financial contracts, asymmetric information (AI) and related features, this chapter analyses the phenomena of equilibrium credit rationing, and elements of financial risk management. Later sections address various mechanisms of financial governance for international coordination, and the role of TC in effecting efficient financial governance under varying institutional arrangements.

1.2 Contracts, Agency and Transaction Costs

An understanding of the economics of contracts, of principal-agent relationships and of TC enables better understanding of the working of financial institutions and financial policies, both domestic and international. The fundamentals covered in this section remain relevant for much of the analysis that follows in this book.

Transaction Costs (TC)

TC include costs of undertaking a transaction, including information and search costs, bargaining costs, as well as monitoring and enforcement costs of executing a transaction. The costs arising out of uncertainty are also considered as elements of TC if the root cause of uncertainty originates in the institutional and informational features relevant in a given policy setting. At the firm level, the roles of TC include their influence the production decisions as well as the debt-equity mix of the firm's capital structure. TC minimizing approach emphasizes the role of agency costs (see definition below) arising out of AI. The optimal capital structure minimizes the sum of the agency costs of debt and equity (for detailed analytical models see Vilasuso and Minkler, 2001). The role of TC remains very significant both in corporate and in government entities, especially in matters of financial governance.

In any formal economic optimization model, TC constitute structural frameworks that must be recognized in the specification of various economic and financial relationships. When TC are added as additional constraints on the system, the optimal solution is generally inferior relative to the optimal solution in the absence of such an additional constraint. In principle, TC should account for all the critical cost elements of financial transactions. However, much of the current methodology in the economics of TC does not explicitly incorporate these costs. Improved methods and applications of TC economics are given in a recent book; see Rao (2003).

Let us first deal with a few basic concepts that lay foundations for financial governance of public systems and their influence on financial capital flows. It is important to note that institutions comprise organizations, their rules of operation, and enforcement of rules and contractual mechanisms. Broadly, market and government institutions span much of the financial infrastructure, nationally and internationally. Institutions comprise both formal and informal rules, their enforcement, and organizational arrangements for the governance of economic and other relationships among individuals and other entities. Functional classifications of institutions admit one or more of the following (in addition to several other classifications, not necessarily mutually excusive): formal/informal, legal, political, administrative, private/public, centralized/decentralized.

As a specific case of focus, financial institutions (FI) are economic organizations that possess potential for economic and financial efficiency with risk management and operational efficiency. Besides, operational efficiency is affected by their economies of scope, economies of scale, and economies of functional specialization, among other features. Chapter 2 explains the role of TC in the formation and functioning of the FI as well as their relationship with economic growth and development; a few salient features are summarized below. Box 1.1 provides some of the important definitions.

Box 1.1: Main Concepts and Definitions

Agency cost: this is the difference between an ideal maximum performance with zero informational asymmetry and attained performance level reflecting the consequence of informational asymmetry between the principals and agents operating an economic entity.

General finance: this includes all forms of financial transactions, including project lending, portfolio investment, private debt (usually non-guaranteed), other private sector financial activities, joint ventures, and foreign direct investment (FDI).

Complete market: a market where commodities and services can be priced under all contingencies for all situations in a competitive sense. An idealized set of market configurations for every possible commodity or factor under all states of uncertainty comprise such markets.

Contract-intensive money: this comprises all monetary instruments that involve institutions or individuals, and are essential for the formation of FI; the value of this collection depends on the macroeconomic policies of the government as well as the adherence of economic actors to their implicit and explicit contracts. This is highly correlated with investment.

Credit formation: transactions leading to voluntary exchange of capital transfer; this includes relevant information processing and screening for effecting a transaction.

Credit view of monetary transmission: this view is based on the assumption that governmental monetary policy affects the terms and availability of credit for new loans and influences short-term interest rates directly and indirectly.

Externality: the effect of actions/inactions or transactions that generate purportedly unintended consequences to different parties that are not directly involved in the transactions.

Positive externality: this refers to the role of an externality in its positive contribution in relation to a specific objective.

Negative externality: the negative contribution of an externality to a specific objective.

Network externality: an economic entity depicts network externality when its value to the participant of the network is a function of the number and type of use of other participants.

Financial liberalization: the removal of controls affecting the interplay of market forces in the financial sector or capital market, thus facilitating capital flows from transnational financial organizations.

Financial repression: distortion in financial systems by tax and nontax measures adopted by the government to insulate the financial sector or capital markets from market forces.

Market failure: the inability of market institutions to attain economically or socially desirable efficiency objectives such as welfare maximization.

Money view of monetary transmission: regarding monetary policy affecting aggregate demand, this view poses that higher interest rates restrain demand because of the role of higher costs of capital relative the return on capital. It is based upon the assumption that all non-monetary assets are perfect substitutes.

Pareto-optimality: a situation whereby all parties gain and further improvements in the welfare of some is likely only at the expense of some others.

Perfect capital market: a perfectly competitive capital market where prices fully reflect demand and supply factors; the TC are assumed negligible and informational asymmetries cannot prevail.

Principal-Agent (PA) theory: when there is an informational asymmetry between different economic or other entities, the primary functionary or entity (principal) can monitor and steer the activities of an agent assigned for fulfilling the objectives of the principal only to a limited extent; thus, a potential discrepancy could prevail between the objectives and functions of the principal and agents.

Traditional finance: financing provided to the public sector or government entities; this bears public obligation, either guaranteed by the government or otherwise.

Transaction Costs and Financial Institutions

In general, FI effect promotion of financial and economic efficiency and savings through their contribution to the reduction of TC. The scope of FI needs exploration in terms of their potential contribution to such cost savings and enhancement of efficiency, among other factors. Details of related roles of FI are given in chapter 2. As a basic phenomenon, financial relationships between FI and their customers involve a "mechanism of commitment" (Hellwig, 1998) that varies across different institutions and their legal and other institutional environment. In such a broad framework, the lowering of TC is a necessary, though not usually sufficient, requirement for achieving economic efficiency. The role of government in this regard at the general level is to provide relevant legal and institutional structure. The assignment and enforcement of property rights is a critical part of this infrastructure that allows economic activities to flourish.

The role of enforcer of property rights is usually a fundamental function of the state. As North and Thomas (1973, p.8) observed, "governments take over the protection and enforcement of property rights because they can do it at lower costs than private volunteer groups." The main issue here is to ensure that transactions take place in a TC minimizing sense. The critical role of falling TC in enhancing economic growth in western economies during the past several decades is now well recognized. It is useful to decipher various important components of TC as they apply in each system and each class of transactions. The roles of search, enforcement, measurement, and other components of TC are to be examined separately (and in terms of interdependencies) for devising cost-effective strategies. Some of the costs of governance can be economized with the participation of user institutions themselves, in combination with effective supervision from the state. The role of the New York Stock Exchange or the Chicago Board of Trade as simply that of monitoring and supervisory entities serve as examples of use of delegated powers for TC minimization. At the international level, the role of banking and other financial norms and standards across countries is important in effecting reduction of informational problems and in the consequential TC. In addressing some of the relevant issues, the International Monetary Fund (IMF) issues Reports on the Observance of Standards and Codes that describe various member countries' specification and observance of financial sector standards and relevant institutional infrastructure. Other international financial institutions and coordinating agencies such as the Bank of International Settlements (BIS) also provide guidelines in this direction; chapter 4 deals with more details.

Financial and other contracts lay foundations for the functioning of various institutions. The structures of these contracts need attention, explained below.

Economics of Contracts

The role of design and enforcement of contracts is critical in the formation and development of institutions for financial and economic governance. Firms and markets are viewed as an appropriately defined nexus of contracts. 'Perfect contracts' may not exist, but a variety of relatively efficient and workable contracts do exist. There is need for greater attention to the law and economics of contracts since most of financial and other transactions are either explicit or implicit (or a combination of both) contracts. These contracts may be complete contracts or incomplete contracts, explained below.

1. A contract is complete if there is an explicit specification in the contract that addresses every possible contingency or a situation as it arises. In general, complete contracts do not exist, given the complexity of comprehending and specifying all relevant details. Thus, almost all contracts remain inevitably incomplete.

2. A contract is legally incomplete to the extent that its terms require of the parties to the contract to condition themselves on 'unverifiable information'. At times judicial or mediatory institutions (such as arbitration panels) seek to fill in contractual gaps and offer remedial measures.

The critical issue in this context of contractual governance is to balance the costs of contract design and contract enforcement at varying levels of contractual incompleteness. At a general level, non-market institutions can also be examined in terms of constellations of different incomplete contractual arrangements (and their enforcement). Often, the administrative and legal infrastructure of a society plays an overarching role in the effectiveness (including cost-effectiveness) of different institutional and contractual configurations.

The elements of financial contracts usually include, in addition to repayment of principal and interest according a specified time schedule, collateral requirements and specifications of contract enforcement as well. In assessing the desirability of a relatively complete contract, the relative costs (*ex ante* costs) of designing a comprehensive contract need to be balanced against costs (*ex post* costs) of enforcement of a less comprehensive contract. Ideally, a judicious mix of optimal comprehensiveness and effective enforcement is required in the mechanisms of contractual governance. Incomplete contracts and AI (defined in section 1.3) lead to one set of TC, whereas behavioral opportunism or lack of commitment among parties to contractual specifications leads to another additional set of TC. These two groups of TC are not mutually exclusive, however. The common underlying foundation that affects these relates to the role of law and custom, since these two factors influence the choice of actions under varying circumstances. The role of TC surfaces again in terms of the costs of provision and enforcement of legal arrangements. A clear understanding of the underlying components of TC is important here. Besides, an analysis of TC provides a link in the issue of organization and the design of institutions with appropriate provision of explicit and implicit contracting.

Are multi-period contracts adding to a specific time interval T superior to single period contracts for the same duration T? Multi-period contracts are mutually beneficial to contracting parties, relative to a sequence of single-period contracts, when private information or AI prevails among some parties and/or when verification of information across parties involves high costs (Townsend, 1982). Besides, the specifications or the structure of an optimal contract is highly sensitive to the time horizon under reference, and the role of time discount factors of participating entities. Lack of uniform ranking of preferences among parties for different time intervals in the future affects the post-contractual performance of parties to a contract (see chapter 6 for more detailed analysis in the context of sovereign debt contracts). Reputation and credibility becomes important as a dynamic incentive mechanism in a repeat transaction multi-period setting when positive reputation of previous intervals enables better credit and credibility for later periods. If decision makers discount future costs and/or benefits excessively then their effective horizon of interest is merely the initial period of contract. Similarly, if some of the parties to a contract do not consider themselves accountable (possibly because they may be transferred to other tasks or relieved of their duties relatively soon) for relevant consequences over a longer horizon, including the one spanning a multi-period contract, their decision making may be subject to high discounting of future consequences. Analogous predictions hold good when there is a high likelihood that the parties are not functioning in a repeat transaction setting and perceive themselves acting in a one-time transaction.

Contract design and enforcement issues deserve particular attention in relation to applicable costs of undertaking these transactions. Formal and informal methods of enforcement make a fundamental difference in the characterization of modern and less modern societies. The role of informal economies, informal constraints and related characteristics in the minimization of TC for the design and enforcement of contracts is noteworthy. The pervasive TC phenomenon adversely affects the economic efficiency and welfare of the society as a whole. Thus, it is important to see the issue of TC minimization in the context of welfare maximization or in a Pareto-optimal sense. The evolution of formal institutions in the western economies has been a significant factor in the reduction of TC; these elements enhanced economic growth in the current developed economies of the western world. Financial institutional development is one of the important aspects of this process. More details linking financial institutional development and economic progress are given in chapter 2. An additional perspective for the analysis of efficient financial governance emerges from an understanding of the working of principal-agent relationships, explained below.

Principal-Agent (PA) Theory

The issue of financial contracting has attracted great attention since the contribution of Jensen and Meckling (1976). The role of agency cost in the framework of Principal-Agent (PA) theory suggests that the agency cost, in the context of financial firms, is often a function of the type and extent of informational asymmetry, and monitoring and information costs. The PA theory was originally proposed by Ross (1973), and later extended by Jensen and Meckling (1976). The PA theory is one of the important approaches for the analysis of policy and operations of financial institutions, including the analysis of external aid and aid effectiveness. Agency costs are highly sensitive to the specifications of the law and contractual structures.

The agency cost is the difference between the value of the firm under perfect information scenario and that under AI and imperfect enforcement of contracts. An operational definition of the concept, given by Jensen and Meckling (1976, p.308) states:

> "the agency cost comprises the sum of the monitoring costs by the principal, the costs of bonding the agent to perform tasks in conformity with the performance objectives of the principal or the economic entity, and that of residual losses that are attributable to the divergence of the optimal decisions effected by the agents in contrast to those that could have been taken by the principal if directly involved in the decisions".

Jensen and Meckling (1976) also showed analytically that external equity finance and external debt finance have agency costs arising from informational problems, as well as from the separation of corporate ownership and control. The role of agency costs in external financing is thus one of net addition to the costs of capital, relative to that of corresponding internal capital deployment, other factors remaining the same. This corporate finance insight is largely relevant in the context of development finance at national and international levels.

Thus, the role of AI remains important, both in the design and in the implementation of contracts, in PA relationships and in influencing the incidence of TC generally. The following section summarizes some of the relevant concepts of the economics of AI.

1.3 Asymmetric Information (AI)

Lack of equivalence of information contents between parties to a common issue that affects each other's interests constitutes an informational asymmetry. A generalization of this concept would also include unequal capacities among parties to a common issue to process a given set of information. This aspect has not been recognized in the literature on the economics of information. It is not only the differential information content as an input but also its effective contribution to an output or an optimal decision that constitutes the essence of AI.

Banks and aggregative markets (including the insurance industry) are contributory participants in the allocation of various types of risks in a financial system. The design and effectiveness of risk-sharing arrangements (both explicit and implicit risks, as well as explicit and implicit contracts governing the same) is an important aspect that affects the efficiency of a financial and economic system. Critical in this configuration is the role of AI among entities involved in financial decision-making. Box 1.2 summarizes some of the important concepts and definitions relevant in the economics of information.

Box 1.2: Economics of Information: Concepts and Definitions

> Adverse selection (AS): this occurs *ex ante* in an interaction among parties leading to a lending decision, contracting or other event, based on information available by the time of the event.
>
> Certainty equivalent: this is the assessed value of an uncertain prospect under a given probability distribution of states and payoffs. If the expected value of a random variable X is given by,
>
> $E(X) = C$, then X is considered the certainty equivalent of C.
>
> Expected value: this is the added sum of the products of quantities with their corresponding probabilities of occurrence.
>
> Moral hazard (MH): this arises *ex post*, after decision to lend, issue contract or other event, has been arrived at among interacting parties based on information available until that event.
>
> Nash equilibrium (NE): this is a situation in a game with participants, where each participant chooses an action strategy that offers each player the highest payoff, given the strategies chosen by the other players.

> Price dispersion: the simultaneous prevalence of multiple varying prices (rather than single market clearing price at a given point of time or in a small region) for a specific commodity or service of comparable quality, even the market is in equilibrium in terms of the equality of demand and supply.
>
> Risk: in a decision problem, if the probabilities of occurrence of plausible events are known, it is called a risk-based decision. If the corresponding probabilities are unknown, it is one of uncertainty-based decision-making. Portfolio theory is concerned with financial decision making under risk and/or uncertainty.
>
> Risk premium: this is the difference between the expected value of payoff of given action or activity and its corresponding certainty equivalent.

The roles of moral hazard (MH) and adverse selection (AS) become relevant in credit markets whenever there are at least three features relevant for the financial system: a) AI; b) positive probability of default; and c) the costs of enforcement of repayment obligations (or contractual specifications, in general) are very high. The role of AI is such that it leads to contractual incompleteness because of inevitably high TC in the presence of AI. Besides, the existence of private information leads to pre-contractual opportunism and thus to AS. On the other hand, unobservable hidden information and/or nonverifiable actions lead to post-contractual opportunism and thus to MH.

In the background of AI, FI emerge as a mechanism to reduce AI and TC. However, FI still have to deal with AS, MH, and agency costs. The functioning as well as the efficiency characteristics of financial markets (inclusive of FI and trading institutions) are affected by the following features:

AI, TC, incompleteness of contracts and of markets (especially with respect to contingent claims or related markets), and behavioral traits of the economic agents (or economic entities) such as 'herd behavior' (HB).

HB is defined as the large scale flow of activities/transactions in the same direction as that of a limited few others preceding these. If a few traders, for example, start selling stocks of a specific class even at very prices, many others in HB do the same, thus in effect substituting their own rational judgment in terms of the predecessor entities involved in the transactions under reference. Founded on the prevalence of AI, HB precipitates financial crises whenever financial systems are less than fully developed and robust with strengths of liquidity. HB is usually procyclical and often effected with very little advance alertness of participating economic entities. Surprises in cause and effect relationships (characterized by nonlinearities and discontinuities of applicable mathematical functions), and financial shocks are rather common occurrences in situations with AI. These factors lead to the following specific behavior relationships affecting the financial systems (see also Rodrik, 1999):

a) AI leads to MH, AS, and to excessive lending for risky projects;

b) short-term liabilities cast disproportionate shadows on long-term assets and their worth;

c) FI become vulnerable to panic attacks or market shocks; and

d) AI exacerbates market volatility and HB.

The role of AI is fundamental in limiting the realization of maximum welfare potential in a situation involving more than one economic entity, explained below.

Welfare Maximization

If we raise an analytical question as to whether there is a possibility of joint welfare maximization of both creditors and debtors involving various debt borrowing and repayment transactions under AI, the answer is in the negative. The following proposition is established analytically; see Box 1.3 for details. Policy implications of these negative assertions include the need for the following actions:

a) reduction informational asymmetry among parties, and

b) reduction of inequities in the information processing capabilities among various entities contributing to agreements or contracts.

These implications suggest the role of improved data and information management, capacity building (wherever necessary), and greater coordinative role as well as transparency of financial institutions involved in lending and borrowing.

Proposition 1.1

Intertemporal social welfare maximizing solutions do not exist for the international credit markets; informational asymmetry aggravates potential deviations from balancing the preferences of creditors and borrowers.

Analogous rigorous results on the impossibility of joint utility maximization in decentralized institutional regimes in a multi-period setting are derived by Hurwicz and Mazumdar (1988) for resource allocation mechanisms.

Similarly, Laffont's (1985) results, based on Rational Expectations Equilibria (REE), also lead us to the non-existence conclusion if the events and their (expected) probability values are not shared truthfully, i.e., without any strategic distortions, among the negotiators (creditors and borrowers). Here REE is defined as the equilibrium condition resulting from so-called rational expectations that maximize expected utility for each participating economic entity over a relevant time horizon.

The following section builds on the concepts laid out thus far in this chapter, and elucidates the functioning of capital flows and the phenomenon of credit rationing as well as its implications.

Box 1. 3: Mission Impossible: Social Welfare Maximization

Expected utility theory shows that each person's preference may be represented by a utility function defined by the domain of alternatives. These utility functions are expectational: if an alternative has uncertain results, its utility is the expectation of the utility of its possible results. Preferences are considered 'coherent' if they satisfy the axioms of expected utility theory, so that the preferences can be represented by an expectational utility function. 'Paretian' social preferences can be represented by a utility function U, as a function of individual utility functions,

$$U(A) = W(U_1(A),...U_n(A)) \forall A,$$

where $\partial W / \partial U_i$ increases with U_1 (i = 1,...,h).

As a general rule, we have no reason to expect preferences of various economic agents to agree about probabilities of stochastic events. The Probability Agreement Theorem (below) tells us that unless individuals (including 'principal' and 'agent' in the credit market) agree about probabilities, there can be no coherent Paretian social preferences; and when these do exist, they must all agree about probabilities, and they must be utilitarian (i.e., the social preference function is the simple additive representation of individual expectational utility functions).

Probability Agreement Theorem (Broome, 1990, p. 479):

Suppose that each person has coherent preferences. Then if social preferences are coherent and Paretian, the individual and social preferences must all agree on the probabilities they assign to every event.

If we consider a social welfare function consisting mainly of arguments in terms of utilities of commercial bank lenders, borrowers, and official creditors, the roles of their varying expectations about the credit markets tend to suggest that a social welfare function could not exist. Alternatively, if all the players in the credit market share identical information and assess the likelihood of events (and their consequences) separately or collectively and agree on the same, a possibility of obtaining joint welfare maximizing optimal credit transactions exits.

1.4 Capital Markets and Credit Rationing

Financing economic development becomes feasible when there is greater mobility of capital as well as effective resource utilization that enhances economic development. Limitations regarding the availability and access to credit form constraints in the optimal capital use for enhancing economic growth and development at the potential recipient country level. The potential for perfect capital mobility and complete globalization remains constrained in relation to the role of TC involved in undertaking various transactions. This is one of the primary factors for the phenomenon of differential interest rates (nominal and real) even in equilibrium (short-term as well as long-term). This is the phenomenon of price dispersion in credit markets.

The incomplete financial markets literature starting with Arrow (1964) did not fully recognize the role of TC in the nonexistence of complete markets. While pointing to the inefficiency of markets that fail to provide for all contingencies, these studies presumed costless information and enforcement of contracts. After we take into account the costs of creating such state-contingent claims, market costs are significant and the net result of incurring these costs may or may not always lead to Pareto efficiency.

Credit Rationing

Market clearing equilibrium price of capital (based on the equalization of demand for and supply of capital) does not exist in the credit markets. This is because credit lending is not an auction in a competitive setting, and does not occur at one event or time instant to determine the interface of the demand and supply factors. The Walrasian concept of market equilibrium is simply inapplicable in this context where we deal with a continuum of economic elements defined over time and incomplete information regarding future states.

There has been considerable literature since 1970s on the theme of credit rationing. Traditionally, credit rationing has been assumed to occur when lenders provide smaller loans than those requested by the borrowers even when lenders determine the applicable interest rate (Jaffee and Russell, 1976). Even under this restrictive notion of credit rationing, it is not reasonable to conclude (as did Jaffee and Russell, 1976) that pure lender monopoly implies no credit rationing, for the following reasons. Even a pure monopolist lender, who can extract usury rates or take temporary advantage of the severity of capital needs at the borrower levels, will not normally be able to sustain high volume of such markets, high interest rates and their validity for a long period. Enforcement problems remain prohibitively costly too. Finiteness of capital resources or their relative scarcity constitutes ample justification for the existence of the phenomenon of credit rationing. In the credit market scenarios, the role of risk leads to imposition of credit limits in relation to specific categories of borrowers.

Enhanced lender interest rate may not automatically lead to improved profitability for the lender because of the endogeneity of debt repayment as a function of high interest rates. These interest rates may lead to the selection of borrowers with greater risk taking behavior and accentuated problems of enforcement of debt repayment. Increases in loan rate can lead to increased loan repayment risks or substantial loan defaults because of one or more of the following factors:

- adverse selection of loan applicants with relatively less commitment for loan repayment even when agreeing for explicit commitments;
- their excessive risk-proneness in financial decision-making; and
- ex post financial inefficiency following loan borrowings.

In terms of formal economic modeling, preliminary analytical models of credit rationing under imperfect information and uncertainty were advanced by Jaffee and Russell (1976). These models, however, reflect various relevant features in a simplistic manner (and admittedly, actual loan markets are quite different from the markets examined in their paper). In a later paper, Stiglitz and Weiss (1981) structured models that find it optimal for the lenders to ration credit because of problems of asymmetric information between lenders and borrowers. Among the relevant features of the loan market that have been considered in their models included: the endogeneity of riskiness of loan repayment in relation to interest rates, and the roles of enforcement costs.

Among the important features relevant for formal equilibrium modeling of credit markets are the following:

a) the incentive / disincentive effects of interest rates and TC in obtaining loans;

b) costs of enforcement of loan recovery under varying mechanisms and loan contracts; and

c) impacts of loan repayment actions of the borrowers on their minimum consumption requirements in various intervals with fluctuating incomes; this feature is particularly relevant for borrowers at household and individual levels (where substance consumption requirements interfere with their fulfillment of loan repayment obligations, or steady income flows are uncommon for most economic activities) in developing countries and their rural institutions.

Formal models have not accounted for the above features so far, and further studies in these directions are necessary. Box 1.4 summarizes important facets of equilibrium credit rationing, subject to this limitation.

Box 1.4: Equilibrium Credit Rationing

The dictionary meaning of credit indicates its emergence from Latin *creditum*, and implies the critical role of trust and/or credibility. Continued commitment of the borrowers to repay at agreed intervals the assigned sum (under almost all circumstances) is one of the prerequisites of credit market activity and its sustainability.

Stiglitz and Weiss (1981) observed that there are no equilibrium interest rates at which demand equals supply in the loan market, even when the market is competitive. They defined credit rationing as the phenomenon where either a) among seemingly similar loan applicants some do not obtain credit at any interest rate; or, b) some identifiable potential borrowers do not obtain credit even though they would with greater supply of capital at the lender level. Credit rationing is an equilibrium phenomenon (Stiglitz and Weiss, 1981).

Capital markets are usually imperfect, and substantial credit rationing occurs for a number of reasons. The role AI is such as to induce either MH or AS or both in some of the borrowers. The role of TC in the monitoring and information processing activities of the lenders is such that it offsets potential gains of higher interest rate-induced problems of AS in most cases when these tasks are undertaken beyond an economical level.

Higher interest-based lending generates AS effect as well as adverse incentive effect at the borrower level, thus posing problems of loan recovery for the lender. There exists an AS effect when borrowers are risk preferring and accept higher interest rates. An adverse incentive effect becomes operative when borrowers adopt excessive risk taking behavior in their operations because of desperateness to meet obligations of higher costs of capital. The result for the lender could be a reduction in the expected yield because of higher interest rates in lending beyond a threshold level of credit and rate of interest.

Most credit markets remain imperfect with features that include: a) AI, b) price discrimination, c) MH, and d) AS. These features lead to equilibrium credit rationing; the phenomenon may not always be the consequence of (c) and/or (d) only (as suggested in part of the related literature).

The role of credit rationing deserves further scrutiny in terms of realistic institutional configurations.

The following results have been obtained by Stiglitz and Weiss (1981):

Theorem 1

As the interest rate increases, the critical value below which potential loan applicants do not apply for loans also increases.

Theorem 2

The expected return on a loan to a lending (typically banking) institution is a decreasing function of the riskiness of the loan.

The above results do not fully account for information costs in particular, and TC in general. Most of the arguments that Stiglitz and Weiss suggest for interest rates (taken at their face value or nominal rates) need to be extended to comprehend the total cost of borrowing per unit capital, and the total cost must include applicable TC. The quality of the loan from the perspective of the lender is affected not only by the nominal interest rate as posited by the authors but also by the total costs, direct and indirect, inclusive of the TC.

The following propositions reflect the realistic settings that incorporate TC:

Proposition 1.2

The demand for loan is a function of both its nominal interest rate as well as TC that include *ex ante* and *ex post* costs of loan transactions, including costs of risks that arise from capital utilization.

Proposition 1.3

Reputation, credibility, collateral and positive network externalities – all contribute to reduction of TC and augment demand for credit for a given level of interest rate and specified time horizon for repayments.

In one of the extensions of Stiglitz and Weiss (1981) study where interest rate is the only policy instrument of market functioning or its efficiency, Besanko and Thakor (1987) suggested that lenders compete in a four-dimensional space: interest factor, loan size, collateral requirement, and probability of granting credit. They expressed credit policy in terms of all credit contracts offered by lenders. These formulations did not consider the role of TC, however.

To complete the specifications of the loan market, it is necessary to characterize the features of the borrower market. This aspect has received very little attention in literature. Any description of the equilibrium markets remains incomplete if relevant features of the borrowers that affect the demand for credit are not properly reflected in the derivation of the equilibrium levels of demand for and supply of loans.

Berger and Udell (1992) have challenged the view that equilibrium credit rationing constitutes a major economic process. This is primarily due to the existence of contractual mechanisms that mitigate some of the problems of AI, and these include the role of collateral for loans and the role of other forms of loan commitments or linked transactions in the loan and other markets.

An empirical study in the US markets (based on the Federal Reserve's Survey of Terms of Bank Lending data for the period 1977 to 1988) lead to the following findings (Berger and Udell, 1992):

a) commercial loan rate is sticky relative to changes in open-market rates, suggesting the role of equilibrium credit rationing; but this stickiness arises from loans made to commitment borrowers (about 50 percent) who receive loans as a result of contractual specifications;

b) secured loans have slightly stickier rates than unsecured loans;

c) the quantities of new commitment loans as well as noncommitment loans increase with open market rates; and

d) committed proportion of new loans does not increase with real open-market rates.

The last two features are especially inconsistent with the credit rationing phenomena. Empirical analyses of credit rationing phenomena suggest that such rationing may not constitute a major segment of credit market characteristic, and plays a much less role than initially projected in simplistic theoretical models of credit markets. What can we say about the validity of similar results for less developed countries? Paucity of data seems to constrain carrying out comparable studies but the ones that are done seem to suggest significant roles for informal lending and reduction of segmentation of markets for credit lending in many regions.

Regarding loan contract and its flexibility features, it is meaningful to include the provisions for renegotiation of loan agreements after a certain time interval. This is because loan contracts cannot address the specifications of all states of nature or contingencies. One of the theoretical investigations suggests that self-selection of loan repayment rescheduling penalties may induce borrowers to reveal more information and thus contribute to reduction of AI. The provision of optimal incentives for contract compliance seems to mitigate the problems of MH and AS in some scenarios; see Zou (1992) for an analytical treatment of this problem. For more details of analytical and applied aspects of loan/debt contracts see also chapter 6.

1.5 Risk Management

Risk management is the process by which different risk exposures (along with their sources) are identified, assessed, and contained (or controlled). Development of FI, financial contracts and their enforcement are among the prerequisites for the reduction of TC and management of risks. Financial institutional development in general and financial risk management functions of these institutions in particular, have been recognized as the primary engines that led industrial revolution in England in the eighteenth century (Hicks, 1969, pp.143-145). Several recent studies in a number of countries also support this position; relevant details are given chapter 2. This section provides some of the important highlights of financial risk management methods. The relevance of these methods is not confined to the area of development finance only but is relevant in all aspects of financial governance.

Risk management (with or without AI) has been the main role of FI. These risks include credit and liquidity risks, interest rate and foreign exchange rate fluctuations and event uncertainties and other major disturbances or shocks to the financial and economic systems. Types of financial risks include the following: market and/or price risk, credit risk, liquidity risk, and operational risk. Other related financial business risks include: financial product (or its performance) risks, macroeconomic risks, and technical risks. In addition, the role of systemic risk needs attention. This risk is defined as a financial risk with the potential that any financial entity may contaminate the entire financial system with a domino effect and threatens the stability of the system or its subsystems.

The elements and categorizations of risk factors for different financial instruments differ, however. The role of counterparty credit risk, settlement risk and other features need to be recognized in less traditional instruments, such as those of the financial derivatives arising out of some financial product innovations. We do not detail all these elements here. We now turn to an important tool of financial risk analysis, explained below.

Value-at-risk (VAR)

VAR is a concept that enables measuring financial market risks. This concept, developed in the 1990s, has since been increasingly popular in adoption. VAR is being utilized for the control and management of credit risks and operational risks as well. For a detailed explanation and application of the concepts and methods surrounding VAR, see Jorion (2001).

In its most general form, the expression for VAR as a risk measure is given in terms of the probability distribution of the future value of portfolio $f(w)$.

For a specified or chosen confidence level c, we need to assess the worst possible realization of portfolio value w^* to equate c with the cumulative probability:

$$\int_{w^*}^{\infty} f(w)\,dw$$

In such a method the probability of a value lower than w^* is then given by the relation

$$1 - c = \int_{-\infty}^{w^*} f(w) = P(w \leq w^*) = p$$

This number w^* is called the quantile of the distribution which is the cutoff value with a fixed probability of being exceeded.

In functional terms, VAR summarizes the expected maximum loss over a target horizon for a specified statistical confidence level or interval. The main steps involved the assessment of VAR are the following:
- identify the relevant risk factors;
- valuation of current portfolios or 'mark to market';
- measure the variability of risk factors;
- set the relevant time horizon for assessment;
- set the confidence level; and
- assess the maximum loss or VAR.

Four desirable properties of risk measures have been suggested by Artzner et al (1999). A risk measure can be viewed as a function of the distribution of portfolio value V, denoted by $P(V)$. The requisite properties are:

a) Monotonicity: if a portfolio has systematically lower returns than another for all states of the world, its risk must be greater

$$P(V_1) \geq P(V_2) \text{ if } V_1 \leq V_2$$

b) Translation invariance: adding cash k to a portfolio should reduce its risk by the amount k

$$P(V + k) = P(V) - k$$

c) Homogeneity: increasing the size of a portfolio by a factor d should imply scaling its risk by the same factor

$$P(dV) = dP(V)$$

d) Sub-additivity: merging portfolios cannot increase risk

$$P(V_1 + V_2) \leq P(V_1) + P(V_2)$$

The quantile-based VAR fails to satisfy the sub-additivity property (Artzner et al, 1999). However, under the assumption that the returns obey Normal Distribution properties, the VAR that uses the standard deviation obeys this property.

Capital Asset Pricing Model

Much of modern finance theory relies on the role of Capital Asset Pricing Model (CAPM). This model defines the relationship between the risks and returns on financial assets under a set of assumptions. The model relates risks and corresponding sensitivity implications in relation to a 'market portfolio'. Unless the latter represents all states of the market, any analysis dependent on it remains incomplete. Lack of sufficient integration of global markets in any specific context of capital markets is often a critical shortcoming of this approach. Yet, for want of better alternatives, this model remains largely in use.

The CAPM states that the required rate of return (ROR) on a project should be the sum of the risk-free rate r_f and the market risk premium $r_m - r_f$ times the project's systematic risk β and is given by the following:

$$r = r_f + \beta (r_m - r_f)$$

The above model has been widely developed in financial management literature and its applications. It is not proposed to provide additional details here. Suffice it state that modern tools of risk management can be and should be adopted more widely in developing countries as well. This becomes feasible with developed capital markets and financial information systems, in addition to regulatory improvements on a pragmatic basis (rather than on financial repression standards).

Broader issues of financial crises and their management are summarized below.

Financial Crises

A financial crisis in the context of a capital-constrained economy is defined as a gradual but substantial or sudden net capital outflow transacted by the financial intermediaries and individuals even when a small change occurs in the economic factors.

Two major categories of explanations are relevant in explaining and/or predicting financial crises (see Chan-Lau and Chen, 2002, for a mathematical model of financial crisis). These categories are:

1. Economic fundamentals-based determinants:

    these explain crises as the consequences of changes in economic factors governing the financial and economic system; and

2. Behavioral expectations-based determinants:

    a) these explain crises as the result of economic decision makers' expectations and sometimes self-fulfilling prophecies actions (including crisis-precipitating bank-runs); and

    b) these include MH factors that lead to crises based on informational asymmetries in financial lending and securitization or other actions.

Often, banking and financial crises operate in a mutually aggravating manner when either of these crises cross certain critical threshold limits. These limits depend on specific systems and their features of resiliency. There are normally quadruplet components of crisis that coexist: banking crisis, currency crisis, loss of access to external finances, and lowered credit rating. The last two are highly correlated, as are the first two. However, all these tend to coexist with multiplicative effects leading to the joint crisis; each feature exacerbates a potential crisis whenever a critical threshold is crossed.

The following section summarizes important aspects and determinants of capital resource transfer to the developing countries.

1.6 Domestic and International Capital Flows

The role of TC remains significant in the efficient mobilization and utilization of financial resources, including international capital inflows. This section summarizes the role and limitations of foreign direct investment (FDI) as a source of development finance, and describes the broad features of developing country credit markets and their access to international capital.

Foreign Direct Investment (FDI)

In general, FDI emerges as a byproduct of global equilibrium of demand for supply of investment capital. A country may devise attractive policies for FDI and still lag behind because of the relative attractiveness of better alternatives provided by some competing countries or other countries. Often, the effects of tax concessions or other incentives are insufficient to result in favorable inflows of FDI. Competing to attract FDI is not a typical game of pure competition either, nor a race of some sort that leads to predictable investment flows under the FDI category. The motivation and considerations for FDI in a specific country or project include the role of market and nonmarket factors. These latter factors include the roles of existing infrastructure, TC, and the credibility of institutions including features governing the implementation of various contracts.

One of the commonly believed properties of FDI is that it is less prone to capital reversals and volatilities that are often associated with short-term capital flows or portfolio movements. Accordingly, FDI is considered a safer form of investment. However, Fernandez-Arias and Hausmann (2001) investigated some of the empirical data and observed that the coefficients of variation within the FDI activities are not much different from those of total net flows of capital for Latin America. The volatility of FDI has been on the rise during the 1990s. In general, for developing countries their non-FDI exposure of financial liabilities increases the probability of currency crises- while FDI effects on their economies are either neutral or lowering the magnitudes of crises. It is therefore possible that FDI is somewhat of an economic shock absorber and has an added feature to promote economic growth in the host country.

It is of interest to note the recent trend that the net FDI dropped from a peak in 1999 at $179 billion to the level $143 billion in 2002. The developing world has become a net capital exporter: during 2002 the developing countries paid $9 billion more on old debt than they received in new loans; similar phenomenon has been observed in respect of the World Bank portfolios as well. Besides, these capital flow reversals occurred when financial inflows to developing countries declined under the official development assistance, thus aggravating potential problems of poverty alleviation and economic development; "…the developing world has become a net capital exporter to the developed world." (World Bank, 2003, p. 1). The latest phenomenon is hardly sustainable, and there is need for both developed and developing countries to devise strategies that promote sustainable capital flows and expansion of the global economy.

FDI influences economic growth in different ways compared to comparable magnitude of domestic investment. Using FDI flow data for 69 developing countries during the period 1970-89, Borenzstein et al (1998) observed that FDI is an important vehicle for diffusion of technology and industrial management. They noted that as long as the level of human capital (which largely influences the resource assimilative capacity) in the recipient country is not too low (below a threshold level); the role of FDI has the effect of a positive economic multiplier. FDI remains an important source of development finance despite some of its limitations in directly addressing some of the problems of economic development such as poverty reduction.

Developing Countries and Credit Markets

Imperfect credit markets that typically operate in developing countries, alternatively viewed as imperfectly developed credit markets in these cases, lead to high TC and thus limit their economic growth. Greater role of the government institutions in such situations is inevitably important to develop the financial systems and enhance their productivity. Thin, fragmented, informal and unstable credit institutions characterize many of the developing country systems, and government financial institutions often feed to the rich and powerful, even though publicly declared policies are often drawn in favor of the poorer segments of the population.

Most developing countries comprise credit market features of both formal and informal financial institutions (such as the private moneylenders). Borrowers tend to form their own loan portfolios and recognize both the TC and enforcement features of loan repayments. The repayment process often accords priority for the informal sector because of severe enforcement capabilities of the lenders. Informal markets operate in spatially segmented markets and are usually very thin and discriminatory. Some of their activities are legal, and are complimentary to the role of formal institutions. A substantial segment of these markets is not functioning efficiently in many developing countries. The interactions of formal and informal financial sectors and other details of informal lending are explained in chapter 3. The roles of TC, social collateral and related factors in group-based lending schemes are also explained in chapter 3.

Majority of the asset-poor in developing countries rely on the informal sector, despite the high incidence of interest rates. Rich farmers and others in the rural areas have better access to formal institutions and at lower rates of interest. These resources are often recycled for lending to the poor, except that in this case the financial intermediaries do not belong to the formal financial structure as often interpreted. During the mid-1990s, about 80 percent of rural borrowing in Nepal was from informal sources of credit, and about 30 percent in Nigeria was of the same class (World Bank, 2002). Formal lenders usually insist on creditworthiness and secured loan transactions for the relatively non-poor. Even the latter may not seek loans from the formal institutions in cases (rather common in some countries) when the TC including corruption and delay factors in loan transactions effectively raise the costs to levels that are above the high interest loans from the informal lenders (with least delay and bureaucratic procedures or other costs of transactions).

At the macroeconomic level, developing countries face an upward-rising supply curve of capital funds. The marginal cost exceeds the average cost for a borrower country. This has been interpreted as a (Harberger, 1985, p.236) "negative externality that in principle justifies a tax on foreign borrowing (that is, each additional foreign loan tends to increase the country risk premium to be paid as other foreign loans are renewed or new ones made)". This externality feature of foreign borrowings needs to be weighed against effective utilization or marginal productivity of capital, so that the total costs of borrowing are meaningfully compared with total gains (at a given level of borrowing and its increments). The role of levying risk premium or equivalent tax may be meaningful after such an assessment. The borrowing entity's contribution to both costs and benefits also require quantification. This can provide answer to the question: who pays for the incremental costs? Further studies (analytical as well as empirical case studies) are relevant to answer this question. A comprehensive investigation of costs and benefits of borrowings in relation to enhanced financial risks (or country risk assessment) and contribution to development potential (including effects on various sections of the society) is expected to shed more light on these issues.

Regarding a country's access to international credit markets, Lensink and van Bergeijk (1991) found that the combinations of per capita gross domestic product (GDP), the net-debt-to GDP ratio and the investment share predict substantial cases of borrower's credit access in the international capital market. They also observed that there exists critical threshold below which marginal improvements in domestic economic policies do not seem to matter for enhanced credit access in the short-run. This analysis suggests the need to identify relevant critical thresholds specific to each economy and its institutions.

1.7 Concluding Observations

Financial institutional development in general and financial risk management functions of these institutions in particular, are the primary engines that led the industrial revolution. The role TC remains very important in the formation and evolution of financial institutions.

One of the robust prescriptions of the economics of TC is this (Rao, 2003, p. 173): comprehend the relevant TC and assess feasible/pragmatic alternatives among a continuum of institutional arrangements.

Contractual completeness for credit agreements are usually incomplete for a variety of practical reasons, including the prohibitive TC in the complete contract formulation. The role of trust and credible commitment are important. These features contribute toward reduction of TC and enhancement of economic efficiency.

The logical impossibility of joint welfare maximizing with informational asymmetries between creditors and debtors has been observed from an analytical perspective. However, an approximation closer to the ideal optimal solution is feasible by devising mechanisms for reducing informational asymmetries and for motivating involved economic entities to function in accordance with the objective of Pareto-welfare improvement for all parties. Some of these issues are examined further in chapter 6.

AI needs to be interpreted not only in terms of asymmetry of information available for processing among parties to a decision but also in terms of unequal processing capacities for a given level of symmetrically distributed information among parties to a decision. This interpretation has its implications for capacity building in developing countries for improved external and domestic debt management, credit market efficiency and financial institutional governance.

It important to recognize that the demand for loan is a function of both its nominal interest rate as well as TC that include *ex ante* and *ex post* costs of loan transactions, including costs of risks that arise from capital utilization. This feature alone justifies the role of dualism in credit markets, the ones with low nominal interest costs but high TC in obtaining the loan, and others with high interest rates but low TC in obtaining the loan.

Credit markets are imperfectly competitive markets. Equilibrium credit rationing and price discrimination are rather typical features of credit markets in many countries. The roles of AI and TC are important in the efficient governance of credit markets.

Much of traditional analysis treated AI as the most important determinant of the phenomenon of equilibrium credit rationing. However, in reality, both the roles of TC and AI are separately and jointly important for explaining the phenomenon. Market clearing may not exist in the sense of equating demand for and supply of credit at any interest rate because of the role of TC, even if there is no AI.

Interest rate dispersion and discriminatory lending are rather common in credit markets. Important determinants of these patterns are lenders' perceived risks, the role of AI between lenders and borrowers, and TC.

Policy imperatives for enhancing market efficiency and welfare of creditors and borrowers include designing transparent financial institutions, reduction of TC from the perspectives of both lenders and borrowers, infrastructural improvements including the design of improved information systems that identify and match these two sections of players in the credit market. The significance of these infrastructural features becomes clear in the analysis of later chapters as well.

Review Exercises

1. Discuss the validity or otherwise of the following suggestion: in a world with greater market transparency and efficiency, financial intermediaries may constitute endangered species.

2. Do the accelerated capital outflows from developing countries during the 1990s represent one of the characteristics of 'integration with the global economy', or is that a price to pay for achieving the latter? If this is an element of such a cost, what potential or realized benefits justify incurring such costs?

3. State the factors that contribute to credit rationing as a relevant phenomenon for the analysis of credit markets. Suggest a quantifiable measure for assessing the magnitude of credit rationing.

4. Examine the ingredients of TC that are relevant in effecting FDI.

5. What are the limitations of the conventional analyses of equilibrium credit rationing?

6. If we define credit market efficiency in terms of the joint welfare maximization of profits or utilities of lenders and borrowers, specify a set of necessary features of the market that facilitate such efficiency enhancement.

7. a) Identify the main elements of cost in the design and enforcement of contracts. What balancing is required in the *ex ante* and *ex post* costs of a contract?

    b) What are the desirable characteristics of an 'efficient' financial contract?

References

Arrow, K. J. (1964): The role of securities in the optimal allocation of risk-bearing, Review of Economic Studies, 31, 91-96.

Artzner, P., Delbaen, F., Eber, J-M., and Heath, D. (1999): Coherent Measures of Risk, Mathematical Finance, 9, 203-228.

Baker, D., Epstein, G., and Pollin R. (Ed.) (1998): Globalization and Progressive Economic Policy, New York: Cambridge University Press.

Berger, A. N. and Udell, G. F. (1992): Some Evidence on the Empirical Significance of Credit Rationing, Journal of Political Economy, 100, 1047-1077.

Besanko, D. and Thakor, A. V. (1987): Competitive Equilibrium in Credit Market under Asymmetric Information, Journal of Economic Theory, 42, 167-182.

Borenzstein, E., De Gregorio, J., and Lee, J. (1998): How does Foreign Direct Investment affect Economic Growth? Journal of International Economics, 45, 115-135.

Broome, J. (1990): Bolker-Jeffrey Expected Utility Theory and Axiomatic Utilitarianism, Review of Economic Studies, 57, 477-502.

Chan-Lau J. A. and Chen, Z. (2002): A Theoretical Model of Financial Crisis, Review of International Economics, 10, 53-63.

Fernandez-Arias, E. and Hausmann, R. (2001): Is Foreign Direct Investment a Safer Form of Financing? Emerging Markets Review, 2, 34-49.

Harberger, A. (1985): Lessons for Debtor-Country Managers and Policy Makers, in G. W. Smith and J. T. Cuddington (Ed.), International Debt and the Developing Countries, Washington, DC: World Bank.

Hellwig, M. (1998): Banks, Markets, and the Allocation of Risks in an Economy, Journal of Institutional and Theoretical Economics, 154, 328-342.

Hicks, J. (1969): A Theory of Economic History, Oxford: Clarendon Press.

Hulme, D. and Mosley, P. (1996): Poverty and Finance, London: Routledge.

Hurwicz, L. and Majumdar, M. (1988): Optimal Intertemporal Allocation Mechanisms and Decentralization of Decisions, Journal of Economic Theory, 45.2, 228-261.

Jafffee, D. M. and Russell, T. (1976): Imperfect Information, Uncertainty, and Credit Rationing, Quarterly Journal of Economics, 90, 651-666.

Jensen, M. and Meckling, W. (1976): Theory of the Firm: Managerial Behavior, Agency Costs and Ownership Structure, Journal of Financial Economics, 3, 305-360.

Jorian, P. (2001): Value at Risk, New York: McGraw Hill.

Laffont, J. (1985): On the Welfare Analysis of Rational Expectations Equilibria with Asymmetric Information, Econometrica, 53.1, 1-29.

Lensink, R. and van Bergeijk, P. (1991): The determinants of developing countries' access to the international capital market, Journal of Development Studies, 28, 86-103.

North, D. and Thomas, R. (1973): The Rise of the Western World: A New Economic History, Cambridge: Cambridge University Press.

Rao, P. K. (2003): The Economics of Transaction Costs: Theory, Methods and Applications, London: Palgrave – Macmillan.

Rodrik, D. (1999): The New Global Economy and Developing Countries: Making Openness Work, Washington, DC: Overseas Development Council.

Ross, S. (1973): The economic theory of the agency: the principal's problem, American Economic Review, 63, 134-139.

Stiglitz, J. E. (2002): Globalization and Its Discontents, New York: Norton.

Stiglitz, J. E. and Weiss, A. (1981): Credit Rationing in Markets with Imperfect Information, American Economic Review, 71, 393-410.

Townsend, R. M. (1982): Optimal Multiperiod Contracts and the Gain from Enduring Relationships under Private Information, Journal of Political Economy, 90, 1166-1186.

Vilasuso, J. and Minkler, A. (2001): Agency costs, asset specificity, and the capital structure of the firm, Journal of Economic Behavior and Organization, 44, 55-69.

World Bank (2003): Global Development Finance 2003, Washington, DC: World Bank.

World Bank (2002): World Development Report 2002, New York: Oxford University Press.

Zou, L. (1992): Threat-Based Incentive Mechanisms under Moral Hazard and Adverse Selection, Journal of Comparative Economics, 16, 47-74.

CHAPTER 2:

Finance, Economic Growth, and Development

2.1 Introduction

One of the definitions (see a leading book on the economics development, edited by Meier, 1989 at p.6) states that economic development is a process whereby a) the real per capita income of a country increases over a long period of time, and b) the number of poor people and economic inequality in the society do not increase. This definition implicitly suggests the need for relative decline in the proportion of poor people when there is a positive population growth rate (but not otherwise), and remains oblivious to the urgent needs of reducing abject poverty. Since the latter is of importance in any society and since the prevalence of hunger and severe poverty act as major drags on the entire economic system, it is necessary to revise the concept of economic development to reflect these factors.

We define economic development as a comprehensive process that includes improvements in all sections of the society and the well-being of the total population on a sustainable basis, while minimizing abject poverty and economic deprivation for any section of the society. This definition focuses on relative prioritization in the processes of development, as well as on the creation of relevant infrastructural aspects. The infrastructural development include, but not limited to, the following: development of legal infrastructure and adherence to the rule of law, cost-effective provision of goods and services by public institutions, promotion of competitive markets and their regulation, human capital development, and environmental protection. Any indicator of progress in economic development of a country needs to reflect these aspects. The concept of economic growth is defined as the rate of growth of total economic output, inclusive of the contribution of capital accumulation in this output. Growth remains a necessary but not sufficient condition for economic development.

Among the most critical inputs for economic development are financial resources and access to these resources in all sectors of economic activity. The provision of capital for multiple objectives of development is unlikely to be feasible if the resource allocation is entirely left to the capital markets. Finance for economic growth and development is not necessarily provided at socially optimal and sustainable levels if global and domestic capital markets are the primary institutional mechanism for achieving economic development objectives. Therefore, a conscious effort is required in all sectors and segments of the global and domestic economic systems and their governing institutions to steer resources, both directly (as in financial aid) and catalytically (as in the promotion of sustainable capital flows, capital markets and institutions for efficient financial governance).

The role of financial institutions and their policies in the governance of broad-based economic development is often addressed only in partial segments. Stiglitz (2000, p. 1085) raised the question: do the global financial policies that affect "the lives and livelihoods of millions of people throughout the world reflect the interests and concerns, not just of financial markets, but of businesses, small and large, and of workers, and the economy more broadly?" This is a key issue of development finance. Economic development perspectives remain relevant in the design of financial policies and institutions for financial governance. Clearly, the focus of financial institutions and their policies should center on development objectives, supported by the efficient functioning of domestic and global capital markets and institutions. While profit motive for the private enterprise continues to remain the driving force, its sustainability and mitigation of any externalities needs examination in conjunction with relevant activities. Similarly, financial institutions that are directed by government entities need to ensure that their transaction costs (TC) are minimized while delivering socially and economically desirable resources and services.

Of specific interest in this chapter are the issues relating to the role of financial intermediaries (FI) in economic growth, relationships between legal institutions, capital flows, and the impact of these on economic development. Often, although it is clear that greater financial development (FD) contributes to economic development, an understanding of the factors that enable such interlinks and relative effectiveness of instruments of policy is useful for the design and implementation of efficient development finance mechanisms. An examination of the mechanisms by which FI contribute to economic growth is an important aspect of analysis that enables policy formulations. Also relevant are the factors that affect the efficiency of FI, and implications on FD. We examine the interrelationships between financial inputs and economic growth, the role of FI in promoting economic growth, and the links between FD and economic development. A closer examination of the underlying issues, interdependencies, and common links enable the design and implementation of improved policies for effective governance of financial and economic systems.

2.2 Capital Flows and Economic Growth

Capital flows include both short-term portfolio flows as well as relatively longer term investments. Some components of these capital flows directly relate to economic development (as in investments in infrastructure development) but most others merely augment capital resources strictly in relation to short-term financial returns to investments, both in debt and in equity investments. Promotion of capital inflows (typically international), strengthening of capital markets for promoting efficient financial markets, financial deregulation and liberalization are often considered macroeconomic features of an economy in efforts to boost economic growth, and expand resources for development finance. This premise is usually founded on the implicit assumptions:

a) 'orderly' movements of capital flows in tune with the dynamics of capital utilization efficiency;

b) prudent financial management; and

c) supervision at the government level, including the provision of infrastructure for effective regulation of various operations.

There is an externality problem associated with excessive capital inflows and outflows. The externality problem of capital outflows may be summarized as follows (World Bank, 2001): the capital outflows above critical threshold levels that may have adverse impacts on the domestic economy by draining foreign exchange reserves, reducing the resources available for domestic investment, and slowing the development of the financial sector.

It has been suggested that sound economic policies are likely to be the best antidote to large capital outflows. These policies are also equally important for attracting as well as retaining capital inflows. The above summary does not fully cover the externality problem of capital inflows. This problem arises when inflows are excessive relative to the retentive capacity of the economic system and/or when such flows are unsustainable over time.

Liberalization of stock market trading has led to investment booms in some countries such as in much of East Asia during the 1990s (for select case studies see, for example, Henry, 2000). However, capital inflows may not translate into investments leading to economic growth. Economic growth occurs in conjunction with a set of domestic complementarities for capital absorption, retentive capabilities, and consequent impact on production and consumption. The possibility of capital outflow also needs to be recognized, along with the costs of outflows at varying levels in different phases of economic growth. Typically, global financial integration allows greater ease in the entry and exit of capital.

It also appears that capital inflows (but not portfolio flows) have a strong impact on domestic investment, especially in terms of foreign direct investment (FDI) and bank lending. This impact has been observed by Bosworth and Collins (1999). This study examined the relationship between various types of private capital inflows, with a focus on the determinants of variations in investments and savings over time within countries. Similarly, the World Bank (2001) report, using data for 118 countries during the period 1972-1998, found that private capital flows (long-term plus short-term) have a strong relationship with domestic investment. Several empirical studies reported (for a brief review, see World Bank, 2001 at p. 67) that there is a greater contribution of capital inflows in developing countries with relatively higher levels of income, primarily because of the coexistence of improved infrastructure that yields higher productivity of capital.

Yet, there is the question of whether the risks of capital inflows cause economic problems. The risk of short-term capital inflow reversals is recognized when capital inflows are encouraged beyond economic limits. Furthermore, the general tendency of short-term flows is to exacerbate cyclical fluctuations in capital flows rather than attenuate the same. This is partly because of herd behavior in the functioning of financial markets and their agents (detailed analysis may be seen in Bikchandani and Sharma, 2001). Private capital inflows take place at more than optimal levels in good times of the host economy, and at less than optimal levels in bad economic times. Here we define the optimum level in terms of maximization of benefits for the host economy as well as the investors, over a medium time horizon (such as a decade). The cyclical nature of capital flows reflects both the underdeveloped state of domestic financial markets and their degree of integration with the global markets. Volatility is more worrisome for the poorer of the developing countries because of their limited ability to absorb capital shocks and economic shocks. Some studies have identified the role of the financial sector and its development in reducing economic volatility. This reduction becomes feasible with enhanced information processing capabilities of domestic economic entities.

The thrust of financial and economic policies should focus on creating conditions for productive utilization of capital inflows (Schandler, 1994). There has been a strong trend recently at domestic economy levels towards enabling conditions for sustainable and substantial openness and financial liberalization, with the removal of regulatory instruments, including those of risk management. However, in these conditions, short-term capital flows can pose greater risks than rewards if these flows are not properly moderated (Stiglitz, 2000). Foreign investment enhances economic growth only in some but not all cases. Excessive capital inflows can impose significant costs to the recipient country in seasons of global or domestic capital volatility. The World Bank (2001) reports that empirical studies led to the observation that private capital flows are associated with acceleration in growth: 1 percent increase in capital inflow as a percentage of GDP leads to about 0.25 percent increase in GDP growth. The complementary roles of sound macroeconomic policies, efficient resource use, and the adoption of sustainable and credible financial policies at the government level are among the relevant factors that contribute to economic growth.

If we consider the role of external aid as a significant source of development finance, the role of such capital or other resource flows has not been as effective in promoting economic growth and development as once predicted (see chapter 5 for details). As Easterly (2001) examined, the relative ineffectiveness of external aid has been founded on one or more variations of agency costs, including substantial and systemic leakages along the line of delivery and usage of resources. For a more detailed discussion of these issues see chapters 4 and 5.

Financial Stability Forum

Regarding global policy formulations for the efficient governance of capital flows and their potential externalities, the global Financial Stability Forum (FSF) established in its inaugural meeting a Working Group on Capital Flows. This Working Group's Report of 2000 contained a number of recommendations. Two of these recommendations relating to capital flows are summarized below (details at www.fsforum.org).

1. If the risk exposures associated with capital flows are not properly managed, the consequences for creditors and debtors and for global financial stability more generally can be severe. Reaping the full benefits of capital flows will require adopting policies that control the risks associated with them.

2. Abrupt portfolio adjustments involving sudden cessation or reversals of capital flows can lead to costly adjustments in affected countries. Countries with severe debt problems and fixed exchange rate mechanisms are seen as more prone to this phenomenon. The role of prudent management of liquidity and other risks remains important. Recent history provides evidence that countries with fixed exchange rates and large amounts of short-term debt are prone to disruptive volatility of this sort, which can have systemic consequences.

Regarding the scope for using capital controls as prudential measures, the Working Group Report observed:

1. many developed and emerging countries have benefited from capital mobility; however, large-scale inflows may have adverse effects on an economy if, by putting upward pressure on the exchange rate, they complicate the design and implementation of domestic monetary policy;

2. large scale inflows of short-term claims are also a source of potential vulnerability of the financial system, as new inflows may cease or existing claims may not be rolled over; and,

3. capital inflow controls, whenever relevant, are to be implemented in conjunction with certain conditions for their use that can help to increase the likelihood of success; controls can only serve as support for a sound macroeconomic program committed to stability.

To summarize, the role of capital inflows as a source of development finance is meaningful only in conjunction with complementary macroeconomic policies, pragmatic regulation of entry and exit systems for various capital flows, financial risk management, and linking of economic development priorities with capital resource allocations.

2.3 Financial Institutions and Economic Growth

The emergence, formation, evolution and functioning of the financial system constitute major determinants of economic growth and development. Hypotheses of links between these factors has dominated part of the economics literature, but studies in the 1990s demonstrated substantial and overwhelming evidence that in most countries, financial factors such as capital flows, formation and efficient functioning of FI have been playing a significant role in economic growth and development for several decades.

Parallel to the role of money as a means of exchange of goods and services, FI have enabled mobilization of savings deposits, trading, resource lending, contracting and information processing for financial decision making. Most importantly, the role of FI includes their potential contribution to efficient allocation of capital across sectors and economic activities in tune with marginal financial productivities among different alternative uses of capital. This potential to enhance financial efficiency is conditional upon the regulatory and institutional framework that governs these FI. In particular, market imperfections, the role of credit controls, interest rate policies, legal factors affecting lending and borrowing operations (including loan recovery and bankruptcy procedures) are some of the factors that hamper the potential to equalize capital productivity as well its marginal productivity at any specified level. Besides, 'efficient allocation' based merely on financial returns may not always be an economically efficient allocation of capital, and this calls for a benevolent role of the state in providing the institutional and regulatory framework consistent with the development objectives of the society and judicious utilization of resources in that context.

The role of FI is not only to reduce information costs and transaction costs but is also to create new products with value added characteristics. Scholtens and van Wensveen (2000, p. 1250) argued that in the process of "asset transformation with respect to maturity, liquidity, risk, scale, and location" these institutions add value to investors and depositors or savings contributors. Thus, it is suggested, value addition should be seen as a major role of FI.

How is Economic Growth Influenced?

The role of FI has been critical in economic growth and development, as observed over many years in most countries. This assessment took some time for acceptance among economists. In one of the early expositions, Schumpeter (1911) argued that the functions and services of FI are essential for technological innovation and economic development. Among the functions and services envisaged were: mobilizing savings, managing risks, monitoring and evaluating financial transactions, and facilitating transactions among parties.

Capital accumulation and technological innovation affect economic growth in diverse ways. In some of the simplified economic models, financial systems affect growth by altering the savings rate sometimes by their allocation of savings for capital producing technologies (Romer, 1986). Technological transformation is thus affected by the role of financial systems. As a result, the pace of change or growth rate is influenced partly by the TC-minimizing role of the financial institutions.

Credit or other resource allocation processes of financial institutions can, in principle, lead to efficient financial management and enhanced economic growth. The efficiency-enhancing role of FI in credit and capital markets is not automatic. Such a role is accomplished when FI conduct the design and implementation of their operations based on cost-effective mechanisms. These mechanisms should reduce TC in general, and information costs in particular. Provision of finance and FI facilitate entrepreneurship, innovation, improvement of economic productivity, and thus contribute to economic growth. Again, this theoretical link between finance and growth is based on important assumptions such as the rule of law, provision of property rights and their effective enforcement, supervision of financial operations in accordance with a sound set of principles and code of conduct.

Financial Intermediaries and Economic Growth

Financial systems that manage risks efficiently contribute to accelerated economic growth (King and Levine, 1993b). Also, as Levine (1997, p.715) argued, "countries with financial institutions that are effective at relieving information barriers will promote faster economic growth through more investment than countries with financial systems that are less effective at obtaining and processing information." The critical issue here is to design a cost-effective mechanism of reducing informational asymmetries among all parties involved in financial transactions.

Properly designed financial systems ameliorate TC (including information costs) and, by recognizing uncertainties and risks of resource management, facilitate the allocation of resources. These institutions, in the absence of additional scrutiny and governing measures, do not necessarily imply efficient risk management in all cases or all systems. The quality of FI is with reference to their cost-effectiveness in the provision of capital and services. A more developed institution (relative to other institutions in that class of institutions) possesses superior features of TC minimization as well as maximization of the values of the objectives of their functioning. Substantial additional analytical and empirical work is required to quantify the 'quality' aspects of FI, and their role in economic growth.

Do more developed FI lead toward enhanced economic growth? The answer is in the affirmative but the strength of such a correlation depends on a few important institutional factors as well. Well-structured and well-developed FI tend to affect positively the mobilization and allocation of savings for economic activities oriented toward greater productivity while simultaneously mitigating some financial risks and reducing TC. As Levine et al (2000) observed in their empirical study, the effective enforcement of contracts and property rights, in addition to accurate financial accounting and disclosure of financial performance information are contributing factors that enable 'better developed' FI. These same factors contribute to economic growth as well.

Economic development contributes to the development of FI and vice versa; the relative magnitudes of the feedback effects vary with the economic system and time-period. The cause-and-effect relationships in many countries were more pronounced in favor of a greater role for FI: FI led to economic growth. Shan et al (2001) provides a review of some of the related studies. The use of time-series data for different countries may reveal greater linkages than cross-section data for different countries at one time point or time-period. The latter imposes limitations for any meaningful comparative study of countries because of the implicit assumption that the economic conditions and quality of institutions among the countries examined possess similar features (see also Arestis and Demetriades, 1997).

The role of modern FI includes the following: financial product innovation, capital productivity maximization and risk management, entrepreneurship for financial services and relevant product design, and dynamic evolution with changes in the institutions (Scholtens and van Wensveen, 2000). The channels through which FI contribute to economic growth include the following:

- the acquisition and processing of information;
- contribution to innovation and entrepreneurship;
- risk management, returns on investment; and
- efficient resource allocation and risk minimization, in an integrated or jointly interdependent framework.

Higher financial returns lead to changed savings patterns and income and substitution effects. In practice, however, the roles of FI vary with their 'quality'. Higher 'quality' FI are TC minimizing producers of financial products and information, and affect favorable productivity and economic growth. The 'quality' or efficiency of the FI may be seen in terms of their ability to enhance product innovations, and reduce TC (including information costs). There seem to be hardly any empirical studies that have examined these relationships.

Historically, was there a significant role for FI in industrial countries? Rousseau and Wachtel (1998) carried out an empirical study of five industrialized countries USA, UK, Canada, Norway and Sweden for the period 1870-1929. They observed the important role of FI in the rapid industrial transformation of these countries. However, they defined the FI in rather narrow terms, as individuals or institutions that solicit funds for loans from capital surplus units and allocate these funds among capital deficient units whose debt they assume.

Empirical Analyses

The factors that link FI and economic growth remain important aspects of empirical analysis. In their study by Beck et al (2000), private credit has been treated as a broad measure of FI development. It includes all financial institutions, not only deposit money banks. The study noted: a) the correlation between private credit by non-banks and real per capita GDP over the period 1960-1995 was 60 percent; and, b) the correlation between non-bank credit to the private sector and economic growth was 30 percent. Beck et al (2000) found that the route to economic growth is not merely through the enhancing role of FI with respect to savings and physical capital accumulation, but through the enhancement of 'total factor productivity' (TFP) growth. The study lends support to the classical view, often known as the Schumpeterian view, that the level of FI development affects the rate of economic growth by influencing the pace of productivity and technological change. Their study used observations and a regression analysis of 63 countries over the period 1960-1995, and defined the measure for FI development in terms of the ratio of FI credit to the private sector relative to the GDP.

Even after accounting for the role and contribution of physical and human capital, a substantial segment of economic growth rate is often accounted for by a residual, often described as the TFP. Major empirical studies (see for example, Easterly and Levine, 2001) suggest the role of factors other than capital in the accelerated economic growth rates. It has been observed that all factors of production flow to the richest areas. This suggests that the rich areas attained their economic progress because of high 'technical progress', and more generally, because of their high TFP (which includes the role of institutions and organizations) rather than high capital itself. Capital accumulation alone cannot contribute to sustainable economic growth over long intervals but TFP enables economic growth on a sustainable basis. The role of development finance is such that it can contribute to both economic growth and TFP.

Another important study by Odedokun (1996) contained an analysis of 71 less developed countries from the 1960s to 1980s. Based on statistical regression methods (regression equation given below), the findings showed that:

- in about 85 percent of the countries, FI significantly contributed to economic growth;
- the contribution of FI to economic growth are more significant in developing countries relative to more developed countries; and,
- the relative contribution was of the same magnitude as that of expanded exports or the growth of capital formation.

Thus, the growth-promoting effects of FI have been invariant in all regions of the world.

The following regression equation has been used in the above study: using the notation, Y as aggregate output or real GDP, X as exports, F for measure of level of financial development, I as real gross investment, L labor force, and u the error term:

$$(d/dt)(Y) = k + a(d/dt)(L) + b(I/Y) + c(d/dt)(F) + e(d/dt)(X) + u$$

where k is the intercept (a constant), a, b, c, and e are applicable coefficients for empirical estimation.

Some element of correlation between F, the level of financial development and X, exports, cannot be entirely ruled out, however.

How does international trade or trade liberalization affect financial market development and economic growth? The main channel by which trade liberalization affects economic growth is via its positive effect on the growth of investment, according to one of the empirical studies by Levine and Renelt (1992). Also, international trade plays an important role in enabling greater access to international capital markets, and thus influences economic growth as well (for a detailed analysis see Lane, 2001). This raises the issue of the roles of exogenous and endogenous influences.

A paradigm developed by Greenwood and Jovanovic (1990) suggests that both the extent of financial intermediation and the rate of economic growth are endogenously determined. FI promotes growth as it enables realization of greater return on capital, and growth in turn supports larger infrastructures for capital management. The widening of economic disparities in the process may be expected, however. Conscious development intervention policies can mitigate the latter problem to enable greater 'trickle down effect' of growth for the vulnerable sections of the society. Beck et al (2000) also found that the financial sector development is significantly associated with faster economic growth. However, for FI to develop, people must trust the third parties to whom they give their money for onward lending or further investments (Keefer and Shirley, 2000). For example, depositors at banks expect the institutions to be able to conform to implicit agreements, in addition to explicit contracts, if any.

Towards a Formal Model

Economic growth rate g is a function, among other things, of the savings, investment, technology of production, and efficiency of resource use. The aggregate output in simplest forms is described as follows. Let Y denote the aggregate output or real GDP, K the capital stock, e the technical progress, and q the assessed quality of FI (including the role of TC), and F an appropriately defined function

$$Y = F(e, q, K)$$
$$g = dY/dt$$
$$= d/dt\,[F(e, q, K)]$$

The above expression shows interrelationships between economic growth and the dynamic changes in e, q, and capital accumulation. System-specific empirical studies are expected to yield relevant estimates of the factors above and provide insight into the specific contributions of FI and other inputs to the economic growth parameter g.

The role of financial systems, including FI, need to be examined in terms of their main features and the traits that facilitate economic growth. This is the focus of the following section.

2.4 Financial Development and Economic Growth

Relevant features of FD include the following:

1. formation and working of financial institutions (including FI) that enhance efficiency and reduce TC, i.e. FD is facilitated when the objectives of FI include: minimization of TC, and maximization of returns to capital allocations; and
2. provision of financial services near optimal levels for all sectors of the economy and all sections of the society.

A quantified index of FD in accordance with this normative specification needs to be developed, however.

FD and formation of infrastructure involving FI facilitates the reduction of informational asymmetries, i.e., the mapping of demand and supply of resources between investors and borrowers, and thus enhances the real rate of return on capital and economic productivity. Firms that are more dependent on external rather than internal (firm-level) capital are generally the ones to benefit most from FI and financial development. In the absence of FI that reduce informational asymmetry, agency costs raise the costs of external borrowings.

The role of FI in FD may be summarized as follows: the mobilization and channeling of savings for investments (including innovation and entrepreneurial development, skill formation), and allocation of capital for projects with the higher expected returns, thus supporting higher productivity.

Although every FD component may not reduce relevant TC, levels of FD beyond a threshold can contribute to the reduction of TC in the financial system, promote financial product innovation and enhance economic growth (for some of the analytical formulations see Pagano, 1993).

The positive contribution that the financial system can make to the process of economic growth depends on, among other things, the design and functioning of the financial system, as argued by Hermes and Lensink (2000, p.509). The selection of a specific institutional and organizational structure leads also to the desired sets of regulatory and supervisory functions of the government or other public bodies. However, a financial system by itself cannot lead to economic growth and development. Several aspects of functioning efficiency are required in order to utilize capital effectively to benefit society. The role of deposit insurance and financial risk management at various FI levels is one such requirement. In addition, the role of asymmetric information (AI) persists, in altered form, even with efficiently functioning financial institutions (see Box 2.1 for an analytical summary of the role expectation formation when AI typically characterizes the basis of economic decision making among different entities). The experience of some of the transition economies suggests such features. Moral hazard and adverse selection problems seem to persist in many of these cases.

As Hermes and Lensink (2000) noted, the banking systems in some of the countries are dragged down by the inheritance of preexisting bad debt portfolios and have stronger incentives to excessive risk taking behavior (perhaps to the situation of being desperate). In the absence of a strong resource base for the government or any other lender of last resort, the weakness of the financial system extends negative externalities to the rest of the economic system.

Box 2.1: The Role of Expectations

Rational expectations (RE), where rationality is in relation to commonly observed and expected vents, can lead to self-fulfilling prophesies of failure if these expectations are founded on past experiences of failure and cynicism. By definition, RE are formed in a way that is stochastically expectation-equivalent to the behavior of observed states with specific parameters under reference. Muth (1961) was among the first to formalize this behavior. McCallum (1980) and several later authors contributed to the applications of the RE concept in macroeconomic stability models. However, as Akerlof (1970) argued, the traditional result that economic efficiency can be achieved with perfect information is generally a myth.

When information asymmetrically distributed between different parties in a transaction, there may not be a single market clearing pricing mechanism; as a result of this feature, social efficiency cannot be attained. Yet, in the context of financial markets and credit markets, the role of FI is to reduce informational asymmetries and thus to minimize TC. The efficiency of credit formation or other functions of capital then are dependent on the role of the FI. Financial contracting is also an important means of achieving TC reduction. The structure of financial contracts and their enforcement influences the TC-minimizing role of the FI.

The rate of capital accumulation and the utilization efficiency of capital are enhanced by the development of financial services (King and Levine, 1993a). Several significant empirical studies followed in the 1990s. Among the important features of FD examined in a few studies for their contribution to the economic growth rates are: the size of the formal FI sector relative to GDP; the relative roles of banks vis-à-vis the central regulatory bank; the ratio of credit allocation to the private sector to GDP, and the percentage of credit allocated to the private sector from the total credit (King and Levine, 1993a).

FD has been assessed as an important determinant of economic growth and its variations among countries. The dependence may not be linear and there could be country-specific threshold levels for positive linkages between financial development and economic growth. For more details on these lines see Berthelemy and Varoudakis (1996).

Empirical Studies

Although empirical studies have established a strong, positive link between FD and economic growth (though not economic development in some cases), wide variations exist among countries in causality factors and their relative contributions. The financial policies, and functioning efficiency of FI explain most of the variations. Besides, the direct costs and economic consequences of banking crises, which arose from time to time has been very significant. Furthermore, financial liberalization has not been implemented without its own consequential costs. In most cases, institutional and policy reforms are required prior to implementing financial reforms.

The broad-based question of whether FD leads, or slows, or synchronizes with, economic growth has been investigated in several empirical studies. It has been observed, based on a cross-country regressional analysis, that (King and Levine, 1993a, p.717-18):

> "higher levels of financial development are significantly and robustly correlated with faster current and future rates of economic growth, physical capital accumulation and economic efficiency improvements."

In a recent study (Shan and Morris, 2002), it was concluded that financial development by itself does not necessarily lead to economic growth, except possibly when the level of FD exceeds a threshold, as in many western countries. Earlier studies by Arestis and Demetriades (1997), and Demetriades and Hussein (1996) concluded that the positive correlation between FD and economic growth is country-specific and it is likely to be affected by the differences in economic structure and institutional characteristics. The link between FD and international trade (exports and trade balances) seems to be a relevant issue here as well (see Beck, 2002, for a preliminary empirical study).

Methodological Issues

Among the analytical and methodological problems in the study of the structures of financial systems in their relationships to economic growth and development are the following:

a) the diversity of composition of the current varying financial structures, the variations in their regulatory controls from time to time for a given country and across countries over time, do not enable a simple relationship for estimation purposes;

b) most institutions operate with initial endowments or some preexisting traditions and implicit norms of operation that are not reflected in formal institutional assessments of their operations (for example, the roles of goodwill, reputation, and consumer confidence, with or without any form of deposit insurance);

c) the composition and roles of banks, insurance companies, stock markets, and other FI; the relative degree of private ownership and nature of private and public control of these institutions; and

d) macroeconomic policies regarding openness and access to external finance, and the role of international aid and credit flows in some developing countries.

At a general methodological level the following conclusion of one of the major founders of neoclassical economic growth theory must be noted. Growth theory was originally conceived as a modeling exercise for an industrial economy, and may not readily extend to underdeveloped and partially monetized economies. Solow (2001) expressed doubts on whether using cross-country regressions involving diverse countries with varying institutional evolution can lead to meaningful comparative results, and he suggested that "comparative studies should focus less on the growth rate and more on comparing and understanding whole time paths." (Ibid, p. 288). Most of the published empirical studies in the interrelated areas of financial development, economic growth, and economic development need to be viewed in this light.

Endogenous Growth

According to the endogenous growth approach, economic growth occurs even in the absence of external factors, affecting increase in economic productivity – because of increasing returns to scale that accelerate economic growth (Romer, 1986). This growth could occur due to enhanced human capital or other infrastructural resources provided beyond a critical threshold. However, some of these phenomena may be viewed as positive externalities. The new endogenous growth models seek to explain the role of government policies or other resource provisions that could have sustained growth implications (Lucas, 1988). Furthermore, the role of a minimum threshold level of infrastructure of resources that enable increasing returns and the existence of endogenous growth is an area that deserves further attention. In other words, an entity must be sufficiently well endowed, *ab initio*, in order to be able to generate more dividends. Alternatively, a prerequisite for the generation of such benefits is the existence of positive externalities in the financial and economic configuration within an economic entity. This clearly is predicated on the ability of a collective institution such as the state or a conglomerate with network externalities to lead to the desirable scenario.

The functional or microeconomic role of FD needs to be viewed in terms of the following:

- a source of entrepreneurship and managed risk-taking;
- financial resource for technical change, transfer of technology and human capital transformation with potential for long-term economic growth;
- adoption of technical change within the financial sector to minimize TC and enhance economic efficiency; and
- integration with the global economy so as to augment relevant complementary resources for economic growth.

Can FD constitute a source of comparative advantage in international trade and finance? Rajan and Zingales (1998) pointed to an important aspect of international trade economics, not discussed in much of related literature: the existence of a well-developed financial market represents a source of comparative advantage for a country in its ability to compete in global trade in its favor. This could constitute yet another source of economic growth for such a country.

Another issue is whether industries that are more dependent on external (not necessarily foreign) financing grow faster in countries that are financially more developed, *ab initio*. Rajan and Zingales (1998) found, using data for the period 1980 to 1990, that FD has almost twice the economic effect on the growth of number of firms as compared to the effect on size of firms. FD was measured in terms of the following indicators: total capitalization in the stock market, bank debt levels, adoption of proper accounting standards, and a combination of these indices. The authors observed, "…the ex ante development of financial markets facilitates the ex post growth of sectors dependent on external finance. This implies that the link between financial development and growth identified elsewhere may stem at least in part, from a channel identified by the theory: financial markets and institutions reduce the cost of external finance for firms." (Ibid, p. 500-501). Beck et al (2000) found that financial sector development contributes to enhanced economic growth.

It is useful to summarize this section with the following:

FD contributes to economic growth firstly through the reduction of costs of provision of capital, and secondly through enhanced entrepreneurship; these factors promote innovation, and offer an economic infrastructural base for the promotion of international trade and finance; both these are additional sources of economic growth. These features, in turn, imply augmentation of resources for economic development. Other sources of finance include capital inflows, especially in the form of foreign direct investment (FDI). These flows accrue to those economies that have or create efficient governance structures for financial and other institutions (for an empirical analysis see, for example, Globerman and Shapiro, 2002).

The role and limitations of capital flows in their potential contribution to economic growth is examined in the following section. The role of FD in the broader process of economic development deserves further scrutiny. This is the focus of the next section.

2.5 Financial Development and Economic Development

In the early stages of relevant analyses, applied studies and empirical works of Patrick (1966), Goldsmith (1969) and McKinnon (1973), among others, demonstrated the close links between financial and economic development in most countries over the years. Patrick (1966) concluded that causation runs from financial to economic growth as a supply-led relationship in the early stages of economic development, but the direction of causation reverses in relatively more advanced stages of development. However, Jung (1986) tested data for 19 developed and 37 developing countries and found supply-led relationship in all stages of development. This was in contrast to the assertions of Goldsmith (1969) who traced the relationship for 35 countries over the period 1860 to 1963. Since the samples of countries, periods of analysis and statistical methods differ in these studies, a robust conclusion may not emerge. But the close association between FD and economic growth was not investigated.

What are the common characteristics of the countries that have better developed FI? Levine et al (2000) conducted an empirical study of economic growth and FD features of several countries. They concluded that countries that have 'better developed FI' or higher quality FI are those which:

a) provide greater priority to investors that belong to the class of secured creditors;

b) have a legal system that enforces contractual agreements vigorously; and

c) have accounting standards that produce comprehensiveness and transparency.

The World Bank in its 2001 report of global development finance repeatedly asserted the role of the legal institutions in promoting FD and economic growth. Some of the relevant extracts are given below:

1. "Policymakers should consider improving the legal and regulatory environment rather than building a particular financial structure. What is important is to have secure rights for outside investors and efficient contract enforcement mechanisms – central theme of this report." (p. 76).

2. "Policies to promote financial development are likely to be more effective if efforts are directed at developing the legal and regulatory environment to support the natural evolution of financial structure. Financial system development depends critically on the protection of private property." (p. 78).

3. "Building financial institutions requires policymakers to focus on the fundamentals: property rights and the enforcement of those rights. This is true whatever the level of income and regardless of the political and macroeconomic environment of the country." (p. 79).

The legal framework under which financial transactions occur has a major effect on the extent of financial market development and economic growth. The role of creditor and investor rights, and their enforcement, is a major feature that influences external private capital flows. The financial contracts and their enforcement are thus critical in the mobilization of external finance. Financial institutions tend to seek shelter under reduced uncertainties. Laws that ensure transparency of dispute resolution mechanisms are a part of this requisite safety mechanism. Box 2.2 summarizes the role of legal and institutional infrastructure in attracting and sustaining external commercial finance for economic activities.

Box 2.2: Law and External Finance

The rule of law has been seen as an important element of the determinants of external commercial (non-concessional) finance. Using the 'law and order' assessment (given by the country risk rating agency International Country Risk, ICR) as a measure of the rule of law, in combination with related parameters including corruption, risk of appropriation, and efficiency of the judicial system, La Porta et al (1998, p. 1151) conducted their empirical study of corporate finance in 49 countries. They found that legal protection of shareholder rights affects the degree of concentration of ownership, and adversely influences access to equity financing. Good financial accounting standards and shareholder protection measures are found to be associated with a lower concentration of ownership. Ownership is apparently a response to the type and degree of legal provisions. Countries with poor investor protection measures have been found to have significantly smaller equity and debt markets. Financial instruments, in general, and securities in particular, do not themselves carry legal rights in any system. The provision of broader laws of financial contracting and enforcement affect the quality and efficacy of these instruments.

At a more general yet empirical level, Keefer and Shirley (2000) showed that the rule of law factor reduction by a measure of one standard deviation (using empirical data of ICR) could induce a decline of 2.8 percent in the rate of investment in a typical economy. The role of corruption is also about the same. Corrupt functionaries are unlikely to pay enough attention to the protection of property rights, investor rights or other contractual enforcements. Investment and economic growth are both adversely affected by the absence of well-defined property rights and appropriate legal infrastructure supporting their enforcement. Countries that failed to provide proper legal mechanisms, including secure property rights did not succeed in reaping the advantages of so-called market-friendly policy reforms.

Specifically in the banking sector, only some studies shed light on legal determinants of sectoral development. Notable among these is the study by Levine (1998). The study examined empirical relationships between legal systems and banking development during the period of 1976-1993 for several countries, based on the applied definition of banking sector development as the portion of credit allocated by commercial and other deposit-taking banks to the private sector, relative to GDP. The results suggested that countries where the legal system emphasizes creditor rights and ensures compliance with contracts have better developed banking institutions. Differences in the legal rights of creditors, and the efficacy with which legal systems enforce those rights account for over half of the cross-country variations in banking development. Further, this feature of legal environment is positively correlated with per capita income growth, physical capital accumulation and productivity growth.

The roles of the following main features of creditor rights have been found to make a difference in the outcome: whether a country's laws impose an automatic stay on the assets of the firm upon its filing a reorganization petition (whereby banks cannot gain possession of collateral or liquidate the firm to meet loan obligations), whether the firm itself or some other court-ordered team manages the firm during the process of reorganization, and whether secured creditors have seniority over others in the distribution of proceeds of the firm in the event of dissolution. The latter is material only when the rule of law enables enforcement of such rights. This factor is also incorporated empirically, based on quantified assessment of the risk that a government might dilute the original terms of contract, and other assessments of ICR. Moreover, as noted in La Porta et al (1998), countries that have English common law are found to emphasize creditor rights to a greater degree than French, German, and Scandinavian countries. In terms of contract enforcement, countries with German and Scandinavian legal traditions tend to be the best. Overall, the importance of legal reforms in several countries aiming for banking sector development and economic growth seems clear.

Macroeconomic Openness

The role of financial liberalization, sometimes called macroeconomic openness, is to promote capital flows toward productive activities, and attract inflows from international capital markets. Thus, in principle, financial liberalization can lead to enhanced investments and increases in factor productivity. However, in practice, this prescription has less than universal relevance. A few important clarifications regarding the role and limitations of financial and economic liberalization, also referred to as openness of an economy are relevant here. These are:

a) openness by itself is not a mechanism to ensure economic growth, while it does lead to enhanced risk exposure (Rodrik, 1999);

b) requisite complimentary provisions for economic development include an appropriate domestic investment strategy (which includes creation of institutional arrangements, including those for dispute resolution at different levels) (Rodrik, 1999).

The role of stakeholder participation in any major policy decisions, especially that which concerns the role of major capital borrowings from external sources (including the multilateral organizations such as the World Bank or the IMF), remains an important factor for ensuring productive utilization of financial resources that entail long-term liabilities. If external resource flows dampen internal resource mobilization and capital use efficiencies, then the role of the former is one of substitution rather than supplementation. Such a role would only imply added costs to the system as a consequence of such openness or financial liberalization.

Bosworth and Collins (1998) observed, in their empirical study covering several countries, that foreign borrowings and/or capital inflows may not usually be sustainable, after a threshold level. A period of unsustainable borrowings can only lead to unsustainable repayments of loans. This process in turn leads to lowered credit ratings and higher costs of capital, possibly creating a chain of adverse effects. The critical issue is to decipher the threshold limits of inflows and debts in relation to productivity of these resources, and to stay within those limits.

Inefficient use of capital inflows and/or capital inflows beyond an optimum level, and herd behavior of investors, could exacerbate any downturns in the macroeconomic scenarios and lead to multiplicative or nonlinear relationships among financial resource inflows and macroeconomic crises. Thus, openness of a financial and economic system needs to be governed in such a manner as to safeguard its stability and to reap the benefits of openness while minimizing potential costs or risks.

The role of information costs, monitoring or other components of TC is such that more developed capital markets enable endogenous evolution of efficient markets for financial instruments, including those for debt and equity. In such an advanced framework, debt and equity markets function as complements rather than substitutes (for more details in this direction of inquiry see Boyd and Smith, 1996).

2.5 Concluding Observations

Financial institutions (intermediaries included) have emerged as a means to facilitate financial transactions. The costs of these transactions, including information costs, contract and enforcement costs and other relevant elements of designing and implementing eligible transactions, determine the choices of institutional ingredients.

FI have the potential to minimize the costs of acquisition and processing of financial information relevant for decision-making and exchange of transactions. In addition, FI networks decrease TC directly and through network externalities.

They enhance consumer welfare when made accessible in close proximity to the public, thus enhancing savings, endogenous growth, and reducing monopolistic features of credit transactions (for details see Amable and Chatelain, 2001). Their role in reducing uneconomic levels of liquidity in the household system promotes economic growth with better mobilization of capital for productive use. Optimal expansion of the FI can also reduce welfare loss that results from imperfect competition in the banking and related sectors.

Financial resources, instruments, markets and institutions contribute to the reduction of TC and raise resource use efficiency both in the short-run and in the long-run. The functions of financial systems include collating and processing of relevant information, facilitating transactions, risk management, trading of risk as an element of risk management, capital allocation, mobilization and steering of resources (savings from domestic economy and external financial resources), and enabling financial contracts and their enforcement. None of these functions are attainable on their own, nor otherwise done in any automatic sense.

FD contributes to economic growth mainly through:

a) reduction in the costs of provision of capital, and

b) enhanced entrepreneurship.

Both these factors promote innovation, and offer an economic infrastructural base for the promotion of international trade and finance. These constitute additional sources of economic growth and augment resources for economic development.

Other sources of finance include capital inflows, especially in the form of FDI. These flows accrue to those economies that have or create efficient governance structures for financial and other institutions.

The role of legal and other institutional infrastructure is critical for efficient functioning of the system. The role of government in providing macroeconomic policies that are conducive to the productivity of financial institutions while balancing the interests of the society as a whole in the social welfare maximizing sense are also important requirements that enable efficient economic growth and development.

Review Exercises

1. What are the important prerequisites for FI in order to improve their quality, and to contribute toward economic growth?

2. Explain the concepts and their interrelationships:

    a) financial intermediaries and financial development;

    b) economic growth and economic development; and

3. financial development and economic development.

4. a) Elucidate the externality problems of capital flows.

    b) What prudent measures are useful for minimizing negative externalities? Examine these measures in terms of their cost-effectiveness in the short-run and long-run, using costs that include relevant TC.

5. Why is an endogenous growth theory explanation of economic growth relevant in linking FD and economic growth?

6. How do FI contribute to: a) enhance TFP; and, b) reduce TC?

7. What specific functions of the government contribute to enhancing the efficacy of FI?

8. What is the positive role of macroeconomic openness in promoting economic growth? What are the main limitations of extending openness beyond critical threshold limits? What are the economic and institutional factors that determine these limits?

References

Akerlof, G. (1970): The market for 'lemons', Quarterly Journal of Economics, 84, 488-500.

Amable, B. and Chatelain, J-B. (2001): Can financial infrastructures foster economic development?, Journal of Development Economics, 64, 481-498.

Arestis, P. and Demetriades, P. (1997): Financial Development and Economic Growth: Assessing the Evidence, Economic Journal, 107, 783-799.

Beck, T. (2002): Financial development and international trade: Is there a link?, Journal of International Economics, 57, 107-131.

Beck, T., Levine, R. and Loayza, N. (2000): Finance and the sources of growth, Journal of Financial Economics, 58, 261-300.

Berthelemy, J-C. and Varoudakis, A. (1996): Financial Development Policy and Growth, Paris: OECD.

Bikchandani, S. and Sharma, S. (2001): Herd Behavior in Financial Markets, IMF Staff Papers, 47, 279-310.

Bosworth, B. and Collins, S. (1999): Capital Flows to Developing Countries: Implications for Savings and Investment, Brookings Papers on Economic Activity, 7, 143-169.

Bosworth, B. and Collins, S. (1998): Capital Inflows, Investment, and Growth, Washington, DC: Brookings Institution.

Boyd, J. H. and Smith, B. D. (1996): The Co-Evolution of the Real and Financial Sectors in the Growth Process, World Bank Research Review, 10, 371-396.

Clague, C., Keefer, P., Knack, S., and Olsen, M. (1995): Contract-intensive money: contract enforcement, property rights and economic performance, IRIS Working Paper, University of Maryland (cited in Keefer and Shirley, 2000).

Demetriades, P. and Hussein, K. (1996): Financial Development and Economic Growth: Cointegration and Causality Tests for 16 Countries, Journal of Development Economics, 57, 387-411.

Easterly, W. (2001): The Elusive Quest for Growth: Economists' Adventures and Misadventures in the Tropics, Cambridge, MA: MIT Press.

Easterly, W. and Levine, R. (2001): It's Not Factor Accumulation: Stylized Facts and Growth Models, The World Bank Economic Review, 15, 177-220.

Globerman, S. and Shapiro, D. (2002): Global Foreign Direct Investment Flows: The Role of Governance Infrastructure, World Development, 30, 1899-1919.

Goldsmith, R. W. (1969): Financial Structure and Development, New Haven, CT: Yale University Press.

Greenwood, J. and Jovanovic, B. (1990): Financial Development, Growth, and the Distribution of Income, Journal of Political Economy, 98, 1076-1107.

Henry, P. B. (2000): Do stock market liberalizations cause investment booms?, Journal of Financial Economics, 58, 301-334.

Hermes, N. and Lensink, R. (2000): Financial system development in transition economies, Journal of Banking and Finance, 24, 507-524.

Jung, W. S. (1986): Financial development and economic growth: International evidence, Economic Development and Cultural Change, 35, 333-346.

Keefer, P. and Shirley, M. M. (2000): Formal versus informal institutions in economic development, pp. 88-107, in C. Menard (Ed.): Institutions, Contracts and Organizations, Chetenham: Edward Elgar.

King, R. G. and Levine, R. (1993a): Finance and Growth: Schumpeter Might be Right, Quarterly Journal of Economics, 108, 717-738.

King, R. G. and Levine, R. (1993b): Finance, Entrepreneurship, and Growth: Theory and Evidence, Journal of Monetary Economics, 32, 513-542.

Lane, P. R. (2001): International trade and economic convergence: the credit channel, Oxford Economic Papers, 53, 221-240.

La Porta, R., Lopez-de-Silanes, F., Shleifer, A. and Vishny, R. W. (1998): Law and Finance, Journal of Political Economy, 106, 1113-1155.

Levine, R. (1998): The Legal Environment, Banks, and Long-Run Economic Growth, Journal of Money, Credit, and Banking, 30, 596-613.

Levine, R. (1997): Financial Development and Economic Growth: Views and Agenda, Journal of Economic Literature, 35, 688-726.

Levine, R., Loayza, N. and Beck, T. (2000): Financial intermediation and growth: Causality and causes, Journal of Monetary Economics, 46, 31-77.

Levine, R. and Renelt, D. (1992): A Sensitivity Analysis of Cross-Country Growth Regressions, American Economic Review, 82, 942-963.

Lucas, R. E., Jr. (1988): On the Mechanics of Economic Development, Journal of Monetary Economics, 22, 3-42.

McCallum, B. T. (1980): Rational Expectations and Macroeconomic Stabilization Policy, Journal of Money, Credit, and Banking, 12, 716-746.

McKinnon, R. I. (1973): Money and Capital in Economic Development, Washington, DC: Brookings Institution.

Meier, G. M. (1989): Leading Issues in Economic Development, Fifth Edition, New York: Oxford University Press.

Muth, J. F. (1961): Rational Expectations and the Theory of Price Movements, Econometrica, 29, 315-335.

Odedokun, M. O. (1996): Alternative econometric approaches for analyzing the role of the financial sector in economic growth: Time-series evidence from LDCs, Journal of Development Economics, 50, 119-146.

Pagano, M. (1993): Financial markets and growth: An overview, European Economic Review, 37, 613-622.

Patrick, H. T. (1966): Financial Development and Economic Growth in Underdeveloped Countries, Economic Development and Cultural Change, 14, 174-189.

Rajan, R. and Zingales, L. (1998): Financial Dependence and Growth, American Economic Review, 88, 559-586.

Rodrik, D. (1999): The New Global Economy and Developing Countries: Making Openness Work, Washington, DC: Overseas Development Council.

Romer, P. (1986): Increasing Returns and Long-Run Growth, Journal of Political Economy, 94, 1002-1037.

Rousseau, P. and Wachtel, P. (1998): Financial Intermediation and Economic Performance: Historical Evidence from Five Industrialized Countries, Journal of Money, Credit, and Banking, 30, 657-678.

Schadler, S., 1994, Surges in Capital Inflows – Boon or Curse?, Finance & Development, March Issue, 20-23.

Scholtens, B. and van Wensveen, D. (2000): A critique on the theory of financial intermediation, Journal of Banking and Finance, 24, 1243-1251.

Schumpeter, J. A. (1911): The Theory of Economic Development, Cambridge, MA: Harvard University Press.

Shan, J. Z. and Morris, A. G. (2002): Does Financial Development 'Lead' Economic Growth?, International Review of Applied Economics, 16, 153-168.

Shan, J. Z., Morris, A. G., and Sun, F. (2001): Financial Development and Economic Growth: An Egg-and-Chicken Problem?, Review of International Economy, 9, 443-454.

Solow, R. M. (2001): Applying Growth Theory Across Countries, The World Bank Economic Review, 15, 283-288.

Stiglitz, J. (2000): Capital Market Liberalization, Economic Growth, and Instability, World Development, 28, 1075-1086.

World Bank (2001): Global Development Finance 2001, Washington DC: World Bank.

CHAPTER 3:

Microcredit and Inverted Banking

3.1 Introduction

The main objective of microcredit schemes is to provide sustainable microfinance with economic development goals. If credit lending institutions can operate profitably and efficiently by targeting lending priorities for the asset-poor in order to elevate the economic status of such borrowers (often to remain above applicable poverty line) and without dependence on any significant financial subsidies, then the microfinance scheme may be deemed to operate as a sustainable microfinance.

In general, microfinance or microcredit is defined as the provision of credit on a small scale to individuals, households and other economic entities that qualify under relevant norms for lending. Microcredit institutions, as a special category of financial intermediaries, have been in operation for several decades in a few countries. Yet, there are very few formulations of formal models of organization that ensure either stability or expandability of these institutions. This is because of relative uniqueness of the institutions that depicted 'success' or 'efficiency' features, and also because of their vulnerability to a wide variety of social, political and economic disturbances. These institutions usually operate on a relatively small volume of lending per borrower but the multitude of borrowers remains large; often they operate on group-based lending and thus economize on transaction costs (TC) through lower costs of information, contract design and enforcement in credit transactions, including loan recovery. They rely on informal and implicit contracts and draw upon local characteristics of 'private ordering' (defined here as the conformity of members of the group to expected norms and the influence of social pressures for deviations from expected performance of members) as the main mechanism of conducting credit and loan recovery activities. These institutions function under the shadow of the domestic laws of local and national relevance but usually do not seek recourse under extensive litigation for loan recovery.

About one-half billion individuals and microeconomic entities have been participating in the micro-credit revolution of recent years. Microfinance or microcredit programs draw attention for a number of important reasons within the context of development finance. In theory and in practice these approaches have assumed prominence during and after the 1980s, especially noting the success of models such as the Grameen Bank of Bangladesh (GBB) (see details in later sections).

Microfinance is often considered a 'bottom-up' approach in the sense that the critical entity is the eligible household that is entitled to credit facilities in order to elevate itself from poverty or raise its standards of living from the existing status. Most often, the individual loan borrowings range from $50 to $1000. Noteworthy schemes in this approach, in addition to GBB are Banco Solidarion (BancSol) of Bolivia, Bank Rakyat Indonesia (BRI), Kredit Desa Indonesia, and Finca in Peru, and others in countries including India, Malawi, and Thailand. Some of the microfinance schemes are not necessarily aimed at reduction of poverty. BancSol and BRI have target clients for lending that are largely non-poor, with an average loan size $1000 with nominal interest rates in the range 30 to 50 percent per annum. Most schemes do not require collateral but BRI does; most are based on group lending but not BRI. In the group lending mechanism, individual borrowers are subject to peer monitoring and loan repayment enforcement. These mechanisms are parts of a larger network called a credit cooperative or credit institution. These groups provide conduits for information and peer pressure for compliance with credit terms, relating to both formal contracts and implicit agreements that promote the objectives of the credit cooperative.

This chapter examines the following issues: the roles of formal and informal sources of development finance for credit operations, credit market imperfections and the roles of the government or other institutions, the role of social collateral in lieu of the traditional banking concept of creditworthiness, important features of model cases of microfinance and group-lending, and a case study of the example of GBB for drawing lessons of experience. Applications of information economics and the economics of TC are very relevant here in the analysis and policy design for microcredit institutions.

The notion of inverted banking comes from credit lending to households, individuals and economic entities based on prospective economic benefit to the borrowers, and this notion does not rely on considerations of initial creditworthiness of the borrowers (which is more of an indicator of the past financial achievement). It is important to recognize that all microfinance or microcredit schemes do not necessarily rely on this inverted banking approach. The inverted banking approaches are usually motivated by the objectives of poverty alleviation and socio-economic development through the productive use of financial resources.

3.2 Social Collateral and Inverted Banking

There have been numerous contributions to the debate on microfinance. Some document varied experiences in different regions and countries (see, for example, Otero and Rhyne, 1994; Ledgerwood, 1998), and some focus on ad hoc analytical issues (several articles in journals fit into this category). However, a common comprehensive and prototype model for micro-credit cannot be suggested as an 'efficient' and workable market model for different socioeconomic and institutional systems. This is because of the complexity of issues and diversity of socioeconomic and institutional settings in which credit models at the grass root level are required for operating efficiently.

The role of peoples' institutions or group-based credit operations in the provision of microcredit seems to have its origins in the 19th century experience of German credit cooperatives. In these cooperatives, members often deposited their own savings with the institution. The credit and interest terms of borrowing members and nonmembers varied to depict advantages of belonging to the cooperative network. About a third of all German rural households belonged to one credit cooperative or another by the beginning of the 20th century. However, some of the cooperatives discouraged the very poor from joining the cooperative network. Based on a review of the experience of the German cooperatives before World War I, Guinnane (2001) noted that among the main explanations for the success and stability of credit cooperatives were their ability to undertake the following tasks:

a) capitalize on access to decentralized but superior information; and

b) enforce sanctions on defaulters at least cost.

Normally, banking activity involves those who hold some assets that already possess market value. The asset-poor do not become eligible for conventional bank loans for lack of any collateral. Inverted banking, as in the case of the GBB, is precisely the feature that targets people with few assets and provides credit facilities for the purpose of raising incomes, thereby upgrading standards of living. Social collateral has been the facility or resource that contributed directly to loan repayment of individual borrowers based on the enforcement capability at the group level. Normally, there are comparative advantages of loan contract design and its enforcement based on the use of social collateral, relative to traditional methods of material assets-based collateralization.

Social collateral generated with group formation and imposition of joint responsibility at the group level may be deemed as an effective substitute for conventional creditworthiness; this collateral offers guarantee for loan repayment and minimization of potential loan defaults. Group monitoring of individual borrowers and enforcement of the terms of the loan contract, especially for loan repayment, provide avenues for effecting cost savings in credit lending and loan recovery operations. Similarly, the costs of loan processing and evaluation are also reduced under this mechanism. For borrowers the TC are reduced because of simplified procedures that often characterize group-based lending; timeliness of loan advances enables better use of such financial resources relative to cumbersome and delayed loan approvals faced traditionally by eligible creditworthy borrowers from formal banking and other financial institutions that operate in credit markets.

Gender and Credit

Credit advanced to women has been often a better mechanism of alleviation of poverty at the household and individual levels. The GBB case and a few other cases in Africa illustrate this phenomenon. The gender aspects of financial credit and financial crises are two different but related issues in the welfare of households and women. The implications of financial crises are more severe for women than for men. Financial market liberalization often improves women's access to credit but this liberalization needs to be devised with mitigating provisions (such as some form of insurance or flexibility in the schedule of loan repayments) to offset adverse consequences of any potential downfall in cash flows or other financial risks. Greater risk exposure with greater access to credit may not always reduce gender gaps in the absence of prudent measures for risk management. For a formal model depicting some of the relevant features, see Floro and Dymski (2000).

With group-based lending, the roles of social collateral and inverted banking are influenced by the roles of innovative and informal sources of finance. The main components of credit markets, their imperfections and relative roles of formal and informal financial institutions in the provision of financial resources are the issues of focus in the following section.

3.3 Credit Markets: Formal and Informal Systems

Credit markets in developed countries are usually dominated by formal credit institutions and corresponding financial intermediaries. In developing countries, the role of informal finance and credit market activities is very significant. Credit markets in developing countries usually consist of both formal and informal sources (such as private moneylenders). The coexistence of formal and informal credit markets suggests both direct and indirect interdependencies of policies affecting one market to the other. In general, market failure features dominate rural credit markets in most countries. This may not automatically justify the direct role of government-controlled credit supply, however (Besley, 1994). The cost of provision of resources and the efficacy of loan recovery, ease of contract enforcement, accountability and performance efficiency are some of the important aspects for consideration in the design of appropriate financial systems.

If we take into account the number of customers rather than the monetary value of credit transactions, the percentage of borrowers from the informal credit sector has been at least as significant as that of the formal banking and non-banking financial institutions in most of the developing countries. The trends during the 1980s and later suggested some declines as the role of the formal sector has been expanding in almost all areas. The main issue here is the interactive effects of formal and informal credit flows and markets.

Credit Market Imperfections

Credit markets are generally both imperfect and inefficient because of problems of asymmetric information (AI) between entities that supply credit and those in demand of credit resources. Besides, contract design specifications are usually incomplete (see chapter 1 for the role of TC in this context) and contract enforcement is usually costly.

Mechanisms that possess the potential to mitigate credit market inefficiencies include the following:

1. optimal loan contract, its design and enforcement;
2. the provision of optimal incentives and disincentives for contractual compliance;
3. monitoring and information processing; and
4. minimization of TC in the processes of credit creation.

In addition to these features, methods such as collateral requirements, flexibility in the choice of loan repayment horizon, and contract renegotiations are also relevant in this context. Trust and credible commitments in loan contract implementation play important roles in repeat transaction settings and form inputs enhancing credit market efficiency.

Since loan contracts tend to be incomplete in terms of linking with various states of nature or economic scenarios, contract renegotiation options in relation to plausible economic contingencies at the borrower level may be included as part of the initial contracts. Ex ante self-selection of loan repayment default penalties may induce borrowers to reveal more information about themselves, contribute to reduction in informational asymmetry, and mitigate problems of moral hazard and adverse selection (if appropriate incentives for compliance with contract terms are offered (for an analytical model, see Zou, 1992). This feature becomes relevant only when cost-effective enforcement of default penalties is feasible.

Borrowers formulate loan portfolios that take into account factors such as access to formal sources of credit, interest rates and relevant TC in the two channels of credit. Loan repayment features include according highest priority for the informal sector. This is generally the result of availability of effective enforcement methods at the lender level. Informal credit markets, although significant, operate with substantial thinness and segmentation, i.e. the lenders and of borrowers are small in numbers, and small adjacent regions possess large variations in interest rates and in the terms of lending. These markets remain sensitive to various interventions in the formal financial institutions and in interest rates.

If the benefits of lower interest rate on institutional loans were not eroded by the incidence of higher TC for obtaining the loans, borrowers would seek institutional finances at applicable maximum limits as their first choice in the portfolio of alternative lenders. Credit rationing by institutional lenders results in spillover demand for the informal credit market. However, the two features stated above are not the only determinants of the demand for credit from private moneylenders. Sometimes any requirement of collateral is waived for the purpose of borrowing. The possibility of quicker or timely access to credit can also influence the loan decisions. The demand for borrowings from the informal market may largely be derived from the residual market, i.e. derived demand. The converse seems to hold good when it comes to repayment of the loans: the borrower tends to accord high priority to repay the loan to private lender and only the residual, if any is offered, is paid to the institutional lender. Then the role of the institutional loan in such situations is to improve the moneylender's expected returns from his loan. Therefore, this configuration leads to the following.

Proposition 3.1

a) The prevalence of institutional credit rationing, especially under-financing in relation to financially justified needs of rural borrowers engaged in productive activities drives borrowers to resort to borrowings from informal credit markets; the former segment of borrowings then act to ensure against high degree of borrower risks, given the preference and prioritization of repayments in favor of the informal lender.

b) Alternatively, the opportunity cost of capital at the margin (beyond the rationed limit of the institutional credit) is captured by the private money lender, and the gain for the borrower in using the informal credit market is simply to sustain productive use of the partial credit offered by the institutional lenders.

The logical policy implication of this phenomenon is that the institutions must meet the credit gap in order to fulfill the credit requirements of the borrower so that the borrowers as well as the credit institutions may share the gains of an improved credit allocation mechanism. Institutional and organizational arrangements that minimize TC at the lender and borrower levels remain key requirements and these constitute important prerequisites for the success and sustainability of credit lending institutions and promote their efficiency.

The conventional economic wisdom often over-simplifies the problems of correcting externalities caused by market failures. The usual remedy tends to center around automatic involvement of government for mitigating the externality effects. The experiences in the erstwhile institutions in highly regulated economies suggest the government control and regulation may not be cost-effective. The role of multiple and competing institution needs to be explored, with catalytic and supervisory activity for the government and other coordinating agencies.

3.4 Rural Credit Markets

The coexistence of formal institutional and informal private credit via moneylenders has been a longstanding feature of the rural economy in many developing countries. The relative shares, however, have been undergoing changes in favor of the former. There has been significant decline of the latter in many developing countries. Until and unless the high TC in the formal sector are brought down and the credit constraints reviewed to meet the realistic requirements of credit in specific activities, there exists continued role for the private moneylenders.

Several studies (see e.g. Ghatak, 1983) argued that as development progresses and average income levels increase, the imperfections of rural credit markets would diminish. It has been argued that a high interest rate is the effect of high-risk premium that the village moneylenders usually charge for lending to the peasants. After the loan transaction, the growth of real income and repayment of the farmers should reduce the probability of default and risk premium. If this holds true, the interest rate (at least in respect of good borrowers) should be lower. This premise remains largely hypothetical, however.

The risk premium in interest rates points to the feature observed elsewhere by Rothschild and Stiglitz (1976): high-risk individuals cause an externality; the low-risk individuals are worse off than they would be in the absence of high-risk individuals. This is an important externality in the context of any proposed group lending (including the widely publicized pattern of the GBB), and the externality has different dimensions for the formal lending sector as well as the informal sector.

When credit lending is largely in the agriculture sector or when the major segment of borrowers are from the agricultural households, factors such as bad weather or low rainfall adversely affecting agricultural incomes could lead to low recovery of loans. There may be no escape for the cooperative credit institutions in the affected area from resorting to additional borrowings from the apex organizations of the financial system. The rationality for the latter to continue lending is largely analogous to the international credit market system: it is a Pareto-optimal solution to provide additional credit (thereby improving loan recovery) rather than to foregoing past loan amounts that may not be recovered otherwise.

Rural Credit Environment

Lack of assets and collateral and lack of access to credit affects most agricultural households in rural regions of the developing world. Even in rare cases where credit may be available, in poor countries, food-deficient households have not been able to bear the risks associated with borrowing on credit. In some of the countries such as Malawi (see Lele, 1992) about 75 percent of small farmers cannot undertake farm operations or use farm production inputs such as fertilizers at optimal levels because of severe credit constraints. Potential borrowers perceive that risks associated with credit borrowing can be minimized when there is an organizational network whereby the borrowers can draw upon proper guidance for resource allocation and marketing of economic output.

Important features of rural credit markets include the following:

1. The formal institutional sources of credit coexist with informal sources of credit controlled by private individuals levying much higher interest rates relative to the former sources;

2. Interest rates are not market clearing; credit rationing exists at any level of interest;

3. Spatial segmentation of sources of credit and volume of transactions as well as the loan sizes contribute to thinly segmented and fragmented credit markets;

4. Cumbersome procedures and loan processing delays are often a common feature in formal lending institutions; these cumbersome procedures and rents created by nominal interest rate subsidies contribute to high transaction costs for the borrowers in the formal institutional set up;

5. Information and enforcement problems pose more serious constraints for the formal institutions relative to the informal ones;

6. The lending norms and methods used by the formal financial institutions are such that the resulting loan amounts for most borrowers fall short in meeting the genuine loan requirements for productive economic activities (such as crops and grain storage); the residual demand for credit then is frequently met by the informal lending institutions; borrowers pay higher interest rates when the marginal productivity of capital is rather high and the formal sources of credit are unable to fulfill the credit requirements.

7. The informal lenders retain senior claim to receive debt repayments even though this source may be the last in the line of lending in relation to a specific set of activities.

Role of Information Economics

A number of studies in recent years emphasized the significance of Information Economics. The "new views" of rural credit markets are summarized by Hoff and Stiglitz (1990), based on the paradigms that emphasize the problems of imperfect information and imperfect enforcement:

1. Screening Problem: Borrowers differ in likelihood that they will default, and it is costly to determine the applicable risk factors;

2. Incentive Problem: It is costly to ensure that borrowers take those actions which make repayment most likely; and

3. Enforcement Problem: It is difficult to compel repayment.

Solving these problems may be necessary but not sufficient for ensuring proper repayment of debts or efficient governance of credit markets. Additional set of requirements would include: a) ensuring the financial viability of the borrowers; and, b) recognition of motivational factors based on borrowers' expectations regarding the future streams of credit borrowings at successive time points after the loan borrowing event. Continued relationship or repeat transactions into the future remains an important motivational factor that would ensure that the borrower does not discount the future too steeply, i.e. not to exclude costs of non-compliance with loan terms or of inefficient utilization of borrowed funds. It is important to examine these features in terms of TC applicable to different economic entities at various levels, and the role of TC as a behavior modifier. Here again, TC minimization remains an overarching policy requirement from a public policy perspective.

The following section examines the issue of the design of rural credit institutions and their desirable characteristics.

3.5 The Design of Rural Credit Institutions

Credit cooperatives are a major socioeconomic institution in many countries, developed as well as developing. The common arguments for promoting cooperatives as instruments of development are under the themes of economic democracy, community participation, economies of scale, and relative efficiency in the resource allocation process and in information processing for decentralized economic decisions. Despite their apparent advantage, credit cooperatives have led to mixed results in different countries. One of the important aspects of rural credit lending is the role of *ex ante* transaction TC, given the diffused nature of customer base and usually low volume of capital per transaction. Consequently, economies of scale are usually unrealizable in such markets.

An argument that favors group-based lending has critically linked the role of groups as entities for effecting reduction of TC. The role of *ex post* TC become significant if the loan repayment and compliance with debt contract terms is influenced by the mode of loan delivery, its monitoring and compliance. Group-based lending tends to reduce these TC as well, because the group as an information acquiring and processing entity reduces TC. Some of these cost reductions are the results of a reduction of informational asymmetries between lenders and borrowers. In addition, the effective implementation of compliance and loan recovery is feasible through a *de facto* decentralization mechanism that operates under the group-based lending system.

In many credit transactions, these costs spill into either lenders or borrowers or both, as long as TC are not minimized in the chain of transactions leading to financial decisions and their effective implementation. Peer monitoring reduces TC, as seen in the GBB and a few other similar cases (explained later in this chapter).

Bhatt and Tang (1998) argued that the limited success of group lending programs in several countries might be attributable to their failure to minimize TC. They distinguished three stages of credit management: pre-loan disbursement, loan approval process, and loan recovery. In relation to each institutional environment, it is desirable to seek TC minimization in each of these stages as well as in their interrelationships of transactions among all stages. Formal analytical models will be useful for deriving greater insights and for their possible use in the design of appropriate systems.

Problems of AI and unobservability (especially the problem of verification as a cost effective mechanism) constitute the foundations of suboptimal performance in group-based activities. Analytical formulations of team behavior and contracting aspects (see McAfee and McMillan, 1991) suggest that the unobservability of team members' efforts is not necessarily the main problem of team inefficiencies. The sources of inefficiency are relative risk seeking/aversion attitudes of members, and their collusion features that may not be observable. However, if costs accumulated by these choices are internalized (as in the case of the GB of Bangladesh) and the costs are common knowledge both for the principal and the agents or the team members, the latter are expected to act 'rationally' as perceived by the principal.

Institutional Credit and TC

Small loans typically involve processing costs in the range of 15 to 40 percent of the loan size (Braverman and Guasch, 1989). These costs vary with institutional infrastructure and methods of processing. The above estimates are not usually inclusive of TC at the borrower level. Most organizations simply ignore the role of these costs, despite the fact that these costs are very significant at the borrower levels and affect loan decisions as well as financial viability of entrepreneurial activities. In addition to the above elements, conventional bank loans may entail private compensation to bank officials, another component of TC for the borrower. The GBB model surmounted these excessive cost barriers by taking loan processors to the potential borrower level directly and eliminating graft for processing loan application. This is among the most innovative aspects of credit administration that has been somehow least emphasized in the literature on microcredit policies and their governance. Due consideration of TC at the borrower level and at the lender level remains an important aspect of any integrated assessment of policy and its effectiveness.

TC have an impact on net profitability and financial sustainability of the credit institution, and on choice of credit channels and quantum of loans (including inclination to participate in the loan application process) for the potential borrower. In general, economic efficiency is enhanced by the process and product of TC minimization (for detailed analysis and applications of TC see Rao, 2003). System-specific analysis enables pragmatic interventions to realize such gains.

Based on a sample survey reported from Gujarat State in India, an estimate of TC applicable to rural borrowers of credit using a typical formal source of finance range from about 3 percent (for miscellaneous types of loans, 6.7 percent) for crop loans, to about 11.3 percent for livestock loans, all averaging to about 4 percent (Shiyani and Bhatt, 1990). If the average needs to be more realistic, one would take it as the lower bound of the TC; it could be higher for many other regions in India that are relatively less developed. Besides, the sample survey makes no mention of bribes that may have to be offered at various stages for obtaining loans. Corrected for this factor, the total TC could well be about an average 8 percent or more. If the interest rates offered by the private moneylender do not exceed the rate offered by the institutional agencies by more than this additional percentage, the former could well be the first choice of the borrower. Usually, the latter rate adds up to about 19 percent (including the adjusted TC), and that of the former exceeds 24 percent. The difference is the margin that seems to attract the borrower to the institutional credit system as his/her first preference in most situations. The above illustration does not arise from a group-based lending activity as in the GBB case, and thus the costs in informal lending do not fully reflect economies in TC.

Group Lending

Experiences in group-based lending in developing countries are varied, although there exist a very few 'success' cases like the GBB. However, issues like joint liability for loan defaults (and hence internalizing potential externalities) prohibit borrower participation in many other regions and countries. Yet, group lending promises the potential to partially offset the problems of the lack of sufficient collateral in the case of poor borrowers for the material collateral requirements. In some societies, precedents like loan waiver schemes in the formal sector send perverse signals on repayment commitments and possible 'soft state' in this regard. This is not to suggest that loan waivers in all cases are improper, however.

Important characteristics and relevant properties for a 'successful group loan contract' (Devereux and Fishe, 1993) are the following:

a) group members are homogeneous with respect to their socio-economic characteristics;

b) some reasonable magnitude of group-specific capital or equity participation is required at the group level;

c) group size is small enough to ensure consistency with the group-specific capital requirements;

d) joint liability for credit recovery is assigned to all or lead members of the group; and

e) security deposit or margin account is maintained to cover any loan defaults.

The Design of Cooperative Institutions

One of the important requirements for sustainable group behavior is the 'exclusiveness property'. In the present context, this may be expressed in terms of the following features. A set of necessary (but not always sufficient) conditions for the "successful" participation in cooperative societies may be stated:

a) those who participate as members of the cooperative society gain (relative to their own standing without the society);

b) non-members in the given area perceive relative deprivation of the gains compared to members.

Let us examine the applicability of these properties for group lending. In general, group borrowers save on fees for registration of collateral, expenses on loan applications and some of the other transaction costs. However, the group organizers could incur uncompensated non-monetary costs. Besides, "the cost of individual members may outweigh the cost of individual borrowing if any members default and others are held liable for their share" (Huppi and Feder, 1990).

Role of Joint Liability

The success of group lending ventures depends, according to Huppi and Feder (1990), on the following:

a) participation by homogeneous borrowing groups that are "jointly liable" and that assume managerial and supervisory responsibilities; and

b) ability of the lending agency to deny access to future credit to "all group members" in case of default by "any member".

However, the above proposals seeking to internalize possible externalities to the broader system are themselves built on uncompensated externality mechanisms. Besides, the above features, which violate the Exclusiveness Property, tend to counter the philosophy of economic democracy – the foundation of cooperative institutions.

It may be convenient from the viewpoint of an external or domestic financial institution to recommend joint liability, but the prescription goes against the norms of economic democracy. If the credit loan recovery is the sole objective or the percentage recovery the success indicator, we may be achieving these at the expense of a major compromise on the foundation principles of cooperatives and liberally spreading externalities within the cooperative units across its members. It is not difficult to visualize such features acting as entry deterrents for group formation or enrollment of members in many of the developing countries.

The above discussion brings us to the point of characterizing the specification of the explicit and implicit liability features in the design of cooperative institutional mechanisms. Joint voluntary liability of the type suggested by Huppi and Feder

(1990) is inconsistent with principles of individualism. Besides, any joint mandatory liability scheme wherein each of the members is not only denied credit because of default by one or more members but also remains liable for others' loans is often an 'entry barrier' for effective group formation and group-based lending.

A Heuristic Model

One of the heuristic models, based on practical experience in some of the developing regions, and on the logical insight works follows (Malhotra and Rao, 1992). Let us use the notation:

$C(t)$ the initial credit limit or creditworthiness of a group,

$R_1(t)$ amount of credit advanced to the group members,

$R_2(t)$ the observed amount of loan recovery against the credit after a unit interval of time (for example one year),

n total group members

m the number of defaulters in the total group members n

At time t, the eligible members for credit borrowings is restricted to $n-m$ (by excluding the defaulters) and the allowable credit limit reduce to $C(t) - D(t)$,

where $D(t) = R_1(t) - R_2(t)$.

This method of variable credit rationing at the group level with a variable size provides incentives for compliance by members with the required financial discipline as their continued eligibility to benefit from the credit facilities of the cooperative system depends on the same, in a dynamic repeat contract system.

Although it may be expected, in the long run, that m reduces to d ($<m$) and that n increases, there exists a problem of threshold size: criticality of the size of n. If m is large (or d is large), the criticality lingers on n as well as $C(t)$. This formulation can be strengthened to reflect the objectives of sustainable microfinance as well as to incorporate relevant structural equations governing the demand for and supply of credit.

Some of the important features of the above model are the following:

a) financial viability of the cooperative institution at the aggregate level is viewed in terms of the financial viability of individual borrowers, thus enabling micro-macro consistency;

b) the approach minimizes negative externalities of joint liability, and thus enable reduction of entry barriers to potential new members; and

c) the model possesses potential for replicability among different economic settings and recognizes the need for financial sustainability of the institution.

An illustrative 'successful' example of a microcredit institution arises from the case study of GBB. This case study is relevant for an understanding of the contributory factors for potential successful functioning of the institution, and for drawing a few lessons of experience for future institutional developments. This is the focus of the next section.

3.6 Model Case: Grameen Bank of Bangladesh

Since its inception in 1976 as an experimental project and later in 1983 as a formal financial institution, about 2.5 million borrowers from over 37,000 villages took loans from the GBB, with an average loan of about $60 (about a fifth of annual per capita income). This rural credit lending institution provides credit and organizational umbrella of infrastructural assistance to the rural poor who generally lack access to credit from the conventional credit systems since they lack asset collateral. Despite the lack of such collateral, loan defaults are negligible; further, there are no direct subsidies for the programs of the Bank. GBB believes in 'inverted banking' – poverty and lack of asset collateral is usually the main criterion relevant for an eligible borrower. The success of the Bank inspired several countries around the world to launch similar credit institutions for the small borrowers and for helping reduction of poverty in various forms.

The GBB devised its methods of handling problems of AI and enforcement of loan repayments. It offers group-based lending to individual borrowers so that their access to credit is linked to group's repayment conduct, and peer monitoring as well as peer pressures ensures compliance with stipulated utilization of loan funds as well their repayment.

There are special components of the bank funds that both motivate borrowers to repay and facilitate financial stability to the lending entity. Borrowers are required to make savings regularly and contribute to designated accounts. About five percent of the loaned amount of each borrower has to be contributed to the 'group fund' and 25 percent of total interest due on loan is deposited in an 'emergency fund'. Savings mobilization is considered an integral part of lending at the GBB. Several studies, particularly Khandker et al (1995), documented important aspects of the Bank operations.

The main objective of GBB has been alleviation of rural poverty with the provision of microfinance for entrepreneurial activities. Credit-based poverty alleviation has been its focus, with women constituting about 95 percent of borrowers. The repayment rate ranges in the interval 92 to 98 percent, among the highest of any lending institution. This contrasts with many developing countries that lack the focus for developing women and thereby alleviating poverty. It also contrasts with various government schemes that provide institutional credit through costly financial intermediaries, leading to inequitable access to asset-rich populations and not addressing the poverty reduction with proper provision of credit for directly productive activities.

Regarding some of the special features that contributed to economic efficiency in the GBB case it is useful to recognize that unlike many other rural scenarios of developing countries, the rural density of population is very high and this enables a good degree of economies of scale in the loan transactions (even though the size of a typical loan is small). Besides, the relative ease in the skilled labor market with plenty of graduate young population facilitates access to low cost skilled staff for performing different activities of the GBB.

In terms of operational features and financial results of the GBB, the following points are noteworthy. Most loan terms are for a year and carry an interest rate of about 20 percent. The membership went up 1200 percent from 1985 to 1996, and the loan portfolio rose from $10 million to $271 million in the same period. A small element of subsidy arose from the donors' lending terms offered to the GBB, and this subsidy may be of the order of ten percent, according to some estimates (Morduch, 1999). Net profitability could be a small loss of the order of $34 million for the period of 1985 to 1996 if the bank had to rely only on income from lending operations and returns from investment. Despite some of these downward revisions in the assessment of financial performance, the fact remains that the GBB made financial and economic contributions to the poorer sections of the society and thus remains a very important model institution for the efficient provision of microcredit and of development finance.

A few other case studies also seem to converge on some of the main characteristics that describe the GBB. Based on survey data and analysis for the western region of Guatemala, Wydick (2001) observed the following:

a) Peer monitoring and access to affordable credit sources enable timely repayment of loans;

b) After their selection, substantial screening of borrowers occurs in the form of expulsions from applicable groups;

c) In very poor areas, the moral hazard problems are better characterized by borrower diversion of loans from investment activities in favor of consumption; and

d) Intra-group insurance mechanisms or risk aggregation (largely informal) for loan repayment are important.

Most of these observations seem relevant for group-based credit institutions in several of the developing countries. The design of effective rural credit institutions and sustainable microfinance schemes continues to be an area of incessant interest in developing countries.

3.7 Concluding Observations

Traditional economic models focus mainly on the role of AI, and consequent problems of moral hazard and adverse selection. These have used simplistic assumptions such as the following: a) negligible TC; b) insensitivity to dire needs of consumption in poorer systems; and c) the role of time discounting as perceived by the borrowers in the loan market.

Comprehensive models reflecting these features need to be developed for analytical and policy purposes. These improved models and corresponding analyses are expected to be useful in examining the implications of recognizing the above features on the design of credit policies as well as microcredit institutions.

Among the common prerequisites for an efficient functioning of the financial system at national and local levels are: well-defined property rights regimes and their effective enforcement; effective corporate/financial governance and prudential management; efficient financial intermediaries that provide services at least total cost (including various TC), and public disclosures of policies and operations. In the microcredit institutions case, provision of services at the least total cost remains the key for success and sustainability.

In most of the developing countries, the traditional financial intermediaries have been the main channels of supply of credit. Institutional finances, controlled by the government or its entities, included an element of subsidy for the poor. However, these resources have not reached the eligible and target groups to a significant extent; instead, these facilities have largely benefited the rich and powerful. In this context, launching of a series of self-sustaining microfinance institutions such as the GBB remains a viable alternative for the provision of development finance and for achieving the objectives of economic development.

The successful models of rural lending are very few and do not seem to be replicable in a variety of socioeconomic and financial systems. Thin and segmented credit 'markets' in rural areas suggest the role of institutional factors beyond market characteristics that affect efficient provision of rural credit.

Credit lending institutions have an improved likelihood of self-sustenance if they also mobilize members' savings and if members hold a stake in the equity, in the sense of careful scrutiny of internal governance and not a distant or remote control sense with mere holding of less than first seniority claims to assets. Governments need to play a catalytic role in promoting policies and institutions that enable provision of sustainable microfinance. This would constitute a major source for poverty eradication and efficient provision of development finance.

Both credit lending and loan recovery mechanisms are founded on the structures of explicit and implicit contracts. Both entail varying TC. The critical issue is to devise policies and programs that minimize TC as well as maximize social welfare affected by the choice of institutions and policies. In this context, the incentives for loan repayment and compliance with terms of contract need to be specified in conjunction with the provision of disincentives for repayment defaults and for non-compliance with terms of contract or other forms of agreement in credit transactions.

Review Exercises

1. If the private moneylender is in a position to extract the first claim from the income generated by the borrower's activities (as is often the case), is it correct to conclude that any preexisting or concurrent institutional credit tends to enhance the expected returns from loan portfolios of the moneylender?

2. If voluntary and involuntary choices of loan repayment need to be distinguished in relation to the role of economic shocks to borrower's economic entities, what arguments support the joint liability provisions of group lending in the GBB model?

3. Explain the role of TC in the loan recovery system as it pertains to formal financial institutions and provide the TC rationale for group-based lending.

4. If there is an inverse ranking of borrowing and repayment hierarchies in the credit markets of the formal and informal sectors, what factors can bring about a closer similarity between the two sources of credit supply?

5. What are the main characteristics of a 'successful' group-based microcredit scheme? Interpret these in terms of the approaches of the economics of TC.

References

Besley, T. (1994): How do market failures justify interventions in rural credit markets?, World Bank Research Observer, 9, 27-48.

Bhatt, N. and Tang, S. (1998): The problem of transaction costs in group-based microlending: An institutional perspective, World Development, 26, 623-637.

Braverman, A. and Guasch, J. L. (1989): Institutional Analysis of Credit Cooperatives, in P. Bardhan (Ed), The Economic Theory of Agrarian Institutions, Oxford: Oxford University Press.

Devereux, J. and Fishe, R. P. H. (1993): An Economic Analysis of Group Lending Programs in Developing Countries, The Developing Economies, 30, 102-121.

Floro, M. and G. Dymski (2000): Financial crisis, Gender, and Power: An Analytical Framework, World Development, 28, 1269-1283.

Ghatak, S. (1983): On Interregional Variations in Rural Interest Rates, Journal of Developing Areas, 18, 21-34.

Guinnane, T. W. (2001): Cooperatives as Information Machines: German Rural Credit Cooperatives 1883-1914, Journal of Economic History, 61, 366-389.

Hoff, K. and Stiglitz, J. (1990): Imperfect Information and Rural Credit Markets- Puzzles and Policy Perspectives, The World Bank Economic Review, 4, 235-250.

Huppi, M. and Feder, G. (1990): The Role of Groups and Credit Cooperatives in Rural Lending, The World Bank Research Observer, 5, 187-204.

Khandker, S., Khalily, B. and Khan, Z. (1995): Grameen Bank: Performance and Sustainability, Washington, DC: World Bank Discussion Paper #306.

Ledgerwood, J. (1998): Microfinance Handbook: An Institutional and Financial Perspective, Washington, DC: World Bank Publications.

Lele, U. (1990): Structural Adjustment, Agricultural Development and the Poor – Some Lessons from the Malawian Experience, World Development, 18, 1207-1219.

Malhotra, V. and P. K. Rao (1992): The Design of Rural Credit Institutions, Unpublished manuscript, Center for Development Research, New Jersey.

McAfee, R. P. and McMillan, J. (1991): Optimal Contracts for Teams, International Economic Review, 32, 561-577.

Morduch, J. (1999): The Microfinance Promise, Journal of Economic Literature, 37, 1569-1614.

Otero, M. and Rhyne, E. (Eds.), (1994): The New World of Microenterprise Finance, West Hartford: Kumarian Press.

Rao, P. K. (2003): The Economics of Transaction Costs: Theory, Methods and Applications, London: Palgrave-Macmillan.

Rothschild, M. and Stiglitz, J. (1976): Equilibrium in Competitive Insurance Markets – An Essay in the Economics of Imperfect Information, Quarterly Journal of Economics, 90, 629-650.

Shiyani, R. and Bhatt, B. (1990): Cost of Farm Credit – A Case Study of Commercial Bank in Junagadh District of Gujarat State, Indian Cooperative Review, 28, 1-10.

Wydick, B. (2001): Group Lending under Dynamic Incentives as a Borrower Discipline Device, Review of Development Economics, 5, 406-420.

Zou, L. (1992): Threat-based Incentive Mechanisms under Moral Hazard and Adverse Selection, Journal of Comparative Economics, 16, 47-74.

CHAPTER 4:

Global Financial Architecture

4.1 Introduction

Resource flows, design and implementation of development policies, and the governance of the economy and institutions in the developing countries are significantly influenced by the operations and mechanisms of policy coordination at national and international levels. The previous chapters have examined, among other issues, the role of information, transaction costs and institutions in influencing financial development and economic growth of developing countries. Since global financial policies and institutions hold potential for significantly affecting the provision of resources for development finance, and thus for financial and economic development, it is important that we examine these policies and institutions. Also of interest in this chapter are the implications of currently popular economic paradigms. A brief background on the working features and an evaluation of the international financial architecture is provided below. The next two chapters are founded partly on the analysis given below.

Global financial organizations provide (at varying levels of efficiency) financial guidance and regulation that affect most countries, and more specifically the developing countries. Their coordinating roles in minimizing financial risks at national and international levels, to promoting financial and economic integration among countries, and their policies affecting financial resources for development, are of interest in this chapter. Among the key components of international financial architecture are crisis prevention and crisis management in economies and financial institutions, reform of institutions with the objectives of fostering economic development and providing financial resources and services at minimum cost, and reform of multilateral financial institutions. These issues remain the concern of this chapter; the theme related to debt crisis management is explored in chapter 6.

Financial governance is a prerequisite for the provision of financial resources for economic development. Risk management is an important aspect of this process of governance. Some of the elements and tools of risk management have been briefly presented in chapter 1. Yet there is an aspect of risk management that deserves attention for international coordination. Section 4.2 below examines the international norms for capital management in the banking sector along with methods of minimizing financial risks associated with some of the problems of capital illiquidity of the banking sector. Also summarized are criteria for the assessment of financial soundness of systems and implications for credit ratings. The phenomena of globalization, which includes financial and economic liberalization, have both merits and limitations in fulfilling economic development aspirations of developing countries. These aspects are discussed in section 4.3 below. Later sections deal with a recent major international agreement, the Monterrey Consensus (constituting a new international 'soft law'), a critical assessment and reform proposals for the international financial architecture.

4.2 Capital Adequacy and Financial Soundness

Developing countries lost over a trillion dollars as a result of banking crises in the 1980s and 1990s; this approximates to the quantity of total Official Development Assistance (ODA) from 1950 to 2001, according to the World Bank Annual Report 2002. Thus, there is a significant need for improved quality of financial institutions at national and international levels for sustained financial stability and economic development. This requires greater national and international coordination efforts and the use of financial norms for efficient management.

Global coordination of some of the standards for financial governance is required in managing financial risks and other economic shocks arising from sources both within a domestic economy and from global interdependencies. The role of a few important organizations is relevant here. These organizations are the Bank of International Settlements (BIS), the Financial Stability Forum (FSF), the International Monetary Fund (IMF), and the World Bank. BIS, the oldest international financial organization, with the active participation of more than fifty national central banks or monetary authorities, commenced its functions in 1930. This organization facilitates supervision and coordination of banking and interbank transactions. The most recent ad hoc organization is the FSF, launched in 1999 at the initiative of industrially advanced G-7 countries with the objective of promoting international financial stability and improving the functioning of financial markets. The IMF and the World Bank are the main Bretton Woods Agreement institutions launched soon after the end of World War II and these have been assigned roles to facilitate international economic and financial development functions. This section outlines some of the important recent guidelines provided by these organizations.

Financial Soundness Indicators (FSI)

FSI include both aggregated information on financial institutions and the markets in which these institutions operate. Macro-financial analysis relies on FSI and assessment of other macroeconomic institutional and economic information. The IMF has been making progress on devising a "Compilation Guide on Financial

Soundness Indicators" for their adoption in the near future. In this context, Sundararajan et al (2002) suggested a 'core set' of indicators for the banking sector, and a supplementary 'encouraged set' of indicators that extend to all other related sectors of the economy. The authors stated that an adoption of this approach of two-tiered information tides over the much criticized 'one-size-fits-all' approach often used in the IMF transactions with developing countries. The desired flexibility in the assessment of overall FSI for each country is useful, although a single index for a simplified decision making based on weights for different components of the FSI system may not emerge.

The 'core set' of indicators include assessments of the following for the banking institutions:

- capital adequacy (regulatory capital and risk-weighted assets),
- asset quality (including nonperforming loans, and net loan provisions), earnings and profitability,
- liquidity and sensitivity to market risk (duration of assets and liabilities and foreign exchange exposures).

Besides, the 'encouraged set' includes, *inter alia*, the following:

- relative distribution of loans across regions,
- foreign currency-denominated loans and liability relative to their respective totals,
- average ask-bid spread in the securities market,
- total corporate debt and equity, returns on equity,
- household debt as a percentage of the annual GDP, real estate prices and loans (residential and commercial), and related information.

Credit Ratings and Financial Management

The role of credit rating agencies is critical in the attempts to reform bank policies. The relationship between sovereign credit ratings and debt repayment risks are not well established in emerging market economies. More significantly, the ratings could be procyclical as they move in the same direction as the volatility of short-term features affecting debt repayment constraints, rather than based on longer horizon economic fundamentals. This process can often worsen the plight of a distressed economic or financial entity, and even facilitate transformation of a short-term crisis into a longer term financial disaster. Can lowering of ratings constitute self-fulfilling prophesies for relatively weak economies? It is hypothesized here that the answer is in the affirmative. This is both an analytical and empirical question, and has not been fully addressed in relevant literature so far.

On the issue of capital reserve and capital adequacy requirements, it is desirable that capital requirements should be countercyclical (Monfort and Mulder, 2000): during a normal downturn in the economic business cycle, country capital should be available for meeting other productive purposes beyond insuring against potential insolvency. Monfort and Mulder (2000) also noted that it is meaningful for the credit agencies to focus on expected losses (recovery rate) rather than on the probability of debt default. Thus, their ratings may not be very appropriate for use in assessing capital requirements.

Definition of Credit Ratings

Let us briefly review definitions of credit rating offered by two important organizations that provide credit ratings affecting capital movements and cost of capital borrowings.

Standard & Poor (1997) defines sovereign credit ratings as, "an assessment of each government's capacity and willingness to repay debt according to its terms." Often, it is the measure of 'willingness' to repay (in accordance with presumably inflexible original schedule of payments) that remains highly subjective.

Moody's (1995) defines this as a, "measure of the ability and willingness of the country's central bank to make available foreign currency to service debt, including that of the central government itself" and asserts that the objective of sovereign risk assessment is to examine the issue of "what is the likelihood of an international default".

Here again, a quantified assessment of 'likelihood' of default is usually based on questionable presumptions about the borrower. Even though the output of credit rating analysis is quantified either in terms of credit rating grades (A+, B- etc) or in terms of scores, the input that goes into these analyses is largely subjective and fuzzy (more precisely, unquantified fuzziness rather than using meaningful applications of Fuzzy Mathematics – now a developed branch of mathematics). This deficiency portends major problems in light of new guidelines offered by the international coordinating and supervising agency BIS for expanded use of credit ratings for banks and related financial institutions (details given below) in the context of capital adequacy guidelines. Accordingly, there are analytical gaps and policy gaps that need to be addressed in order to ensure greater objectivity and predictability of credit ratings in relation to financial stability of the specific economic entities. Most importantly, the excessive role of compliance with debt repayment in accordance with a rigid (and possibly inefficiently drawn repayment) schedule in determining the health of an economy needs to be curtailed; other fundamentals of the economy and institutions need to be objectively assessed and incorporated into the ratings analysis. Chapter 9 reflects on these issues in greater details.

Capital Adequacy Guidelines

The Basel Accord of July 1988 under the aegis of the BIS has been adopted by more than 100 countries. This agreement sets a minimum target for bank equity capital of 8 percent of the bank's risk-weighted assets. The Credit Risk Charge (CRC) is thus given by:

$$CRC\ =\ 8\%\ *\ (risk\text{-}weighted\ assets)$$

Among the criticisms of this norm included the following:

a) inadequate differentiation of credit risks (there are only four categories);

b) lack of recognition of market risks assumed by the banks, as well as of risk mitigation methods such as collateralization or other securitizations; and

c) failure to recognize the risks of short-term capital flows.

The 1988 Basel Accord was amended in 1996 to include market risk charge (MRC), by adding a capital charge based on either of the following two approaches:

a) trading book: the bank portfolio containing financial instruments that are intentionally held for short-term resale;

b) banking book: loans and other instruments.

$$The\ new\ total\ risk\ charge\ =\ CRC\ +\ MRC$$

Rather than adopting strict uniform norms, banks have been allowed to deploy their own objective-tailored models in their assessment of the capital requirements. This posed its own problems in financial reporting and management of risks. Lucas (2001) observed that Banks have been prone to underreporting their true market risks (i.e., the existence of the moral hazard problem) under the 1996 Basel Amendment. Here the market risk has been quantified by the use of the Value at Risk (VAR) method (see also chapter 1): assessment of the maximum loss that can occur during a certain time-period for a specified confidence level (expressed in statistical terms).

New guidelines, devised by the BIS in 1999, improve the risk classifications and their weights, and greater differentiation of risks in the lenders' portfolio, using five categories of risk weights, based on credit ratings. The use of credit ratings by third parties remains a contentious issue for the borrower countries, however. Details of the New Basel Accord are given in Box 4.1.

The new proposals are based on three 'pillars':

- minimum regulatory requirements (CRC, based on credit ratings);

- supervisory review (using internal capital assessment processes);
- market discipline (including scope for shareholder scrutiny and transparency).

While international coordination and development of norms for financial institutions remain relevant for reducing financial risks and enhancing financial stability, a basic approach to the role of markets and other institutions in the promotion of financial and economic development remains an important aspect of global financial architecture. The current popular economic paradigm favors market-based financial resource flows and global financial integration. The following section examines the role and limitations of globalization, which includes financial liberalization at country levels.

Box 4.1: New Basel Capital Accord

> The Basel Committee in 1999 drafted a new framework suggesting amendments to the 1988 Accord. The implementation of the new Capital Accord is to begin from 2004. The Committee proposed to incorporate differential risks of bank assets and the role of external credit rating agency valuations are proposed to be taken into account, in addition to bank's own internal risk assessment. This has implications for the quality of output from credit rating agencies and formation of governing guidelines as well as incentives for accurate reporting for these agencies as well as banks. The new Accord in its main structure is founded on three 'pillars':
>
> 1. Minimum capital requirement – This requires that the risk-weighted minimum capital requirement is 8 percent. The risks considered are: credit risk (the risk of financial losses arising from defaulters), market risk (the risk of losses in trading when market prices change adversely), and operational risk (direct and indirect losses resulting from inadequate internal processes, governance, and external environment). In order to ensure that risks within the entire banking system are considered, the new Accord extends its assessments to holding companies of banks as well.
>
> 2. Supervisory review process – The new framework requires the banks to develop an internal capital assessment process and set targets for capital that are consistent with the bank's risk profile and regulatory provisions. Greater supervisory responsibilities are expected in this framework.
>
> 3. Market discipline – Effective and enhanced disclosure of financial governance information is expected to enhance market discipline of banking institutions. The new Accord sets forth a core set of disclosure recommendations and methodologies for assessing credit risk, its mitigation and asset securitization.

4.3 Financial Liberalization and Globalization

Although not a popular paradigm in the 1970s, the role of financial globalization in promoting investments and growth of economic output was emphasized in a few studies (see, for example, McKinnon, 1973; Shaw, 1973). However, over time a number of limitations have also been recognized, largely based on practical experiences in various countries during the 1980s and later. When the liberalization process leads to excessive capital borrowings and when external debt is denominated in foreign currencies, a country's exposure to exchange rate risks and costs of debt repayment increases significantly. The latter problems tend to defeat the primary objectives of liberalization process itself. However, this does not imply that financial repression is an alternative policy that is worth utilizing.

The Washington Consensus

The so-called Washington Consensus constituted the basis for many of the controversial globalization principles. This 'consensus' was packaged based on a list of measures for addressing solvency problems of developing countries and thus crept into the loan mechanisms and their conditionalities at the international lending institutions, especially the IMF and the World Bank. The list of measures was primarily advocated in 1989 by John Williams and became the basis for 'structural adjustment' programs of the multilateral lending institutions. In its initial form, the list comprised of the measures:

- Fiscal discipline (including pruning public expenditure)
- Financial deregulation and enhancement of the role of the private sector
- Tax reform including broadening tax base and reducing marginal tax rates
- Trade liberalization
- Reduction of quotas and tariffs unilaterally at the country level
- Liberalizing foreign direct investment
- Privatization and deregulation
- Provision of secure property rights regime
- Elimination of Foreign Exchange rate controls
- Reprioritizing public expenditure priorities

Later, Williamson (2000, p. 258) admitted that his 1989 formulation (see Williamson, 1990) of the so-called Washington Consensus was "flawed in that it neglected financial supervision, without which financial liberalization seems all too likely to lead to improper lending and eventually to a crisis that requires the taxpayers to pick up the losses from making bad loans." Williamson (2000, p.262) suggested that it would be desirable to advance beyond the prescriptions of the Washington Consensus by emphasizing "the importance of the institutional dimension as well as of the sort of policies....that will promote an equitable distribution of income as well as a rapid growth of income."

On the institutional aspect, there is an urgent need for according greater attention to financial supervisory institutions at national and international levels, and for the provision of financial and other complementary resources to promote financial and economic development in developing regions of all countries. The prescription on equitable income distribution goes counter to the full scale market orientation of financial and economic reforms and does not seem to have found favor in capital-rich nations so far. Nonetheless, a modest beginning has been made recently under the Monterrey Consensus; see section 4.4 for a summary of this agreement.

Financial Liberalization and Growth

In theory, financial liberalization can influence economic growth through the following channels:

a) development of the domestic financial sector, if due attention is paid to sustain small and infant financial industry entities;

b) enhanced access of domestic financial and non-financial firms to foreign funds;

c) improvements in the efficiency of capital allocation toward higher productivity; and

d) promotion of institutions for financial governance, possibly through reduction of transaction costs and market development.

Is there a financial liberalization index? Bandiera et al (2000) constructed an index using the following variables: interest rate regulation, capital reserve requirements, directed credit/credit allocation, bank ownership (and state control), prudential regulation, liberalization of security markets, pro competition measures, and openness of the capital account of the country. This study relies on the usage of dummy variables (or binary choices of 0 or 1) to describe the state of each variable and thus falls short in its capture of the full extent of the degree of financial liberalization. Because of these shortcomings, the quality and magnitude of changes that affect the process of financial liberalization are unlikely to remain fully incorporated in their index. Thus, there is a need for developing more realistic indicators for assessing the extensity and intensity of financial liberalization processes.

These limitations aside, the empirical assessment of the study by Bandiera et al, based on a time-series analysis for the period 1970-94 for the countries Chile,

Ghana, Indonesia, Korea, Malaysia, Mexico, Turkey, and Zimbabwe (all these countries have undergone significant but different financial reforms during the period of study) led to the following highlights. Financial liberalization may not lead to increased savings in many cases; there is no evidence of a positive effect of real interest rates on savings. The study also observed that official data on savings could be underestimated since cross-border trade and capital flight are not reflected properly in these statistics in some of the countries. Real estate property booms have been noted in many countries following financial liberalization and diversion of savings into such investments has also been a common practice, thus net realizations might not be accounted for. Such effects belong in the category of transitional rather than permanent effects. The issue then is what makes such booms sustainable, or at the least retain their real net worth of wealth.

Banking Crises and Other Risks of Financial Liberalization

In the absence of efficient regulatory mechanisms to ensure compliance with sound financial management principles, financial liberalization leads to risky lending by banking institutions and this is often followed by banking and financial crises. The most important reason that financial liberalization may not bear a positive impact on economic growth in the short and medium term is that the route to liberalization is often achieved through a dose of enhanced instability. Government policy should aim at the stabilization of capital flows (Stiglitz, 1999, p.1512), "for it is the instability of such flows which generates the high costs and limits their benefits." These required intervention measures include the following: broad and effective bank regulation, risk-adjusted capital adequacy norms, transparency and accountability of financial transactions, and corporate governance. A report of the US Congress argued on the role of the IMF in its promotion of financial liberalization. It has been observed that the IMF advocacy of capital account liberalization even before adequate institutional reforms were in place tended to exacerbate the already existing serious moral hazard issues (US Congress Joint Economic Committee Study, 2001).

Regarding the effects of financial liberalization on banking crises, Kaminsky and Reinhart (1999) offered empirical evidence that banking crises are often preceded by financial liberalization. They examined 76 currency crises and 26 banking crises during the 1970s to mid 90s. Their study included:

a) industrial countries: Denmark, Finland, Norway, Spain, and Sweden

b) developing countries: Argentina, Bolivia, Brazil, Chile, Colombia, Indonesia, Israel, Malaysia, Mexico, Peru, the Philippines, Thailand, Turkey, Uruguay, and Venezuela

They found that banking and currency crises are closely linked in the aftermath of financial liberalization, and that banking crises often precede currency collapse.

The results of globalization are seen as a mixed bag. Promoting market institutions and financial/economic efficiency is a very desirable approach. However, proper attention is required to establish institutional infrastructure (including financial supervision) and to those needs of economic development that cannot possibly be addressed by marketized institutions. On the issues of direct provision of financial resources for poverty reduction and economic development in developing countries, a recent international agreement as a new policy component of global financial architecture suggests a few directions. The details are given in the following section.

4.5 International Financial Institutions

This section is primarily concerned with the role of multilateral financial institutions rather than transnational commercial banks or similar institutions. The level efficacy of capital markets and credit markets is not merely the responsibility of capital providers but also that of the recipients. We consider first the role of borrower states, joint responsibilities of lenders and borrowers, and later we focus on the multilateral financial institutions and on reforms for improving the global financial architecture.

Should the borrower country utilize only state entities and the public sector for external borrowings? Often the issues of legal responsibility for debt repayments and financial accountability suggest an automatic role for the state in these transactions. Cost-effectiveness of this channel (including the role of TC and efficient financial governance) has not been fully examined for any specific public system in published documents. Besides, the magnitudes of economic externalities of public monopolies affecting market inefficiency also deserve to be assessed. In general, the role of financial liberalization is such that it mitigates some of these costs and ameliorates externalities, provided there are proper regulations that are effectively enforced. When the private sector is allowed to borrow credit from abroad it may be private-to-private sector transaction. This does not imply there are no negative externalities in this process. Any contractual noncompliance could bring down credit rating based on country risk assessment and entail costs to future borrowers of the private sector. Often, the government enters a guarantee for private sector loans from abroad, and this entails a separate set of additional costs. The role of private capital flight is another significant problem where the government's regulatory control and supervision of policy effects is relevant.

An important aspect of infrastructural improvements for international finance and financial governance is that of quality of data, deliberated below.

External Finance and Data Improvements

There a number of avenues for strengthening data base and transparency of external financial balances of various countries. The Special Data Dissemination Standards (SDDS) devised by the IMF as a format for comprehensive and timely disclosure of economic and financial data, including on countries' reserve positions may enhance an element of transparency of national financial information. The IMF and its member countries are expected to intensify their efforts to strengthen the SDDS, including by improving the contents of national data on the Internet. Box 4.2 summarizes a set of elements of external finance related data systems that deserve further attention at the country levels.

Box 4.2: Data on External Financial Positions

> Key initiatives to improve data dissemination include steps to enhance the SDDS, and the work of the Inter-Agency Task Force on Finance Statistics (TFFS) on a new guide for external debt statistics.
>
> Regarding measures to improve database and information flows, the FSF Working Group on Capital Flows in its report of 2000 (see details at wwww.fsforum.org) identified a few steps; some of the important ones are summarized below.
>
> *A. National data on international investment position and external debt*
>
> Important gaps remain in national external debt statistics, especially regarding the assessment of liquidity risk: data by residual maturity rather than original maturity; by face value as well as market value; with a distinction by currency as well as residency; information on embedded put options in bond contracts; and amortization schedules (including interest payments).
>
> It has been reported that in order to improve the dissemination of debt data more generally, the TFFS is working on a comprehensive guide for compilers and users of external debt statistics (a replacement for the 1988 "Grey Book"). This new guide intends to set internationally agreed definitions and standards for the compilation of debt statistics.
>
> *B. Creditor and market data on external debt*
>
> In March 1999, four international agencies (the BIS, IMF, OECD, and the World Bank) introduced a new series of quarterly statistics on external debt for 176 developing and transition countries, the Joint BIS-IMF-OECD-World Bank Statistics on External Debt (Joint Debt Statistics). These statistics provide information on components of external debt currently compiled and published separately by the contributing institutions. The data are mostly from creditor sources (e.g., the BIS International Banking Statistics), supplemented by data from market sources (e.g., the BIS International Securities Statistics and the OECD data on nonbank trade credits), and by data from debtor and debt market sources (data on Brady bonds).
>
> The FSF Working Group Report states that this compilation constitutes an essentially creditor-side data, and these do not provide a 'fully comprehensive

and consistent measure of external debt for each country', although these bring together 'the best international comparative data currently available.'

C. Reconciliation between debtor and creditor data

Substantial discrepancies between the creditor-based BIS International Banking Statistics and debtor-based sources need to be reconciled for some countries. The international organizations that utilize and/or publish data need to minimize errors in their publications.

D. Additional Data requirements

National policy makers should give high priority to improving external debt statistics. The measures need to address minimizing current gaps in financial data by residual maturity rather than original maturity; by face value as well as market value; with a distinction by currency as well as residency; and amortization schedules, including interest payments.

Source: Report of the FSF Working Group on Capital Flows, 2000; details at www.fsforum.org

Legitimacy of Sovereign Debts

Whether all debts incurred by borrower countries remain legitimate and whether all such debts are repayable is an important issue. A brief summary of various dimensions of this controversial question is given in Box 4.3. Logical and legal implications of illegitimate debts might include the need for debt waivers in some of the cases. The legal and economic issues and development impact of such waivers requires further study. Some of the major financial institutions participated on a rather systematic basis and with knowledge of large scale siphoning off external financial resources by the ruling elite in some countries. This process raises the need for reform in the governance of these institutions.

Box 4.3: Are All External Debts Legitimate?

Ethically and legally it is necessary to differentiate, to distinguish debt that are genuinely incurred for the borrower countries and debts that are obtained to be substantially misused by the functionaries of the sovereign governments. If we distinguish private citizens and their governments as two separate decision making entities with rather widely varying objectives, many of the insolvent poor countries have been headed by rich rulers who are far from insolvent, at least after they assumed political power. The official data on country balance-of-payments are often flawed in less developed countries; the data are based on significant misinvoicing of exports and imports to evade customs duties and other taxes as well to effect illicit transfer into desired foreign currencies.

Boyce and Ndikumana (2001) estimated capital flight for 25 sub-Saharan African countries, classified by the World Bank as 'severely indebted low-income countries'. Their estimates indicated that the total external debts of the 25 countries stood at $178 billion in 1996, and their cumulative capital flight amounted to about $193 billion or more, thus suggesting that the region has been a net creditor. The authors argued that there exists a 'disjuncture between public external debts and private external assets.' They called for accountability at all levels and debt transactions, including the implicit participation of multilateral lending institutions in allowing some of the ill-managed economies to incur debt on public account when they are not *'bona fide'* debts; repayment burden should not be inflicted upon the impoverished populations when did not enjoy any benefits of such external debts.

Fraudulent loans are not repayable in many countries. In the case of sovereign debts, Kremer and Jayachandran (2002) argued that the legal doctrine of odious debt suggests that sovereign debt incurred without the consent of the people and not benefiting the people is odious; it is not fair to transfer this burden onto the non-beneficiaries if creditors possessed advance knowledge of the fund diversion mechanisms. They also suggested that odious debt contract should be made legally unenforceable.

The IMF

The recent crises in developing and developed countries have demonstrated that international financial globalization has not been matched by commensurate institutional framework to regulate it or be governed by efficient norms of corporate and financial/economic governance. The international financial architecture has exhibited substantial fragility during the past few decades. Major financial crises erupted while the major institutions were 'on the job' of advising and rescuing troubled economies. One of the relevant guiding principles has been suggested by Stiglitz (1999, p.1508): "We should keep in mind that the success of a development or stabilization must be assessed by its impact on the livelihood of the concerned individuals, not by whether the exchange rate has stabilized!" It is important that international financial institutions, in general, and the IMF, in particular, are sensitized to economic development implications of their activities.

It is useful to recall Article Five of IMF Articles of Agreement in stating its Purposes of formation, which reads: "To give confidence to members by making the general resources of the fund temporarily available to them under adequate safeguards, thus providing them with opportunities to correct maladjustments in their balance of payments without resorting to measures destructive of national or international prosperity." This forms the foundation of the lending function of the IMF. However, the role and effectiveness of the IMF in addressing these objectives, and thus in facilitating its contribution to development remains questionable, as documented in several expert reports; some of these are summarized later in this section.

The IMF acts as a 'lender of last resort' when almost all the other financing options are exhausted by a borrower country. This imposes severe responsibilities on the lender, in addition to imposing mechanistic conditions on offering lending support. Because of the pre-specified or preexisting critical state of the borrower economy, relief measures need to address short-term issues on a high priority basis but not to the neglect of long-term aspects of economic stability requirements. The lending packages have not led to significant increases in their investment levels or economic growth rates. Based on empirical studies of involved borrower countries, Bird (1996, p. 489) concluded: "Rather than serving to generate new flows, IMF credits are often in effect repaying other creditors…..IMF involvement was neither a necessary nor a sufficient condition for attracting capital from other sources." It was also suggested that the thrust of economic reforms in borrower countries should start from the notion of an 'optimal adjustment path' and work toward necessary provision of financial resources. Countries should be involved in a phased program that allows much greater flexibility in their selection of menu options in credit eligibility as well reforms of policies that they can own and sustain over time. Policy conditionality in such cases should be a preventive measure against financial crises rather than constituting (although often ineffective or very expensive for the borrower when all costs are added up) corrective actions.

The international multilateral lending institutions make several unrealistic assumptions about different project prospects, offer project advice and impose conditions of reforms without being accountable for the results. Yet, the locus of responsibility and corresponding liability is transferred to the borrower countries. Suzuki (2001, p.321) argued that a developing country's government bears the burden of adjustment under IMF loans in times of financial crises brought about by financial liberalization, "while foreign speculative capital is effectively bailed out…..at the expense of developing countries' taxpayers." Clearly, this phenomenon is not conducive to augmenting economic growth and development in the developing countries.

Poorer sections of the society pay a substantial share of costs of adjustment arising from debt crises. Ignoring such costs has been a norm in the design of debt management policies advocated by the IMF and the World Bank and such an approach distorts objective evaluation of relative merits of alternate policy measures. A transaction cost perspective in this regard is given in Rao (2003, pp.76-84). It has been argued that these international financial institutions have depicted a high degree of inertia and lack of any substantial reform aimed at promoting their development effectiveness. To the extent that the IMF and the World Bank policies impose conditionalities on capital borrowing countries with frequent adverse implications on the poor populations in developing countries, it is fair to seek a degree of risk-sharing between the credit lending institutions and their borrowers.

A vivid description of glaring inefficiencies in the functioning of international institutions including some of the United Nations agencies, the IMF and the World Bank may be seen in Hancock (1989). Several country studies that documented adverse consequences of the IMF-prescribed economic reforms during the 1980s have also been cited. Very little seems to have changed during the past few years in some of these organizations.

Methods of Assessment

Some of the studies (see for example Mosley et al, 1991) found that the World Bank's policy-based lending had a marginal effect on real GDP growth, and a negative effect on investment. The World Bank conditionality mechanisms provide little cause for confidence for private lenders and investors in their expectations about economic growth of the borrower country. However, Bank projects have been seen to lead to additional private capital flows, arising both from foreign direct investment and from private debt flows (Bird and Rowlands, 2001).

The World Bank's method of assessing its own projects is flawed and long-term impact shortchanged; for details see Lerrick (2002). This is partly because the Bank conducts Impact Evaluations only on 5 percent of its programs. Its definition of 'satisfactory' is arbitrary and subjective; the definition of project sustainability states that it is a feature based on the likelihood that the project will maintain its net positive contributions in the future. Only half or less of the projects qualify for the sustainability feature.

In terms of formal economic analysis, the role of analytical models that incorporate debt repayment horizons as a decision variable are relevant if these models recognize the interdependencies of availability of information and its role in effecting project revisions, wherever necessary. Search costs, and more generally, transaction costs are often influenced by the choice of channels of information, quality of information, institutional arrangements and methods of project implementation. Borrower and lender institutions need to consider the role of reduction of various transaction costs in addition to the attainment of stated objectives of undertaking various transactions.

Recommendations on Reform

There have been several efforts to devise and implement reforms in the international financial architecture, especially with reference to the IMF and the World Bank. Some of the important ones are briefly summarized below.

The Bretton Woods Committee Report (1994, p.A-7) stated that these institutions should be more open with current information about operations, and more importantly that they pay "more attention to legitimate public concerns and address them with more commitment." This suggestion seems to have been partly fulfilled but there is a long way for further reform.

The UN Report (1999) suggested some of the key areas of reform of the international financial architecture:

1. Improved consistency (and complementarity) of macroeconomic policies at the international levels, including public scrutiny of the policies and operations of the central banks as well as the IMF;

2. Reform of the IMF to provide for adequate international liquidity in times of crisis;

3. The adoption of improved codes of conduct and financial supervision at national and international levels, in the interests of borrower and creditors;

4. Preservation of relative autonomy of capital account issues in developing countries for appropriate regulation of short term capital flows or avoidance of sudden capital reversals; and

5. Provision of time-bound and focused debt rescheduling, where and when necessary, rather than protracted and chaotic debt renegotiations that aggravate costs of debt crisis to borrower countries.

Most of these recommendations are still relevant for undertaking reforms. We now summarize another recent expert committee report. The International Financial Institution Advisory ("Meltzer") Commission was appointed by the US Congress in 1998 to recommend future US policy toward major multilateral financial institutions. The Commission Report was submitted in 1999. The Meltzer Commission Report (1999) observed that:

a) the World Bank operations are characterized by "high cost and low effectiveness"; and

b) the IMF paid very little attention to improving financial structures in developing countries, and concluded that the IMF "system of short-term crisis management is too costly, its responses too slow, its advice often incorrect, and its efforts to influence policy and practice too intrusive."

The Meltzer Commission Report noted that a wide gap exists between the Bank's rhetoric and performance. Nearly 70 percent of the Bank's non-aid resources flow to 11 countries that already enjoy access to private sector resource flows. The multilateral institutions could serve a better purpose, it has been suggested, if they could efficiently provide a variety of global public goods such as supporting global environmental features and controlling illicit monetary transactions.

The report identified the following main reasons behind the poor performance of multilateral financial institutions and development banks:

1. Large share of the resources flow to a few countries with access to private capital;

2. Host government guarantee mechanisms delink project failure and the Bank's risk of loss;

3. Funds remain fungible at the borrower end and this feature does not allow resource inflows and project effectiveness;

4. Borrower countries hardly sustain policy reforms, even if they temporarily undertake any; and

5. Development projects cannot achieve their objectives when credit recipient countries do not maintain a significant level of commitment.

The above list also suggests the relative contributory roles of the borrower developing countries and the multilateral lending institutions in augmenting development effectiveness of financial resources.

It is also useful to recall that the Finance Ministers of the seven industrially advanced countries (G-7) in their statement of October 30, 1998 agreed to initiate several steps for reforming international financial architecture, including: seeking to minimize the human costs of financial crises and protection of vulnerable sections of the society. This task needs to be fully addressed by the G-7 countries and the international institutions.

Regarding accountability at some of the multilateral institutions, it is worth noting that the IMF and the World Bank do not pay for the costs of their mistakes, developing countries do. These organizations need to function as a subset of stakeholders in the development process (for a detailed assessment see Pieper and Taylor, 1998). The main mechanism of incentives that could enhance the performance and effectiveness of these organizations and their functionaries is to draw relevant parallels from private industry – the entity that these organizations proclaim as the panacea for most problems of the world. This mechanism is to enable devising a 'bottom line' for performance accountability. The incentives should be expressed in terms of development indicators of specific developing countries where the relative efficacy of inputs and advice (including loan conditionalities) provided by these organizations is assessed in quantifiable terms. The design of incentives for improved performance or career advancement of the staffers must also be clearly articulated and linked to the above performance indicators.

4.4 Financing for Development: The Monterrey Consensus

The UN sponsored high-level International Conference on Financing for Development held at Monterrey, Mexico in March 2002 was a first of its kind global event that engaged the attention of the world in addressing issues of global financial governance for development in an integrated framework, especially for its focus on alleviating problems of poverty in developing countries. This Conference led to a Resolution, called the Monterrey Consensus. Some of the highlights of this Consensus are summarized below (UN, 2002).

In its preamble, the Resolution of the Conference stated (UN, 2002): "Our goal is to eradicate poverty, achieve sustained economic growth and promote sustainable development as we advance to a fully inclusive and equitable global economic system." Mobilizing and increasing the effective use of financial resources is considered the first step in achieving this goal. The Resolution urged developed countries to enhance their participation and contribution in ODA and asserted (para 41) that "To build support for ODA, we will cooperate to further improve policies and development strategies, both nationally and internationally, to enhance aid effectiveness." Regarding external debt management, the Resolution recognized that sustainable debt financing is an important aspect of capital flows for investment and suggested (para 47): "Debtors and creditors must share the responsibility for preventing and resolving unsustainable debt situations...."

It was also suggested that the debt relief programs being implemented under the purview of the IMF and the World Bank need to continuously review their underlying assumptions and computational methods in order to remain sensitive to realistic economic scenarios of specific countries, changes in the terms of international trade, and interdependence with the global system. Regarding the role of policy advice and loan conditionalities advanced by the multilateral financial institutions, the Resolution specifically stated (para 56) that the advice should take into account "social costs of adjustment programmes, which should be designed to minimize negative impact on the vulnerable segments of society." In reality, however, these recommendations are not yet meaningfully reflected in the design and implementation of most policies.

Limitations of the Consensus

The Monterrey Consensus, the first of its kind international agreement on development finance issues, was too broad in including comprehensive objectives and fell short on specific actionable programs at national or international levels. Creation of "strong, accountable institutions" at all levels was recommended, but no actionable follow up emerged in the 16 page Resolution. Even after having declared repeatedly its focus on the role of sustainable development, the final part of the Resolution did not mention the role of administrative ministries of the environmental sector when it stated (para 70) that countries resolve: "To continue to improve our domestic policy coherence through the continued engagement of our ministries of development, finance, trade and foreign affairs, as well as our central banks;..." The coherence of laudable objectives and corresponding specification of operational steps is thus lacking.

The next section examines current trends in the operating features and need for reform of some of the important international financial institutions.

4.6 Concluding Observations

Financial liberalization must be attempted only in conjunction with effective financial supervision and application of sound principles and norms of financial governance. Provision of relevant legal and other institutional infrastructure by the state is a required complementary factor for the realization of gains of financial liberalization. The benefits of market-oriented reforms are likely to be sustainable only with the effective supervision and regulation.

The global financial architecture needs reform and strengthening on the following lines:

- improved mechanisms of coordination that include participation of all countries;
- delineation of the role and limits of globalization to minimize costs of financial crises;
- devising improved methods of credit rating for adoption by credit rating agencies;
- focus on financial supervision and assessment of transaction costs of alternative methods of financial governance at national and international levels;
- recognition of the roles of economic development and poverty reduction as the main objectives of financial operations of multilateral financial institutions; and,
- improving standards of accountability and transparency at the multilateral financial institutions.

Credit rating methods need to be improved to weigh in not only debt repayment feature as a determinant of the rating but should objectively assess medium and long term economic and institutional factors as well. Credit rating need not contribute to accentuate financial crises and to conversion of short term liquidity problems into longer term crises. An important analytical and empirical issue for further study is this: is the contribution of lowering of credit ratings a self-fulfilling prophecy?

An important question of global policy and financial governance relates to the provision of incentives for improved performance at the international financial institutions. Can the international financial institutions go wrong and if so who pays for such mistakes? The answer to the first part of the question is yes, and to the second part the question is: borrower countries. Creditor-debtor risk sharing mechanisms need to be explored as a method of encouraging joint responsibility and sustainability of policy advice as well as financial/economic reform.

At the operational level, incentives for improved performance of functionaries of multilateral financial institutions should be linked to the development contributions of specific developing countries where the relative efficacy of inputs and advice (including loan conditionalities) provided by these organizations. The design of incentives for improved performance or career advancement of the staffers must also be clearly articulated and linked to the above performance indicators.

Review Exercises

1. Does financial liberalization lead to banking crises? Is this the same as stating that banking crises are often preceded by financial liberalization? Discuss the differences in these two positions and examine relevant case studies.

2. The reforms included in the 'Washington Consensus' were claimed (Williamson, 2000) as necessary but not sufficient for promoting development. Examine the validity of this statement.

3. Is the role of the World Bank funding and conditionality to induce private capital flows, and if yes, what measures ensure their sustainability?

4. Examine the validity, if any, of the following statement made by the then First Managing Deputy Director Stanley Fischer (statement on October 1, 1998 regarding the need for the IMF conditionality, at the World Economic Development Council, Washington DC; details obtained from the IMF website www.imf.org/external/np/tr/1998/TR981002.htm, visited on 01/05/99):

    "Why is it needed? It is needed because from time to time, for whatever reason, countries get into trouble, frequently because of mistakes in their own policies. But he tendency in those situations is to take measures that would be destructive of their own prosperity or of their neighbors. What measures would be destructive of their own prosperity? It would be to close down the system, to increase tariffs, to impose capital controls...."

5. What are the implications, in terms of lending and borrowing policies (and their contracts as well as conditionalities, *ex ante* and/or *ex post*) of the following recommendation of the Monterrey Consensus:

    "Debtors and creditors must share the responsibility for preventing and resolving unsustainable debt situations."

6. Suggest relevant ingredients and their quantification for arriving at a financial liberalization index.

References

Bandiera, O., Caprio, G., Honohan, P., and Schiantarelli, F. (2000): Does Financial Reform Raise or Reduce Saving?, Review of Economics and Statistics, 82, 239-263.

Bird, G. (1996): The IMF and Developing Countries: A Review of the Evidence and Policy Options, International Organization, 50, 477-511.

Bird, G. and Rowlands, D. (2001): World Bank Lending and other Financial Flows: Is there a Connection? , Journal of Development Studies, 37, 83-103.

Boyce, J. K. and Ndikumana, L. (2001): Is Africa a Net Creditor? New Estimates of Capital Flight from Severely Indebted Sub-Saharan African Countries 1970-96, Journal of Development Studies, 38, 27-56.

Bretton Woods Committee (1994): Bretton Woods – Looking to the Future, Washington DC.

Hancock, G. (1989): Lords of Poverty- The Power, Prestige and Corruption of the International Aid Business, New York: The Atlantic Monthly Press.

Kaminsky, G. L. and Reinhart, C. M. (1999): The Twin Crises – the Causes of Banking and Balance of Payment Problems, American Economic Review, 89, 473-500.

Kremer, M. and Jayachandran, S. (2002): Odious Debt, Finance and Development, 39, 36-39.

Lerrick, A. (2002): Are World Bank Claims of Success Credible? It is time for an External Performance Audit, Pittsburgh: Carnegie Mellon Quarterly International Economics Report.

Lucas, A. (2001): Evaluating the Basle Guidelines for Backtesting Bank's Internal Risk Management Models, Journal of Money, Credit, and Banking, 33, 826-846.

McKinnon, R. (1973): Money and Capital in Economic Development, Washington DC: The Brookings Institution.

Meltzer Commission Report (1999): Report of the International Financial Institution Advisory Commission, Washington DC: US Congress Joint Economic Committee.

Moody's (1995): Global Credit Analysis, New York: Moody's Investor Services.

Monfort, B. and Mulder, C. (2000): Using Credit Ratings for Capital Requirements on Lending to Emerging Market Economies: Possible Impact of a New Basel Accord, IMF Working Paper WP/00/69, Washington, DC: IMF.

Mosley, P., Harrigan J., and Toye, J. (1991): Aid and Power: The World Bank and Policy-Based Lending, 2 vols, London: Routledge.

Pieper, U. and Taylor, L. (1998): The revival of the liberal creed: the IMF, the World Bank, and inequality in a globalized economy, pp. 37-66, in Baker, D., Epstein, G. and Pollin, R. (Ed.): Globalization and Progressive Economic Policy, New York: Cambridge University Press.

Rao, P. K. (2003): The Economics of Transaction Costs: Theory, Methods and Applications, London: Palgrave- Macmillan.

Stiglitz, J. (1999): Reforming the Global Economic Architecture: Lessons from recent crises, Journal of Finance, 54, 1508-21.

Shaw, E. (1973): Financial Deepening in Economic Development, New York: Oxford University Press.

Standard & Poor (1997): Sovereign Credit Ratings: A Primer, New York: Standard and Poor's Credit Week (April 1997 Issue).

Sundararajan, V. et al (2002): Financial Soundness Indicators: Analytical Aspects and Country Practices, Washington DC: IMF Occasional Paper #212. Also available at www.imf.org/external/pubs/nft/op/212/index.htm

Suzuki, E. (2001): The Fallacy of Globalism and the Protection of National Economies, Yale Journal of International Law, 26, 318-323.

United Nations (2002): International Conference on Financing for Development, Monterrey, Mexico, March 2002. New York: UN Conference Document A/CONF.198/11.

United Nations (1999): Towards a new international financial architecture, Report of the Task Force of the Executive Committee on Economic and Social Affairs, New York: United Nations.

United States Congress Joint Economic Committee Study (2001): Recent Bailouts and Reform of the International Monetary Fund, Washington DC: US Congress.

Williamson, J. (2000): What should the World Bank think about the Washington Consensus? , The World Bank Research Observer, 15, 251-64.

Williamson, J. (1990): What Washington Means by Policy Reform, in J. Williamson (ed), Latin American Adjustment: How Much Has Happened?, Washington DC: Institute for International Economics.

CHAPTER 5

External Aid and Development

5.1 Introduction

At a general level, one of the reasons for larger collective institutions functioning as bases for resource transfers stems from Arrow's (1983, p.188) argument: "There are significant gains to social interaction above and beyond what individuals can achieve on their own.... there is a surplus created by the existence of society which is available for redistribution." This argument also holds good when external aid, as an important source of development finance, is properly channeled and efficiently utilized by the recipients. In an ideal situation, such inputs enable relatively poorer societies to tide over financial crises, enhance economic development, promote economic integration with the global economy, and benefit donor nations with markets for their products and services. This chapter examines some of the important constraints in this context.

External aid, in contrast to market-based foreign debt, includes a component of concession or subsidy. The supply of financial and other resources in the form of external aid relative to a national economic system depend on several economic, political, social and other factors. Similarly, the demand for such resources is also subject to a variety of factors but there often exists an 'excess demand' relative to any level of supply. The role of 'price' in this 'market' for external aid is such that it is often fuzzy and uncertain, both *ex ante* and *ex post*. Thus, there is a phenomenon of equilibrium rationing of external aid, given a fixed supply of such resources. Even the existence of 'aid fatigue' is not uncommon when resource-rich countries look upon potential borrowers as endemic deficit entities; some view that subsidies to other countries may not be sustainable and could diminish resources for fulfilling their own domestic requirements. In recent years, the expanded role of globalization and thus market factors has taken over the role of officially directed external resource flows. Selective and diminished external aid is perhaps more conditioned by strategic political considerations (especially in bilateral deals among countries). Besides, a substantial portion may not even be aimed at reduction of poverty and enhancement of economic development; in all such cases, foreign aid may not constitute an element of development finance. To the extent that the remaining economic support from bilateral and multilateral agreements and multilateral as well as regional financial institutions belongs in the development finance arena, the debate in this chapter becomes relevant.

Trends in external finance for the developing countries during the 1990s showed reversal and later stagnancy of net short-term flows, and capital outflows (including 'errors and omissions' of accounting) depicting a rather unwelcome trend: these capital flows amounted to $16.9 billion in 1991, and have since been systematically rising steeply. These estimates represent the capital flight phenomenon, partly due to weak investment climate in the domestic economies. The estimated outflows for later years (in US $ billion) are (World Bank, 2001): 93.1 in 1992, 150.3 in 1996, 246.9 in 1999, and 306 in 2000. It has also been noted that the component relating to errors and omissions is reflective of the "inability of international financial statistics to identify a significant portion of capital transactions." (Ibid, p.34). This limitation needs to be examined by international and national organizations to enable the correct assessment of financial inflows and outflows.

This chapter examines the role and performance/effectiveness of Official Development Assistance (ODA) as a significant source of development finance and of external support for development. Also examined are current methods of assessment of financial needs of developing countries, theoretical arguments on the role of external aid in influencing economic growth of recipient countries, empirical evidence regarding the contribution of external aid to development, the relative merits of policy-oriented versus country-oriented priority in aid resource allocation, and strategic analytical approaches to aid allocation. Major focus of the analysis remains on policy issues and their underlying economic arguments. After a brief analysis of political economy of aid, this chapter proceeds to examine some of the analytical issues relevant to strategic decision-making for near-market capital flow systems, given informational asymmetries and imperfect capital markets. Some of the propositions and findings of Krueger's (1986) analysis are critically examined and improved. This debate provides additional insight into the relative roles of donors and donees, or creditors and borrowers. Besides, creditor-borrower negotiations are analyzed in terms of differential game-theoretic interpretations to reap greater insight into the structural behavior and improvement of policy framework.

5.2 Official Development Assistance

The ODA, referred to here as external aid, consists of one or more of the following:

1. concessional capital flows from individual donor countries, including bilateral ODA (where the grant element is 25 percent or more);

2. concessional capital flows from multilateral institutions (like the International Development Association, World Bank); and

3. approximate market term loans provided by multilateral development institutions and nonconcessional multilateral capital flows (including those of the IMF, World Bank and other financial institutions).

Trends in ODA

Concessional capital flows increased globally (at constant world prices) by 50 percent during 1970 and 1980, and by 32 percent during 1980 and 1990, and dropped by 25 percent during the next decade (World Bank, 2001). ODA to developing countries stood at $43.2 billion in 1990 and at $41.6 billion in 2000 (both in current world prices); bilateral concessional loans during this period dropped from $8.3 billion to $5.1 billion, and multilateral concessional loans hovered around $6.7 billion. The share of ODA in total financial inflows came down from 56 percent in 1990 to 18 percent in 1998, because of decline in ODA and increases in capital flows because of globalization policies in some of the countries (Zedillo Commission Report, 2001).

The recent developments of 2002 Monterrey Consensus (highlights given in chapter 4) led to developed country pledges to increase their respective volumes of ODA relative to the 1990s. A pledge by the USA allows increases by $1.7 billion in 2004, $3.3 billion in 2005 and $5.0 billion in 2006 and beyond, representing a 50 percent increase over the levels of 2002. There is a new element of conditionality of funding: the above additional funds are to be placed in a "Millennium Challenge Account" and funds are proposed to be disbursed to developing countries if they demonstrate a strong commitment to good economic and institutional governance promoting more open markets, entrepreneurship and attention to health and education sectors. The European Union also pledged to increase their ODA by $7.0 billion by 2006.

Rationale for ODA

A paradigm that provides rationale behind resource transfer suggests (Ruttan, 1989): (1) economic and strategic self-interest of donor countries, and (2) ethical and moral sense of responsibility of the richer countries toward the poor countries. Empirical evidence (Maizels and Nissanke, 1984) suggests that donor self-interest plays a relatively larger role in bilateral assistance while the recipients' interest plays a significant role in multilateral assistance. Later, a study by Ball and Johnson (1996) that examined the US government sponsored PL480 food aid to Africa concluded (p. 529), "when we consider all titles of PL480 and all 20 years of our sample, geopolitical interests and surpluses of American agricultural commodities appear to have been the most influential factors in the allocation of US food aid among African recipients."

The most important arguments regarding some of the problems of expanded aid are the following:

1. the ethical responsibility for distributive justice principles could very well apply to individuals or families (especially within the societies of the richer group of countries) rather than to collectives such as nations, since they may not provide sufficient assurance that the needy and deserving people would receive the support (Cooper, 1977);

2. the incentives for efficient allocation of resources to programs at the donor and recipient levels are often distorted;

3. donor countries tend to forcefully extract resources from their citizenry in order to transfer them to foreigners (Bauer, 1981); and

4. aid has been frittered away in several cases through missed opportunities and corruption, and it has not often proved to benefit the poor as the aim of the rulers of some of the recipient countries is not to alleviate poverty.

The relative strengths of arguments contained in (c) and (d) are conditional upon the magnitudes involved (donors – if the extracted resources are significant, and recipients – if the rulers of some countries are less concerned with development than the donors). An additional clarification is useful to note that even in these situations the donor interests may not be sustainable. The features in (b) may still be a relatively small price to pay if the benefits of economic integration (including trade) that accrue tend to more than compensate the citizenry for those costs of resource transfer. Considerable empirical analysis could throw more light on these issues. Reverting to (a), the question of welfare improvement of the deserved sections of the society, domestic or abroad, is not a zero-sum game. External assistance is not necessarily at the expense of the budget for the needy on the domestic front if there are benefits of goodwill, international linkages and enhancement of the demand for products and services from donor economies.

However, if the borrower / recipient countries suffer as a result either of incorrect donor policies and/or lack of proper development efforts by the domestic governments, the combined output of such negative inputs in the production function is an inferior public good that is unable to meet the interests either of the donors or of the borrowers. The process then would involve redistribution of losses rather than gains, equitably or otherwise. This is just the opposite of the basic premise of external aid; thus, aid can negate itself (or self-eliminating) depending on the specifications of the inputs involved.

Traditional foreign aid theory-related arguments are generally focused on aid-savings-economic growth linkages. Riddel (1987) considered several alternative possibilities, including ethical foundations of aid, along with theory and empiricism of aid effects. Similarly, there is little support to the view that (Krueger, 1986) "a recipient's potential welfare could always be increased by a grant, whereas the donor's potential welfare might be reduced." This claim is not generally valid as seen later in this chapter. Since the evidences are mixed regarding the result of success/failure in terms of long-run productivity impact of aid, there is little reasoning in the extreme positions: aid is always mutually beneficial, or aid is always disastrous. It is desirable to examine the milieu of conditions that contribute to productive utilization of resources and the role of external aid as a useful source of development finance.

The next section outlines the basic premise that led to the assessments of external aid in various countries, and points to its limitations as well.

5.3 External Aid and Economic Growth

Two-Gap/Financing Gap Model

The logical foundation of providing external aid (other than specific purpose humanitarian assistance) to developing countries is to facilitate improved economic development, including enhanced economic growth. The presumption here is that external aid generates investment and this leads to economic growth. The technical approach for the assessment of the magnitude of external aid the main basis for this has been the so-called financing gap model or two-gap model of Chenery and Strout (1966). This formulation was based on the classical Harrod-Domar model of economic growth (Harrod, 1939; Domar, 1946). The dominant international financial institutions have used these models widely.

In early formulations relating the role of aid in effecting economic growth Chenery and Strout (1966) suggested the two-gap formula: savings gap and foreign exchange gap. Both these gaps constrain economic growth and the role of aid is largely to fill this gap. This 'aid needs' assessment method is founded on several simplistic assumptions: human capital that has no direct role in economic growth or capital formation, economic uncertainties (exogenous and endogenous factors contributing to these uncertainties); no significant misuse of external resources for the private benefit of the ruling elite or dictators in recipient countries. The formulation does not explicitly recognize the role of external aid in softening the effects of external financial shocks to vulnerable economies.

Aid requirements in the two-gap model are estimated by first prescribing a targeted economic growth rate and then using a constant incremental capital output ratio (ICOR), as well as assessments of private investment and domestic saving, thus quantify the financial resource gap that may be filled by external aid.

The formula, using the Harrod-Domar formulation, is given by the following:

$$s / (ICOR) = g$$

where g is the target growth rate, and s the savings rate.

For a set of specified values of ICOR and target g, the above equation is solved for s. After adjusting for domestic private investment in the magnitude (not the rate) of savings, the resulting magnitude of required 'external financing' or 'financing gap' is estimated.

This traditional financing gap analysis of economic growth emphasizes that savings and foreign investment via borrowing are two of the main influences on economic development (more specifically, on economic growth) in developing countries. The productivity of capital is presumed to be at such significant levels as to contribute to economic growth, net of all costs (including costs of borrowing, transaction costs and capital substitution, if any). White (1992) noted that much of the existing literature on aid and growth is focused on extremely simplistic Harrod-Domar models and that there is need to move further for more realistic models. White concluded: "Most of the literature does not even allow for the differential impact of aid under different binding constraints predicted by the dual-gap model, using cross-section studies that incorrectly assume that aid impact will be constant across countries.....the results....are empirically, as well as theoretically, suspect." (Ibid, p.225).

In the oft-used formulation, foreign aid/borrowing requirements are assumed to simply equal the gap between investment requirement (for a specified economic growth rate) and the available domestic resources (represented by the sum of private financing and domestic savings). These presume that foreign borrowings fill in investment gaps undiminished in magnitude (i.e., dollar for dollar) and that economic growth is directly proportional to investment (at least in the short-run), the constant proportionality factor being the ICOR. These assumptions have no meaningful analytical justification nor have any empirical validity (more details may be seen in Easterly, 1999).

To sum up, 'Financing gap' is a dubious concept and deriving 'investment requirements' based on such 'gap' assessments is full of gaps in the understanding the real economies. But for the major role the concept played for over half a century, the details would not have attracted attention here. Defenders of the financing gap analysis suggest that the magnitude of foreign borrowing estimated on these premises is a 'necessary but not sufficient' element of expected economic growth. This is also a dubious claim, as the economic or other logical foundations of estimating 'necessary' financial requirements are shaky. Foreign borrowings (concessional or other) estimated in excess of US$1 trillion took place during 1960 to 1995 on the basis of the two-gap analysis. The reasons for adoption of the simplistic method seem to be related to the factors: it is easy to calculate the gaps, it has been a matter of habit to use the formula, and the inertia of multilateral financial institutions enabled their continued usage (for more details see Easterly, 1999).

Aid Fungibility

Aid is not necessarily used for intended purposes at the recipient country level, and this is not necessarily a concept that is difficult to comprehend at the donor levels. Aid fungibility is a common element. Among others, Feyzioglu et al (1998) found that most aid is fungible; their study was based on 14 developing countries for a 20-year period. The role of political motivations at both ends as well as the interests of functionaries involved in the aid allocation and utilization game deserve further attention than has been accorded in literature. Knack (2001, p.313) observed: "Aid is commonly used for patronage purposes, by subsidizing employment in the public sector, or in state-operated enterprises, as foreign aid can provide funds for government to undertake investment that would otherwise be made by private investors."

Several studies document the possibility that aid may not significantly enhance development, as the resources are typically fungible. This fungibility lead to decrease in efficiency of investment and states avail this cushion to further their own non-economic objectives; economic development becomes less of a priority. Even with conditionalities specified under different aid schemes, it is often difficult to ensure that the targeted approach is complied at the recipient country level. Sustenance of sound economic policies that are generally influenced by aid policies and conditions stipulated by donor institutions, is often difficult. On the other hand, do donors care to reward states with less corruption and leakages of domestic and external funds? Not likely, according to some of the studies. There is little evidence that donors systematically allocate aid to countries with less corruption (Svensson, 2000).

Aid Experiences

Is there any consensus from theory regarding aid and growth relationships? Hermes and Lensink (2001) argued that because theory appears to be inconclusive, the task of finding relevant answers belongs to the arena of empirical inquiry. The 1998 World Bank report "Assessing Aid" (World Bank, 1998) highlighted the role and importance of the recipient country policy environment for the effectiveness of aid. In an important review of this document, Dalgaard and Hansen (2001) argued that the conclusions of the report are fragile and hypersensitive to data specifications. They also showed that many of the conclusions in the Burnside and Dollar (2000) study (which is closely linked to the above report of the World Bank) are far from robust, as changes in (addition or deletion of) a few observations (or sample countries) led to widely different and opposite conclusions.

The relationship between aid and economic growth has often been assessed as weak or negligible (see, for example, Snyder, 1990). Easterly (1999) examined the economic growth implications of external aid resource flows. Based on data from 88 aid-recipient countries spanning the period 1965 to 1995, it has been observed that only five of these nations had a positive effect of foreign aid on investment.

Literature that argues in favor of extreme forms of role of aid (viz. zero level of aid, or that aid should lead as a major determinant of economic development) does not throw light on realistic issues involved in the aid policies and their impact. Griffin (1970) argued that aid retards development. Similarly, Kohr (1979, p.105) suggested that development without aid is "not only feasible but faster as well as cheaper than the assisted variety", and that foreign aid introduced too early in a country's development could enable "young nations to jump over the identity-shaping hardships of the vital intermediate stages of economic advance without even the benefit of speeding up the process" (Ibid., p. 76). Although Kohr provided some examples of countries, the above claims tend to be more ideological than economic-oriented. Besides, the definition of some of the stages of development is arbitrary. Later, Kharas and Levinsohn (1988) argued that foreign capital inflows jeopardize the creditworthiness both through their negative impact on domestic savings and through the build-up of debt. Based on an empirical study of 26 developing countries for the period of 1961 to 1982, they found that foreign capital borrowing reduced average domestic savings rates and concluded that "only if foreign borrowing can help to achieve structural reform, through raising marginal savings rates, is its impact on creditworthiness substantial" (Ibid., p. 785). The need to incorporate multiple objectives of the donors and recipients calls for "team decision," discussed later in this chapter.

Given the interdependencies of external aid, private capital flows, economic governance features and the resultant economic growth, a comprehensive economic model is required to capture fully, the net effects as well as their sustainability over time. The patterns of flows of aid and of private capital vary with potential recipient country policies as well as the corresponding donor preferences. The impact of 1 percent of GDP in aid leads to increase of 1.9 percent of GDP in countries with good economic management; in countries with poor economic governance, the GDP decreases by 0.5 percent because of 'crowding out', i.e. more capital gets displaced outward because of such aid process when recipient's governance mechanisms are defective. The above estimates are drawn from the World Bank's annual publication Global Development Finance 1999 (World Bank, 1999).

Performance-Based Aid and Conditionalities

Aid with donor conditionalities as well aid without similar conditions – both seem to have led to results at the same minimal levels of effectiveness. It has been observed that imposition of aid conditionalities often leads to temporary changes but not sustainable reforms to achieve the substantive objectives of providing such aid or its conditionalities. As an illustration, the Government of Kenya succeeded in suggesting the same set of agricultural reforms to the World Bank four times during a 15-year interval, and each time reversing its policies after the receipt of concessional loans (Gwin and Nelson, 1997). This illustration raises a number of analytical and policy issues.

Should aid allocation be determined by stipulations of economic performance rather than on instruments of economic and institutional governance? Let us first introduce the definition. Economic performance is the economic outcome of economic growth, poverty reduction, human capital development, and related features. These are not entirely attributable to exogenous factors only. The role of endogenous factors is very important. The level of economic performance is the net outcome of the roles of various influences, adjusted for the impact of external factors (including external shocks).

In broad terms, the dichotomy of stipulating aid conditionalities *ex ante* versus asking for results or output from aid (thus constituting *ex post* conditionality) need to be examined in terms of stipulating a critical combination of both. Any one set alone may not offer sufficient incentives and disincentives for improved performance at the recipient level.

Guillaumont and Chauvet (2001) argued in favor of aid policies that allocate funds according to 'economic performance' as defined by the following criterion: economic growth (or other desirable indicators of economic performance) adjusted for the total impact of the external disturbances (including direct impact and impact through international policies), given the specifications of initial conditions. It has been suggested that aid allocation based on economic performance adjusted for allowable factors (initial structures and external shocks) increases aid effectiveness and offers incentives for improved performance over time.

A normative prescription has been advanced by Collier and Dollar (2002), Their study constituted an extension of the Burnside and Dollar (2000) study. Based on their empirical studies which suggested significant positive roles of institutional governance and sound economic policies in about 50 countries for about a quarter century, Collier and Dollar argued for aid allocation among countries that remain 'poverty-efficient', i.e. for a given level of poverty in the recipient country, aid should increase with policy environment in the host country, and for an index of meaningful policies, aid should increase with levels of poverty. This prescriptive standard does not recognize the role of potential externalities of exclusion of 'ineligible countries'. The problems of inefficient use of aid resources with expectations of continued availability of funds (the endogenity problem) deserves attention in a multi-period policy framework.

Is the excessive use of aid conditionalities counter productive? Collier et al (1997) stated the answer in the affirmative and argued that such an approach could enhance potential ownership of relevant and substantive (in contrast to perfunctory, short-term and make-believe) reform process in the aid recipient countries. Thus, performance conditionality has been proposed as an alternative to the traditional instrument conditionality. It is doubtful if this set of policy instruments alone would deliver the results. The broad analytical problem here is one of designing of a combination of *ex ante* and *ex post* conditionalities and incentives that constitute an optimal solution to the welfare maximizing provision of external resources. Considerable further research is required in this direction for devising useful methodologies and pragmatic policies.

One of the paradigms for external aid suggests that aid should be seen as compensation or a sociopolitical measure to soften negative shocks to the economic and social systems of potential aid recipients, and in that the eligible beneficiaries should mainly be those with 'good governance' of their economic and other institutional institutions. The issue of development effectiveness of external aid has been engaging attention from time to time at the international levels. Some of the relevant features and experiences in this regard are discussed in the following section.

5.4 The Effectiveness of Aid

A few years ago the Report of the World Bank – IMF Task Force on Concessional Flows (Lewis Committee Report, 1985, p.25) observed that despite its flows, the aid revolution has been one of the great innovations and that in an increasingly interdependent and politically fragmented global economy, "the practice of development assistance has raised the norms of international conduct." Much of the debate on the role and contribution of various alternative external aid packages is centered on issues relating to effectiveness of aid and of debt crises problems that affect the creditors and borrowers. In the analysis of the development process at the borrower's end, it is useful to begin with a clarification given in the above report, "aid can be a powerful catalyst for constructive change, but more often than not, it is only one of many factors determining development outcomes" (Lewis Committee Report, 1986, p.17). This assessment reverberates in almost all the recent studies carried out by the World Bank and other organizations, as seen in this chapter.

The Lewis Committee Report (1986) came up with several suggestions for improved framework in the interests of accelerated development effect of external aid, these included operative features of improved information processing, sharing, and decision-making, given below. It is useful to note that much of the current debate in international aid policy focuses on new terminology (capacity building, policy ownership, and policy environment) but deals mainly with the same problems and potential remedies.

1. Joint actions by donors and recipients, with a policy dialogue (this view is rigorously supported by theory, later in this paper);
2. Donors should be more aware of the impact of their policies on the development prospects of recipients;
3. Recipients should use aid resources to complement rather than substitute for domestic resources.

The effectiveness or development impact of external aid has remained a complex issue over the past few decades. Several empirical studies concluded that the effect of aid on economic growth of recipient countries has been generally negligible (see especially Mosley 1987, White 1992, Burnside and Dollar, 2000). If external aid is fungible and governments utilize the resources for less productive activities (economically), or if it leads to crowding out private investments, then it may not lead to discernible impact on economic growth levels (White, 1992). Boone (1996) observed that the macroeconomic effects of aid are generally ambiguous. Nonetheless, it has also been noted (Burnside and Dollar, 2000) that when good policies of economic and institutional governance are in place, the role of aid enhanced economic growth beyond the direct economic effect of aid itself. Based on a cross-country regression analysis for 56 countries during the period 1970-93, Burnside and Dollar observed that aid had a positive impact on real GDP per capita growth only when aid is interacted with a set of influencing factors reflecting the quality of institutions. The latter are represented by the existence of property rights and their effective enforcement, the efficiency of the government machinery (see also Knack and Keefer, 1995) and sound economic governance in various sectors.

There are a few problems in suggested allocation of aid based merely on recipient country policy framework. 'Good policy' orientation received general support from multilateral donors. If aid flows repetitively, a reallocation of aid to countries with 'good' policies would face an endogeneity problem (Langhammer, 2002): as a result of an anticipated rise in the level of aid inflows, policies of the recipients would face a decline in quality simply because of 'crowding out' effects. Thus, country differentiation by policy quality would become intertemporally unstable. Countries receiving more aid on a permanent basis would face strong temptations to operate increasingly 'permissive and populist economic policies' in successive time periods. This behavioral trait renders the country differentiation by policy quality intertemporally unstable. Therefore, it is more useful to focus on issue-oriented rather than country-oriented aid allocation; at the next level of priority, setting the relative efficacy of utilization of aid should be addressed. This approach has the potential to address poverty and human well-being priorities as a matter of universal concern, and offers incentives for improved performance at the recipient country level.

The Role of International Factors

Declining terms of some of the commodities in international trade as well market instabilities leading to export-earning instabilities affect developing countries and adversely affect their economic growth and sustainability. External shocks include both short-term and long-term shocks, reflected in declining real values of exports, systematic adverse terms of trade and related factors. Several authors have examined the role of such shocks in growth and sustainability (see, for example, Collier and Gunning, 1997). One of the paradigms of external aid suggests that it has a major role in smoothing the impact of such shocks in vulnerable countries. However, these shocks do not find due consideration in enforcing debt repayment (including in ODA debts) schedules. Some of the debt management issues are discussed in chapter 6. Suffice it to clarify here that any 'gap analysis' should consider both exogenous and endogenous influences.

In an empirical study, Landau (1990) examined aid-and-effect issues for 60 less developed countries for a span of 25 years, and found:

1. aid is usually used directly on projects to further economic growth, but,

2. the growth-promoting effects of aid are negated by the reactions of recipient governments that reduce other growth-promoting government activities in order to increase "rent-creating" activities (activities that lead to private benefits to some in a position to direct resources at the expense of legitimate and efficient uses of aid).

These observations tend to explain the micro-macro dichotomy of aid effectiveness. A few significant contributions (Cassen et al., 1986, Lewis Committee, 1986, Krueger et al., 1989) address a variety of relevant issues in order to examine the short-term and long-term effectiveness of aid in relation to desirable objectives of ODA for the donors and recipients. The following observations are relevant:

1. "...while it is not possible to document fully the positive contributions of aid to growth, it is also exceedingly difficult to find well-documented instances of aid having a negative impact on overall growth – though surely there have been many cases of specific inefficiencies and counterproductive interventions" (Krueger et al, 1989, p.311).

2. "It is evident that there are a number of instances where a positive relationship between aid and growth cannot be demonstrated. This is especially true for many countries of Sub-Saharan Africa...donor programming and operations also have been at fault; there is abundant room for improvement on both sides" (Lewis Committee, 1986, p.30).

At broader levels that include interdependencies of major international economic influences that led to the demand for aid, the following issues are relevant. To the extent that financing gaps in a developing country are contributed by the trade policies of developed countries (e.g., the coffee commodity price in the early part of the 21st century and its serious impact on coffee exporters), any aid from importing countries (which largely overlap with the set of developed and donor countries) can be partly deemed as a correction factor for offsetting flawed trade terms and inefficient global markets (the role of oligopolistic and monopolistic trade features included). The need for external aid is expected to diminish with improved and fair trade in the international markets. The critical role of external aid then is to reduce any additional shocks to the economies of vulnerable countries due to other factors.

Toward Relevant Theories

On the question of whether official capital flows contribute to the simultaneous improvement of welfare of both donor and recipient Krueger (1986, p.64) suggested the following:

1. The answer to this question hinges on whether imperfections in the market preclude it from equalizing (risk-adjusted) rates of return between donor and recipient.

2. If returns were higher in developing countries, the welfare of both donor and recipient could be improved through official flows. The recipient could service its debt and have a higher future income stream than would otherwise be possible.

It was clarified by Krueger that the conclusion regarding simultaneous improvement of the welfare of both donor and recipient was based on: a) the assumption that the ODA permits incremental investments with real returns at least as good as the return to the donor, and b) the assumption of policy optimality in borrowing countries, even after they received aid. This assertion needs to be read in conjunction with another implicit assumption, viz. that economic efficiency exists in a developing country in the sense that, given resource constraints, domestic policies are consistent with efficient allocation of domestic resources. These are extraordinarily restrictive assumptions for a real economy. These call for resource allocative optimality in both *ex ante* sense as well as *ex post* sense with the additional input under the ODA. This is an impossible configuration except when the additional input itself is a part of a time-consistent optimal solution, i.e. preserving optimality of resource allocations after provision of aid. The creditors or donors in this context are required to ensure such consistency if the resources they provide are to optimize the recipient economic system and its efficiency.

There are serious problems of design and adoption of policies that ensure the existence of such optimality: such policies may not exist! It appears relevant, therefore, to waive the assumption of *ex ante* optimality in a recipient country and to state that *ex post* optimality can be met, in principle, by:

a) appropriate policy reform in the recipient country; or,

b) proper choice of aid bundle offer by the donors (subject to informational limitations); or,

c) a combination of both with a meaningful policy dialogue.

A pragmatic approach would emphasize (c), and encompass elements of (a) and (b).

Reverting to conclusion 2 of Krueger, it needs to be modified to the following: If the risk-adjusted returns to incremental capital flows in recipient countries are r_i and in the i-th country, the welfare of the donors and recipients is improved separately and jointly, if

$$r_i > max\ (r_j,\ r_l)$$

where j is the index set of donor countries, and l denotes alternative opportunity costs of capital in various investment possibilities in the recipient country.

In view of the above analysis, the following "lesson learned," summarized by Krueger (1986, p.74) need not be valid:

> "Because individual projects earn their returns in a milieu influenced by overall economic policy, project financing is not likely to maximize the donors' impact on the recipients growth unless macroeconomic policies are either already appropriate to growth or beyond influence. In the latter case, some types of projects may nonetheless yield positive returns and

thus speed up overall growth (even within the unsatisfactory frameworks), or else lay the foundation for higher growth should policy reform later become feasible."

When macroeconomic policies are 'beyond influence' or disconnected with external inputs, any conjecture about the impact of the latter remains questionable. In addition, Krueger (1987) argued that the private capital market might fail to remain efficient despite the rational behavior of all participants. However, the market failure could be the result of a breakdown of one form of rationality, and not despite it. The above phenomenon is typically a situation characterized by the game "Matching Pennies" (Howard, 1971), which arises because of breakdown of "objective rationality," where it is impossible for all the players (with heterogeneous interests) to be objectively rational or to agree on a common objective. The celebrated Minimax Theorem of Von Neumann in the late 1920s provided a way of dealing with this problem (and marked the beginning of Game Theory).

Box 5.1 provides a brief summary of game-theoretic approaches to the formulation of strategic policies regarding external aid allocations. Clearly, there is scope for further analytical developments in this direction with due recognition of problems of asymmetric information and uncertainty.

Box 5.1: External Aid and Game Theory

A typical multilateral ODA lending transaction obeys a differential game, where the borrowers tend to optimize their objectives based on the known objective of the creditors along with other applicable critical information like interest rates and repayment obligations. These obligations may not be seen as entirely binding on the part of the borrowers influenced by their perception of relevant time-horizon, usually shorter than that of the lending institutions. In this differential game, the creditor ("leader") is restricted to open-loop solutions/decision rules, while the borrower ("follower") may use feedback rules; the leader seeks to announce an optimal rule, knowing that the follower will react on each decision by correspondingly choosing his best response. This game calls for obtaining a Stackelberg solution that could be optimal for both parties. However, a Stackelberg solution fails, in general, to provide an intertemporally stable solution (Mehlmann, 1988), with the implication that multilateral ODA decisions are not necessarily stable. It is also known that time-consistency (or additivity of solutions with respect to time) does not hold for a Stackelberg solution, in general (Mehlmann, 1988). However, a coordinated effort by creditors and borrowers can mitigate this problem. This is because time-consistency of Stackelberg solutions can be assured if the two-player game is converted into a single team problem (Papavassilopoulos and Cruz, 1979), whereby team-optimal joint-decision-making model is solved for common solutions relevant for "leader" and "follower."

> For a collection of techniques of game-theoretic models in different economic problems see, for example, Hamalainen and Ehtamo (1991).
>
> Pedersen (1996) formulated a two-period analytical model involving donors and recipients in the aid process, distinguished different categories of Stackelberg strategies and found that the contribution of aid to economic growth in the recipient economies is likely to depend more on the host state policies than on the strategies of the donors. This conclusion is largely built on the assumed high costs for donors in actively participating in the design and implementation of host country policies.

5.5 Concluding Observations

Most of the aid assessments of the international financial institutions used the two-gap model or minor variations of it for the past four decades. Given the severely restrictive assumptions underlying the models, it is surprising that this method has been used for all these years.

A survey of alternative premises and effectiveness of ODA, including international credit lending through multi-lateral lending institutions, suggests the relevance of continued operations modified in light of additional analytical and empirical insights, combined with an analysis and understanding of experiences. A pre-requisite to enhance the effectiveness of aid is to ensure that aid is a complementary rather than a substitutory input.

In the context of provision of aid (or debt) conditionalities (and incentives for performance or effective use of external resources), an important analytical problem for further investigation is one of designing of a combination of *ex ante* and *ex post* conditionalities and incentives that constitute an optimal solution to the welfare maximizing provision of external resources.

There is significant scope for improvement in the decision-making approaches and strategies for concessional credit lending and borrowing. Among the important pre-requisites for enhanced success of transactions are:

a) reduction in informational asymmetries, and

b) enforceable incentive-compatible credit borrowing and repayment strategy in a dynamic context under changing economic environments.

The determinants of aid effectiveness, in a large part, are policy and economic institutions in the recipient countries, sociopolitical factors, stability of institutions, and the existence of effective legal or quasi-legal mechanisms for the resolution of social and political conflicts.

Review Exercises

1. Identify the elements and the role of transaction costs in the effectiveness of external aid in contributing toward a) economic growth, and b) economic development in the recipient country.

2. Examine the scope and implications of moral hazard dimension of recipient country behavior when the two-gap model constitutes the basis for extending external aid.

3. Discuss the validity or limitations of the following conclusion regarding "lesson learned" in external aid projects, summarized by Krueger (1986, p.74), "Because individual projects earn their returns in a milieu influenced by overall economic policy, project financing is not likely to maximize the donors' impact on the recipients growth unless macroeconomic policies are either already appropriate to growth or beyond influence. In the latter case, some types of projects may nonetheless yield positive returns and thus speed up overall growth (even within the unsatisfactory frameworks), or else lay the foundation for higher growth should policy reform later become feasible."

4. Specify both normative as well as positive considerations in the provision of external aid. What policy and implementation reforms are relevant for the efficient aid packages?

References

Arrow, K. J. (1983): Social Choice and Justice, Cambridge, MA: Harvard University Press.

Ball, R. and Johnson, C. (1996): Political, Economic, and Humanitarian Motivations for PL480 Food Aid – Evidence from Africa, Economic Development and Cultural Change, 44, pp. 515-537.

Bauer, P. T. (1981): Equality, The Third World, and Economic Delusion, Cambridge, MA: Harvard University Press, pp. 86-134.

Boone, P. (1996): Politics and the effectiveness of foreign aid, European Economic Review, 40, 289-329, 1996.

Burnside, C. and Dollar, D. (2000): Aid, Policies and Growth, American Economic Review, 90, 847-868.

Cassen, R. and Associates (1986): Does Aid Work?, Report to an Intergovernmental Task Force, Oxford: Oxford University Press.

Chenery, H. B. and Strout, A. (1966): Foreign Assistance and Economic Development, American Economic Review, 56, 679-733.

Collier, P. and Dollar, D. (2002): Aid Allocation and Poverty Reduction, European Economic Review, 46, 1475-1500, 2002.

Collier, P., Guillaumont, P., Guillaumont Jeanneney, S., and Gunning, J. (1997): Redesigning Conditionality, World Development, 25.

Collier, P. and Gunning, J. (1997): Trade Shocks in Developing Countries: Theory and Evidence, Oxford: Clarendon Press.

Dalgaard, C-J., and Hansen, H. (2001): On Aid, Growth and Good Policies, Journal of Development Studies, 37, 17-41.

Domar, E. (1946): Capital expansion, rate of growth, and employment, Econometrica, 14, 137-147.

Easterly, W. (1999): The ghost of financing gap: testing the growth model used in the international financial institutions, Journal of Development Economics, 60, 423-438.

Feyzioglu, T., Swaroop, V. and Zhu, M. (1998): A Panel Data Analysis of the Fungibility of Foreign Aid, World Bank Economic Review, 12, 29-58.

Griffin, K. (1970): Foreign Capital, Domestic Savings and Economic Development, Bulletin of Oxford University Institute of Economics & Statistics, 32.

Guillaumont, P. and Chauvet, L. (2001): Aid and Performance: A Reassessment, Journal of Development Studies, 37, 66-92.

Gwin, C. and Nelson, J. (Ed.) (1997): Perspectives on Aid and Development, Washington DC: Overseas Development Council Policy Essay #22.

Harrod, R. (1939): Essay in Dynamic Theory, Economic Journal, 49.

Hamalainen, R. P. and Ehtamo, H. K. (Ed.) (1991): Dynamic Games in Economic Analysis, New York: Springer-Verlag.

Hermes, N. and Lensink, R. (2001): Changing the Conditions for Development Aid: A New Paradigm? , Journal of Development Studies, 37, 1-16.

Howard, N. (1971): Paradoxes of Rationality: Theory of Metagames and Political Behavior, Cambridge, MA: MIT Press.

Kharas, H. J., and Levinsohn, J. (1988): LDC Savings Rates and Debt Crises, World Development, 16, 779-786.

Knack, S. (2001): Aid dependence and the quality of governance: a cross-country empirical analysis, Southern Economic Journal, 68, 310-329.

Knack, S. and Keefer, P. (1995): Institutions and Economic Performance: Cross-Country Tests using alternative institutional measures, Economics and Politics, 7, 207-227.

Kohr, L. (1979): Development Without Aid, New York: Schocken Books.

Krueger, A. (1986): Aid in the Development Process, The World Bank Research Observer, 1, 57-78.

Krueger, A. (1987): Debts, Capital Flows and Growth, American Economic Review, 77, 159-164.

Krueger, A., Michalopoulos, C., and Ruttan, V. (Ed.) (1989): Aid and Development, Baltimore: The Johns Hopkins University Press.

Landau, D. (1990): Public Choice and Economic Aid, Economic Development and Cultural Change, 38, 559-576.

Langhammer, R. J. (2002): Halving Poverty by Doubling Aid: How Well Founded is the Optimism of the World Bank? , Working Paper #1116, Kiel Institute for World Economics, Kiel, Germany.

Lewis, J. P. (1985): Committee Report, Task Force on Concessional Flows, Washington DC: The World Bank-IMF.

Lewis, J. P. (1986): Committee Report, Aid for Development – the Key Issues, Washington DC: The World Bank – IMF.

Maizels, A., and Nissanke, M. (1984): Motivations for Aid to Developing Countries, World Development, 12, pp. 879-900.

Mehlmann, A. (1988): Applied Differential Games, New York: Plenum Press, pp. 105-106.

Mosley, P. (1987): Overseas Aid: Its Defence and Reform, Brighton, UK: Wheatsheaf.

Papavssilopoulos, G. P., and Cruz, J. B. (1979): Nonclassical Control Problems and Stackelberg Games, IEEE Transactions on Automatic Control, 24, pp. 155-165.

Pedersen, K. R. (1996): Aid, investment and incentives, Scandinavian Journal of Economics, 98, 423-438.

Riddel, R. (1987): Foreign Aid Reconsidered, Baltimore: The Johns Hopkins University Press.

Ruttan, V. (1989): Why Foreign Economic Assistance?, Economic Development and Cultural Change, 37, pp. 411-424.

Snyder, D. (1990): Foreign Aid and Domestic Savings: A Spurious Correlation?, Economic Development and Cultural Change, 39, 175-181.

Svensson, J. (2000): Foreign aid and rent-seeking, Journal of International Economics, 51, 437-461, 2000.

White, H. (1992): The Macroeconomic Impact of Development Aid- A Critical Survey, Journal of Development Studies, 28, 163-240.

World Bank (2001): Global Development Finance 2001, Washington, DC: World Bank.

World Bank (1999): Global Development Finance 1999, Washington, DC: World Bank.

World Bank (1998): Assessing Aid: What Works, What Doesn't, and Why, New York: Oxford University Press.

Zedillo Commission Report (2001): The UN Commission on Financing for Development, New York: United Nations. Details may be seen at www.un.org/reports/financing/index.html

CHAPTER 6:

Sovereign Debt Management

6.1. Introduction

Sovereign debt management issues include the policy and operational management of capital borrowings by a sovereign state from bilateral and multilateral financial institutions, and of state guaranteed external borrowings by private entities. These borrowings often form an important source of credit for economic activities, including tiding over financial crises from time to time in developing countries. Sovereign debt influences the economy directly through the availability of additional resources under various debt contracts. In this chapter, we examine important implications of various debt management mechanisms.

At the general level of the global economy, an efficient functioning international financial and economic system enables continuous improvements in capital formation and wealth redistribution across countries and sectors. An important facet that affects the efficiency of the global financial system is that of international lending, borrowing and repayment, summarized here as debt management. The players affecting the demand for and supply of credit include both private entrepreneurs and states. The states are obligated to function under various international laws, including the role of state sovereignty. This feature of the state's rights possesses the potential to enhance informational asymmetries between parties to credit transactions, and makes enforcement problems even more difficult. Hence, there is need for a strategic approach in the management global debt issues. These aspects are examined in sections below.

A brief review of historical experiences in sovereign debt and its restructuring is conducted in section 6.2. The economics of sovereign debt contracts (including analytical foundations of optimal debt contracts), political economy of debt relief, and the scope for reforms of sovereign debt rescheduling and management involving borrowers and international financial institutions (including debt reorganization under modified bankruptcy code) are examined in later sections in this chapter. Among the main analytical issues for analysis proposed in this chapter are: 1. Given the theory and practice of debt contracts, is there any scope for reform in the design of sovereign debt contracts? 2. What are the implications of *ex ante* specification of renegotiability of contracts? 3. What are the roles and limitations of incentives and disincentives in debt contracts and debt renegotiations?

6.2 Debt Management – A Historical Perspective

Historically, international credit lending has been a risky business, but perhaps never so risky as to pose 'systemic risk' possibilities. When international lending is subject to sovereign risks of debt repudiation, default or renegotiation, the *ex ante* risk premia are routinely, and quite possibly non-discriminatingly, incorporated in the contracted rates of interest. Lending and contracting process is built around informational asymmetries as well as suboptimal prescriptions of borrowing and repayment. The problem becomes more complex with the additional features of informational asymmetries, differential risk taking attitudes and rates of time preference (and hence differential effective planning and decision-making horizons) of borrowers, levels of efforts in utilizing the externally borrowed resources, and related aspects. Clearly, the real world credit market remains an imperfect, incomplete, and non-stationary international credit market.

Studies that examined the history and management of international debt problems found a repetitive pattern of lending boom and repayment constraints in different intervals of time. Lindert and Morton (1989) documented experiences of the interval 1850 to 1987 and concluded (Ibid, p. 77):

> "On the whole, lending to foreign governments has brought investors a higher real rate of return than the alternative of lending to their own governments, despite foreign defaults."

This assessment suggests that some of the debt write-offs or other waivers to developing countries are merely a reduction in profits of the lending institutions and generally are not net loss resulting activities.

Based on their detailed historical study, Lindert and Morton (1989) argued that the international financial community has often repeated the past rather than worked based on evaluation of experiences. Since 1974, international lending went through another cycle of enthusiasm followed by nonrepayment and creditor revulsion, repeating a pattern that has occurred several times since the eighteenth century. Hence, there is a need for a careful reassessment of analytical and realistic aspects of the design of sovereign debt contracts.

Debt Restructuring Experience of 1980s

From 1976 to 1982 (i.e., predate 1982 Mexican debt crisis) a pattern in debt restructuring appeared. Banks used a short horizon to deal with the problem, as only one to two years of upcoming maturities were rescheduled, amortization and grace periods were very short; the margin over the base London Inter Bank Offer Rate (LIBOR) rate was very high, and commissions were lucrative for creditors. Latin American debt reschedulings in the first round (1982-83), second round (1983-84), third round (1984-85) and the fourth round (1986-87) have the following features:

1. Amortization periods as well as grace periods for new loans were generally less than the corresponding periods for the rescheduled principal.
2. Interest margins over LIBOR as well as Bank commissions for new loans were higher than those for the rescheduled principal.

The higher price of credit in the situation of high uncertainty (that typically characterizes debt rescheduling) has often been cited as a useful instrument to obtain cooperation of small lenders involved in the total set of lenders for a specific country. However, this cooperation can be achieved with non-price incentives as well. The raising of the price of credit in the middle of a crisis could be counterproductive since it increases the burden and reduces the probability of repayment. When a borrower is dishonest, weighing the costs of default versus its benefits, the higher price can simply raise the benefits of not paying (Eaton and Gersovitz, 1981). Raising the price of credit, especially when borrowers are under economic stress, can increase moral hazard, not reduce it (Devlin, 1989).

The above discussion leads us to consider issues that are more fundamental to the design of debt contracts, especially in relation to contingency-based rescheduling with possible mechanisms for cooperative information sharing between creditors and debtors. For a wide variety of reasons, discrepancies between realized and contractually guaranteed repayments exist, thereby opening an avenue for renegotiation – even when the original contract was supposed to be 'renegotiation proof'. These issues are discussed in later sections of this chapter.

6. 3 External Debt and Economic Growth

Is there a possibility that a structure of debt transactions exists so that the welfare of both creditors and debtors is maximized, in a situation typically characterized by informational asymmetry between parties? This issue has been examined in chapter 1 where a general answer was in the negative; more light on potential alternatives to enhance creditor and borrower gains (thus contribute to sustainable debts and economic growth) is offered via debt contract structures, and sovereign debt management reforms, discussed later in this chapter. In this section, we raise the following issues:

1. How does the magnitude of debt affect economic growth for a specified set of economic features?
2. What is the empirical evidence on these issues, even for a segment of borrower countries?

Debt Levels and Economic Growth

When is debt productive in contributing to the economic growth of borrower countries? What are the primary prerequisites for ensuring such a potential positive correlation between debt borrowings and their productive utilization?

These are some of the relevant issues both in theory and in policy we need to examine briefly.

Much of the conventional theory in the past assumed that a country's external financial resource mobilization under international credit markets allows borrowing (with borrower set limits) at world interest rates. Under this simplified approach, credit limits are set by the creditworthiness of borrowers and/or borrower's ability to repay as projected into the next several years of loan repayment, taking into consideration net exports and budget surpluses. Some literature suggests that the net debt should be bounded, as a norm for setting a ceiling on the limits of borrowings, by the discounted value of future trade surpluses. Even this overly simplified approach to external lending is founded on several unknowns and uncertainties in information and events spread over several years. This is a largely untenable proposition because several additional factors are considered by lending institutions in their foreign lending operations. The phenomenon of 'credit rationing' and related features (see chapter 1 for more details) constrain the magnitude of loans.

Total factor productivity (TFP) has been identified as the most important determinant of economic growth (see chapter 1 for some of the relevant studies). The economic impact of excessive debt is generally contributed by the loss of TFP because of the following issues:

1. distortion of productive resource allocation in order to accord priority to loan repayments beyond the levels of marginal productivity of debt,

2. influence in the choice of projects and activities with shorter time horizons and of higher than optimal discount rates (or distorted rates of time preference, not conducive for sustainable economic growth), and

3. loss of incentives for investments (in both their total magnitude and their sectoral allocations).

Why do large magnitudes of outstanding debt reduce economic growth of borrower countries? The main explanation arises from the role of 'debt overhang', defined as the dampening of investments due to expectations that indicate potential inability of the debtor in repaying excessive outstanding debt, and the possibility of rising costs of capital borrowings in international markets (possibly due to country risk ratings and debt valuations). This feature is also related to another issue, discussed below.

The debt 'Laffer curve' phenomenon also has the same effect on borrowings and economic growth. This phenomenon suggests that the magnitude of outstanding debt stocks, beyond an optimum level, is inversely proportional to the probability of debt repayment. In this phenomenon, there is an early phase of debt stocks and debt repayment probabilities, where both can increase and contribute toward economic growth.

Empirical Study

Pattillo et al (2002) examined some of the empirical issues using a database containing data for 30 years on about 100 developing countries (excluding special countries such as those with less than population of 400,000 and those with export of oil as their primary source of revenue). They suggest that debt levels and economic growth are linked by a nonlinear relationship, as is intuitively clear from the reasoning of debt overhang and debt Laffer curve phenomena. In addition to confirming an inverted-U relationship between net present value (NPV) of debt and growth of annual per capita output, they identified two critical points: the overall contribution of debt to growth seems to become negative at about 160 percent of debt to exports in NPV terms. It has been estimated that if the debt burden of heavily indebted poor countries (HIPCs) were lowered to the target of 150 percent of exports, the corresponding economic growth rate could increase by one percentage point. This assessment needs to be seen in close relation to the debt relief measures discussed later in section 6.5.

The following section addresses analytical issues relating to the approximation of long-term contracts in terms of a series of short-term contracts, economic ingredients of optimal debt contract models, and new methods for further analyses.

6.4 Debt Contracts and Renegotiation

Since the emergence of debt repayment constraints in Latin America during the 1980s, several attempts were made to control and resolve a potential debt crisis. Despite a few improvements, some problems remain to be solved as a joint effort of the creditors and borrowers. Continued debt overhang poses several inefficiencies in the credit markets and that debt reduction is an important prerequisite for improved economic integration. There have been some major initiatives, including the HIPC Initiative of recent years for a select group of indebted countries (see details later in this chapter), and Baker Initiative and later the Brady Plan a decade ago for many of the indebted countries (the latter sponsored by the US Government) that attempted to achieve sovereign debt reduction.

For a wide variety of reasons, discrepancies exist between realized and contractually guaranteed repayments, thus providing a potential for renegotiation – even when the original contract was supposed to be 'renegotiation proof'. Renegotiation of explicit contractual agreements can be explained by relating to various problems of complexity and incomplete information. Besides, the process of renegotiation can be availed as a way of exploiting multiple equilibria to provide incentives as efficiently as possible (for analytical details see Pearce and Stacchetti, 1988).

Long Term and Short Term Contracts

The possibility of approximating long-term contracts through a series of short-term contracts negotiated periodically, has been recently examined by Fudenberg et al (1990) and Rey and Salanie (1990). The latter showed that when there is credible commitment, renegotiable short-term contracts would implement the long-term optimum in a multi-period 'principal-agent' framework (see chapter 1 for relevant explanation) when:

a) there exists no informational asymmetry (regarding 'relevant' information) at the contracting dates;

b) objectives are not identical; and

c) renegotiable transfers are non-trivial.

In the absence of credible commitments, short-term contracts would suffice if the following conditions hold (Fudenberg et al, 1990):

a) there exists no informational asymmetry;

b) the 'agent' can access a credit lending institution on equal terms with the 'principal';

c) recontracting takes place with common knowledge about technology and preferences; and

d) the frontier of expected utility payoffs generated by the set of incentive-compatible contracts is downward sloping at all times, i.e., it is composed of separable preferences.

From the above conditions, it is clear that the crucial role of symmetric information in debt contract specifications is a fundamental necessary (but not sufficient) requirement for evolving time-consistent series of short-term contracts that might approximate to a long-term contract. Still the question that remains to be examined is how to meet the symmetric information requirements.

Long-term contractual relationships may help overcome adverse selection problems, just as some of the stipulations governing collateral requirements in lending activities would. An alternative contract system to the sequence of standard-debt contracts may be proposed. In this contract, the payment at the second stage is made conditional upon whether the borrower fails and defaults in the first period; in particular, the second period payment will be higher if the borrower defaults in the first period than if she does not. It then follows that this modified sequence of contracts yields a lower expected return for low-quality borrowers than for high-quality borrowers. This is because the former have a higher probability of default, entailing a lower probability of capturing the lower payments at the second stage. This could lead to reduction of the adverse selection problem. Some of the theoretical underpinnings are offered by Webb (1991).

Analytical Aspects

Analytical formulations of debt models need to reflect that the possibility of renegotiation adds a set of additional constraints in the formal explicit contract design; new contracts should be required to be 'incentive compatible' and 'renegotiation-proof'. Unless these constraints are non-binding in the optimal solution sets, these renegotiability specifications tend to restrict the region of optimal solutions relative to the one without such a requirement. The general issue remains, however: whether one could go for relatively sub-optimal policies in the interests of renegotiation-proof solutions, or, whether any possible trade-off between regions of renegotiation-proof solutions and renegotiable but potential Pareto-welfare improving solutions could exist.

The operational limitations of *ex ante* specification of renegotiation-proof policies are the following:

a) the solutions tend to be relatively restricted or sub-optimal; and

b) there may still be no guarantee (legal or other) that the contract specifications have to be fully realized *ex post*, with no consideration for any changes in the credit-borrower situations and externalities.

The strongest argument against *ex ante* agreement that includes renegotiability is that the possibility of renegotiation can slow down the speed of information revelation (see e.g. Laffont and Tirole, 1988). This requires additional attention for provision of incentives for information revelation, and this is better done via incentives for compliance with *ex ante* contract specifications. An important content of renegotiation can be used to relate to future intensity of incentives to the degree of discrepancy at the end of the first part of the contract term; see also Bolton (1990). An important aspect of such an incentive design is suggested below, which also helps in the selection of preferred borrowers.

Does a comprehensive contractual specification nullify the need for any debt renegotiations? Bulow and Rogoff (1989) observed that 'if loans are perfectly indexed to all possible shocks, then one need never reschedule negotiations' is fraught with significant limitations. These include problems of observability of outcomes, or of dynamic informational asymmetry features, and problems of enforcement of original contracts when the degree of borrower commitment is an endogenous parameter (which is not observable, predictable, contractible or enforceable). This leads us to the pragmatic configuration wherein, despite a comprehensive indexing of contingencies and related contractual terms, there is a requirement of provision of incentives for information revelation and compliance with agreed-upon provisions. Bulow and Rogoff (1989) formulated a recontracting debt contract model of sovereign debt, where the primary motivation for debt repayment is the threat of direct sanctions that lenders can impose by legal methods, and the recontracting exercise is primarily due to interest rate shocks.

While this approach is better than the model that does not allow for such renegotiations after interest rate shocks, the results are of limited value because of the strong assumptions. These assumptions include the following:

a) symmetric information between creditors and debtors;

b) costless negotiation and bargaining among parties involved; and

c) constant time-preference even with changing state actors in the borrower case.

In reality, considerable costs are involved in debt negotiations and reschedulings, including costs of delays (strategic or other delays), and costs of disagreement or crisis potential arising out of breakdown of negotiations (relative to costs of mere postponement or simple automatic rescheduling of repayments or some of the key elements). From a transaction costs perspective it is meaningful to keep the rules and parameters of negotiation and renegotiation simple to minimize total costs of the debt recontracting process.

There remains the general issue: whether one could go for relatively suboptimal policies in the interests of renegotiation-proof solutions, or whether any possible trade-offs exist between regions of renegotiation-proof solutions and of renegotiable but potential Pareto-welfare improving solutions. The operational limitation of *ex ante* renegotiation-proof solutions include the following:

1. the solutions tend to be relatively restricted/sub-optimal; and

2. there may still be no guarantee (legal or otherwise) that the contract specifications have to be fully realized ex post, with no consideration for any changes in the creditor-borrower situations and externalities.

One of the strongest arguments against *ex ante* contractual specification that includes renegotiability as a potential future event is this: the possibility of renegotiation can slow the speed of information revelation (for analytical details see Laffont and Tirole, 1988). This problem can partly be addressed by the specific provision of incentives for information revelation as well, in addition to the specification of incentives for compliance within *ex ante* contract agreement.

Optimal Debt Contracts

At least three types of risks are relevant in international credit markets: solvency risk, repudiation risk, and panic or distress risk. There exists a large gap between theoretical models and their practical usability (Sachs, 1984), and this continues to be a valid constraint even to this day. Most of the technical model formulations seek to obtain partial optimal solutions. The center of focus of such models is an idealized all-benevolent planner or state actor in the borrower country whose objective is simply to maximize the social welfare or the sum of representative consumer utility functions over a time horizon, using a social time preference based discount function. However, there is little agreement regarding the choice of time horizon, discount rate for evaluating future, recognition of relevant costs, and some of the operational constraints. An optimal lending/borrowing model needs to incorporate not only the costs of these risks but also various transaction costs that apply in different stages of the debt market transactions. Currently there are no comprehensive models that recognize all these cost elements and their interactions with various objectives, incentives and constraints. These elements govern debt markets as well as their dynamic efficiency aspects, and hence there is a need for further development of methods and analyses on these lines.

Sovereign debt contracts are typically characterized by potential debt repudiation, rescheduling possibilities, asymmetric information, and limited enforceability of debt contracts. The main ingredients of debt contracts are: loan sizes, interest rates, repayments in different time intervals in the original initial contract and corresponding specifications for subsequent contracts (obtained via recontracting), time horizons relevant to initial contracting and to recontracting, contract compliance and contingency incentives for borrowers, and default penalties for non-compliance with contract terms.

Methodological Improvements

A suitable class of optimal control models is expected to be formulated and analyzed as a part of the modeling effort; new formulations will be especially meritorious in recontracting and rolling plan methods. Box 6.1 summarizes a few perspective directions for further development of analytical methods and applications. In any complex system – with ingredients like uncertainties, strategic behavior, incomplete information, and multiplicity of agents and institutions – it is often difficult to evaluate the probabilities or other features from past occurrences. A methodology to deal with non-probabilistic uncertainties – or fuzziness – of systems needs to be utilized. The 'muddle through' style of public policy decision-making and political instabilities at the national government level in borrower countries is a rather common process. These features provide a substantial structural basis for fuzziness of the systems. Operationally for example, the effective time discount rate of the decision-makers representing individual borrower nations could be stochastic or fuzzy, at variance with nominal or official discount rates. These could involve serious discrepancies in the perceived valuation of resource inflows and outflows, as seen by the borrower country representatives at a given time.

Box 6.1: Improved Approaches and Analytical Methods

For operational purposes, the real division between uncertainties that matter ('severe uncertainty') with fewer consequences ('petty uncertainty') is whether there are chances to correct a decision, or at least to make errors in some unimportant way (Aiginger, 1987, p. 177). This correction can be formulated as a two-stage optimization process: short-run optimization for a given long-term optimization. This suggests the possible use of a 'rolling plan' approach, wherein constant recontracting takes place. Only the first period in a T-period contract (T may be five or more finite number of years) is in effect implemented, and the remaining specifications renegotiated for the subsequent T-period (rolling but fixed horizon). Such a process can possibly reduce informational asymmetry problems as well.

Alternatively, if it were possible to visualize all the possible contingencies, contracting that provides for such contingencies contracts and rolling horizons may provide the optimal contract arrangements beneficial to creditors and sovereign borrowers. An optimal contingent rule may be preferable and workable, formally and empirically. Some of the important foundations have been laid out by Buiter (1981). Choice of contract horizon is a critical issue here. It appears that significantly greater attention is required for further analytical studies and assessment of their implications on the following, with policy implications:

a) acquisition of information for decision-making, verification, and revision;

b) devising optimal contingent rules that take into account both creditor and borrower welfare on a long term basis;

c) costs of undertaking these exercises, and totality of transaction costs; and

d) treating the horizon itself as a decision variable or policy instrument for negotiation, contracting and recontracting.

The addition of choice of time horizon as a policy instrument enlarges the set of meaningful decision alternatives (for technical proof see Rubinstein and Wolinsky, 1992).

If we turn to cooperative games with sequential structures allowing for renegotiation or incomplete information, Harsanyi and Stelton (1989) method is expected to be useful: a game with incomplete information can be transformed into classical cooperative game-theoretic framework by using a probabilistic model to represent the incomplete information. Harsanyi and Stelton theory of solution selection is based on the risk dominance relationship between solution candidates and equilibrium selection. However, the risk dominance ordering is intransitive and this poses serious limitations to the selection of desirable solutions. The concept of Equilibrium Selection Based on Resistance Avoidance (ESBORA) evolved by Guth and Kalkofen (1989) is based on the requirement of 'minimal opposition by all players' to the proposed candidate solution of a player. Generalized Nash property is also included within the ESBORA theory differs from Harsanyi and Stelton theory mainly in that the latter's intransitive relation of risk dominance is substituted by the transitive relation of resistance dominance among solution candidates. These are some of the relevant directions for further research with meaningful applications in debt recontracting and renegotiations.

6.5 Debt Relief Policies

The economic performance of the debtor is mainly the resultant effect of the effort level of the debtor, conditionality set forth by the lending institutions, and economic shocks arising from both domestic and international sources. Next, the debt repayment behavior of a debtor country is the resultant of economic performance, incentives for compliance with debt contracts, and disincentives for noncompliance. Thus, debt repayment features are not necessarily the sole responsibility of the borrowers; the contributions of creditors in any debt default situation must be assessed.

High Indebtedness

Several measures have been proposed in recent years to restore financial standing to some of the poorer countries with heavy external indebtedness. One of the issues related to a form of barter trade. Can counter trade or barter mitigate some of the financial constraints of the highly indebted countries? Barter can solve some of the incentive problems related to resource transfer to developing countries when the promise future goods can be enforced more cost-effectively than the promise of future money. The phenomena of barter trade increased after the 1980s debt crises and expanded during the 1990s East Asia financial crises. Marin and Schnitzer (2002) observed that investment goods and consumer goods have been suitable for barter for countries whose creditworthiness is not too low. The broader issues here are those of debt waiver, debt reduction, and provision of meaningful mechanisms of 'insurance' against international export market – demand and price for some of the primary commodities.

The debt situation of several developing countries attained precarious and unsustainable levels. Interest payments on external debt (IED) exceeded economic growth rates in some countries. Some of the countries where the IED exceeded one percent (this estimate given in bracket) of the corresponding GDP at the end of 2001 are Cameroon (3.5), Guyana (5.4), Madagascar (1.2), Nicaragua (1.2), and Sao Tome and Principe (7.6). Countries whose external debt exceeded 75 percent of their corresponding GDP at the end of 2001 are, in addition to the above, The Gambia, and Rwanda.

The relative debt burden of some of the developing countries is given in Table 6.1 in terms of a comparison of magnitudes of debt repayment, which remains generally at about thrice the level of their corresponding social service expenditures.

Table 6.1: HIPC Countries and Social Services- Select Cases

Country	Basic Social Services	External Debt Payment
Cameroon	4	36
Cote d' Ivoire	11.4	35
Kenya	12.6	40
Niger	20.4	33
Tanzania	15	46
Zambia	6.7	40

Source: UN Secretary General's Report (2001). The numbers denote percentages of country annual budgets for the year 1998.

Recent Developments

A summary of the HIPC Initiative is given in Box 6.2. At the 2002 Annual Meetings of the IMF and the World Bank the Development Committee of these organizations in its resolution of September 28, 2002 (at para 11) suggested that the success of the HIPC Initiative will require:

> "a sustained commitment by HIPC countries to improvements in domestic policies and economic management; capacity building for the management of financial assets and liabilities; full participation and delivery of relief by all affected creditors; and adequate and sufficiently concessional financing by international financial institutions and the donor community."

The IMF and the World Bank have been playing the key role in the implementation of the HIPC Initiative to address the problem of minimizing the burden of external debt in heavily indebted poor countries. The total assistance from donor countries and multilateral financial institutions committed by about the middle of 2002 represents a reduction in the outstanding debt stock of about $40 billion in NPV terms. This constitutes about a two-thirds reduction in the outstanding debt stock of eligible countries. In addition various measures in progress at the IMF and the World Bank for sovereign debt reorganization (see Box 6.3 for details) could effect changes in dealing with the issues of country risk (see also chapter 9) and debt repayment.

Box 6.2: The HIPC Initiative

The HIPC Initiative is touted as a 'comprehensive' approach to debt reduction for poor countries, and involves participation of all creditors. The IMF and the World Bank launched a program in September 1996 to address the problem of excessive and unsustainable debts of poor countries and began this Initiative. To be considered for financial assistance under this program, a country with unsustainable debt burden (after reflecting any debt-relief schemes) is required to establish a track of reforms endorsed by the twin institutions. If the external debt ratio (NPV of debts/ exports) for a country is above 150 percent, the country may be considered for assistance under the HIPC Initiative. In special cases of highly export-driven open economies (with exports-to-GDP ratio above 30 percent); countries may be eligible even when this percentage is lower. Several African countries became eligible for assistance under the HIPC Initiative.

The NPV of debt is defined here: it is the sum of all debt-service obligations on existing debt, discounted at the market interest rate.

By the last quarter of 2002, among the 36 HIPCs 24 countries reached their 'decision point', i.e. these countries have adopted some adjustments and reforms to enable their eligibility for assistance and the IMF and World Bank Executive Boards decide possible endorsement for support. During 2001, an enhanced HIPC Initiative (or HIPC II) was launched to improve and expand the original HIPC Initiative. The total cost of providing assistance to 34 countries under this Initiative was estimated around $36 billion in NPV terms at the end of 2001. By September 2002, 26 countries reached their completion point or are in their interim period after decision point. Of these, the six countries that have reached their 'completion points' for debt relief purpose are Bolivia, Burkina Faso, Mauritania, Mozambique, Tanzania, and Uganda. Their debt service relief total comes to $13.34 billion. Besides, 20 countries that have reached their decision points become eligible for corresponding relief that adds to $27.38 billion. In addition, 12 countries would have been able to seek relief under the HIPC but these are political and social conflict-affected and have complex problems in devising viable reform packages (IMF and World Bank, 2002). Total committed resources for debt relief (as of September 2002) by creditors stood at $41.52 billion.

It is also recognized that debt relief and rescheduling alone do not guarantee that a country will permanently exit from falling back to unsustainable levels of debt; ensuring long-term debt sustainability will require sustainable economic growth and policy reforms, as well as stable export earnings (IMF and IDA, 2002).

Some of the prerequisites for effective debt reduction include: stabilization of the terms of trade affecting developing country export revenues, debt relief contingent upon due efforts by the debtor, and provision of 'interest holiday' and other forms of repayment flexibility (to enable debtors revert to greater financial strength especially in the short run; for analytical models in this line of inquiry see Cohen, 1991).

Analytically, one of the most important aspects of sovereign debt contract formulation and subsequent management is that of provision of incentives for promoting efficient debt governance. The role of provision of penalties or other disincentives is often suggested in the debt literature, but these disincentives are largely unrealistic in achieving their objectives, besides failing to be cost-effective. These aspects, mainly their analytical dimensions, are discussed in the following section.

6. 6 The Design of Incentives

In one of the classical formulations of credit lending (not necessarily in the sovereign borrowing context), Stiglitz and Weiss' (1981) model for conventional credit markets assumed that lenders know the probability distribution of returns on investments, and that borrowers cannot alter the distribution. This would then rule out the role of effort or of positive incentives for enhanced efficiency of the agent in the context of a principal – agent model. However, it was recognized that the perceptions of relevant probability distributions could differ between creditors and borrowers. Subsequently, Stiglitz and Weiss (1983) considered 'incentive' contracts where the threat of termination of contract (which typically falls in the category of disincentives) was considered an incentive to motivate the borrower. Clearly, formulations that are more realistic are required to address the issue of provision of optimal incentives.

The general issue, beyond the analysis of effectively static models of Stiglitz and Weiss (1981), is the incentive problem. This problem poses the question of, in a heterogeneous (finite number of non-identical customers) borrower market, and in a multi-period framework, what would be the dynamic incentive effects of debt forgiveness or other concessions on the distinguishable categories of borrowers such as existing 'well-behaved' borrowers, existing borrowers other than the above, new borrowers, and potential new borrowers.

The provision of a judicious mix of incentives and enforceable disincentives remains a very important dimension of optimal debt contracts. In the reputational approach of Eaton and Gersovitz (1981) and of Grossman and Van Huyck (1988), the debtor's sole incentive to make debt repayments is to preserve its reputation as a good borrower and hence creditworthiness. Alternatively, Bulow and Rogoff (1989) assumed that the primary motivation for repayment is the threat of direct sanctions that creditors can impose, under the assumption that perfect symmetry of information existed between the parties involved. These preliminary formulations of debt models have highlighted only one or two elements of the total set of incentives and disincentives in affecting the borrower behavior after entering into debt contract. More comprehensive formulations and analysis will be useful for the assessment of real world settings.

Role of Sanctions

The legal sanctions available to private creditors could not often constitute disincentives for a sovereign borrower's decision whether or not to default (Kaletsky, 1985). Both the potential defaulters and the creditors are usually aware that the latter may not realize net gains from legal action to enforce debt repayment obligations; some creditors could lose more than the defaulter could – even if their legal actions were to succeed. The analytical and practical role of incentives rather than disincentives in affecting the credit repayment prospects of debtors and the degree of compliance with various terms of debt contracts needs further examination.

The scope for levying revised and differentiated risk premia analogous to the insurance industry (where premia are revised in relation to individual claims, or 'experience rating') has not been fully utilized in the international credit market transactions for the following reasons:

1. re-lending decisions are largely influenced by the official creditors and their governments rather than competitive private banks;
2. higher risk premia tend to worsen the debt servicing situation of the existing constrained debtor, and could possibly lead to the classical adverse selection problem; and
3. international credit lending institutions tend to operate largely according to a few straightjacket methods of uniformity for large classes and categories of borrowers.

The potential efficiency-improving roles of incentives and disincentives are usually better captured by customer-specific treatment rather than uniformity that is unrelated to performance. As suggested by Calvo (1989), objective situations and contracts are clearly not identical across countries; hence, there is no reason to expect that all countries should be subject to uniform debt relief or default penalties. Debt problems and their solutions have not been generally viewed in terms of the more basic problem of enforcement. An analysis for the provision of penalties for debt repayment defaults, and *ex ante* and *ex post* dichotomies in their enforceability is given by Calvo (1989). Varian (1990) argued in favor of the efficacy of provision of greater role of incentives for compliance rather than disincentives for non-compliance.

Some of the major issues that are relevant may be stated: a) If default penalties and other economic sanctions could not be effectively levied on problem debtors, is there room for devising more stringent and legally enforceable measures to ensure compliance with the terms of borrowing. b) Do we, instead, emphasize more on the provision of interest rate subsidy or other types of bonuses as incentives for compliance with various contractual obligations of the borrower? c) Can we evolve a mix of both (a) and (b)?

Another parallel set of issues also needs to be clarified within the above framework. The costs of efficiency, enforcement and monitoring of alternative provisions of incentives and/or disincentives need to be considered. In addition, the major differences in these implications in relation to provisions distinguished by the *ex ante* vs. *ex post*, with reference to debt contract agreements also need to be considered.

Whatever the stringent penalties that might be provided for in the contract specifications, "ex-post, once the country has borrowed and gotten into trouble, the ability to penalize can be harmful" (Froot et. al., 1988, pp. 17). If sovereign debt default is punished by impeded trade or a credit embargo, then creditor countries stand to lose along with the debtor (Eaton, 1990).

Provision and enforcement of penalties has several serious obstacles. These are the following:

1. if the provision of default penalties is such that it does not fully take into account the diversity of risk-averse attitudes (which, by definition, cannot be a uniform factors for all borrowers), this could lead to adverse selection;

2. the enforcement of penalties is fraught with serious legal and practical limitations under sovereign debt;

3. when there are multiple lenders (especially a large number), the potential free-rider problem in the sharing of costs of enforcement inhibits many of the lenders from incurring various (financial or other) costs;

4. inflicting penalties can be like a remedy worse than the disease, especially when there exist externalities, including 'trading externalities', irreversibilities in the debt servicing potential of the borrower and possibly other dead-weight costs, including hurting exporter country/creditor country interests; and

5. this last factor provides incentives for official creditors to step into the debt renegotiation processes and thus relegates original creditors to the historical background.

There are serious limitations of debt research contributions that suggest that countries might take narrow cut-off point decisions wherein debtors compare the costs of non-compliance (including default penalties) with the benefits of suspending debt service payments (for relevant details see Dooley and Svensson, 1990). Continued debt service is rational in cases where the economic benefits and costs of default are likely to be very limited. This is because there are additonally several spillover costs and benefits that deserve attention, including implications on reputation and effects on repeat transactions in various markets.

Incentives

The list of incentives for debt repayment or compliance with contractual obligations could include the following:

1. ensure credit worthiness and regular credit flows – if interested in continued borrowings;
2. reputation to be retained or improved – whether or not continued borrowings are required;
3. conditionality in agreements with creditors that tends to explicitly or implicitly incorporate access to export-import markets;
4. externalities with other potential creditors;
5. cost of penalties: explicit in debt contracts (whether or not they are totally enforceable); and
6. interest rate subsidy (if any) for compliance.

Inclusion of contract duration or time horizon as a decision variable (rather than impose a standard fixed horizon) enlarges the set of feasible alternatives for the borrower and allows realization of rents on private information, just as the accompanying self-selection of penalties for noncompliance with debt contract terms would also achieve similar objectives. Formal analysis on the relative efficiency of provision of incentives and disincentives, or rigorous explanation to the question whether generally the 'carrot is better than stick' for effective enforcement and realization of objectives, requires straightforward application of Generalized Envelope Theorem in an optimizing framework (see e.g. Varian, 1990). There are at least four constraints that are relevant to the creditor's decision-model:

a) obtaining a pre-specified return on capital;
b) borrower incentive compatibility;
c) borrower's information revelation; and
d) minimizing the enforcement costs and other transaction costs.

If we operate in lending regimes that emphasize default penalty provisions as a measure of avoiding non-compliance, should the default occur, the ex post costs of enforcement tend to be very significant (as indicated earlier) and shall constrain the objective function value to higher levels. Let us recall that the definition of incentive compatibility requires that the decision making entities (or borrowers, in the present case) find it to their benefit to comply with the specifications of an agreement. Constraints (b) and (c) are not likely to remain binding for optimal solutions, as fulfillment of these constraints maximizes the utility functions of the borrowers: taking advantage of various incentives by compliance and hence information revelation (see also Pearce and Stachetti, 1988).

The information role of optimal incentive provision is far more significant than the moral hazard or other related problems of provision and enforcement of disincentives. Besides, the cost to the creditor of incentives for borrower's compliance with contractual obligations is transparent and can be assessed with probability one; in the case of resorting to default penalties and other disincentives, the stochastic costs need to be assessed and are likely to possess high levels of mean and variance. Some of these issues require further investigation in the context of a multi-period repeated transaction framework, with or without renegotiation possibilities. Zou (1992) used a static optimization model that included both features of asymmetric information, viz. moral hazard and adverse selection. The desirability of an element of self-selection of penalty for deviations from contract terms has been suggested as a motivator for information revelation. There is a combination incentive problem of provision of incentives for compliance with debt contract terms: firstly for information sharing and secondly for implementation of agreed effort allocations (including resource allocations). The Zou (1992) model uses a number of simplify–ing assumptions, however. These include, the transaction costs of contract design and enforcement are zero; penalties and other threats/ disincentives are enforced with certainty, i.e. these constitute credible threats and are cost-effective.

Regarding the role of provision of contingencies related to debt repayments, it is useful to note that the provision of optimal contingencies eliminates or reduces the default phenomenon. A contingency plan that makes interest rate contingent upon realization of random shocks to the borrower economy is preferable (in the sense of enhancing total welfare) to levying penalty in relation to default rate or magnitude (Aizenman, 1989).

The following section focuses on policy and legal issues relating to sovereign debt restructuring and reform.

6. 7 Sovereign Debt Management

Several policy initiatives are required for improved sovereign debt management in the interests of both creditors and borrowers, so that debt structures remain sustainable. In addition, cost-effective debt reorganization needs to occur wherever and whenever necessary. Some of the suggested policy reforms take the developing country debt situation in a broader context of poverty and human welfare, and some others address the immediate procedural and legal constraints to improved management.

UNCTAD (2001), among a few others, suggested a principle under which a state may impose a temporary standstill on foreign debt servicing at the onset of a financial crisis and subject itself to the scrutiny of independent experts for evolving remedial measures and possibly a consensus-based resolution of the crisis, acceptable to creditors and the debtor country. More fundamentally, the UN Commission on Human Rights (2001) in its Resolution 2001/27 (at paragraph 7) stated:

> "Affirmed that the exercise of basic rights of people of debtor countries to food, housing, clothing, employment, education, health services and healthy environment could not be subordinated to the implementation of structural adjustment policies, growth programs and economic reforms arising from their external debt."

Nonetheless, current debt management policies of international institutions are not yet reflective of these multiple concerns of economic development.

It may be argued that debt reduction is perhaps a necessary but not sufficient condition for improved efficiency of international credit markets. Considerable information sharing, cooperation and renegotiation regarding debt contract specifications and compliance is an important mechanism that could alleviate potential debt crisis and provide improved arrangements for future transactions. A number of varying measures have been attempted since the 1980s to reorganize debt of sovereign states, especially those with high indebtedness or unsustainable debt magnitudes. Debt buyback markets (with or without the use of different debt bonds) were promoted. Some of these involved debtor's resources for buybacks, and some involved buybacks using donated resources. In addition, debt-equity swaps were undertaken in a few Latin American countries. These initiatives were aimed at promoting foreign direct investment, and some swaps involved debt-for-nature that aimed at protecting the environment (in the debtor country with positive environmental externalities or benefits for the global environment) and effectively reduced sovereign debt. A detailed analytical treatment for various debt buyback models may be seen in Eaton (1992).

Sovereign Debt Restructuring

Debt management requires application of prudential governance principles. These principles include assessment of debt structure, borrowing and repayment policies in terms of their combined effect on potential for insolvency and costs of such crises. Dooley (2000) hypothesized that about ten years of depressed economic activity in debtor countries followed the 1982 debt crisis, and that prolonged debt negotiating hurt borrower economies by inducing excessive uncertainties and their multiplier effects. It has also been suggested that:

a) a good loan portfolio is one that balances welfare gains from each activity with the costs generated by that activity's contribution to default risk; and

b) the objective of the state in debtor countries must be managing financial institutions and policies to avoidance of financial crisis.

Until about late 1980s, creditors to developing countries were mainly transnational banks, multilateral lending institutions and bilateral lenders/donors. Later, this situation changed to include diffused groups and institutions, in addition to the above entities. Commercial bank loans moved largely from conventional loans to bonds. Unlike in the previous years this change brought in two main features to the debt markets:

   a) coordinators of the creditors for debt rescheduling for any country is very cumbersome because of the involvement of multitudes of institutions, financial instruments, and their terms of agreement (including widely differing applicability of financial laws); and

   b) many creditors lack repeat ongoing transactions with the debtors and this characteristic requires recognition of significantly varied incentives and disincentives for debt governance at any point of time for any specific borrower country.

A comprehensive sovereign debt restructuring requires coordination and cooperation of several bond issuers, syndicated loan issuers, trade financing entities and multilateral and other lender institutions. The practicability of debt restructuring based on a single indicator such as the NPV of debt becomes less meaningful in this complex scenario.

How is the NPV defined by the IMF and World Bank for the implementing the HIPC Initiative? The NPV of debt is expressed as (IMF, 2002): "the sum of all future debt-service obligations (interest and principal) on existing debt, discounted at the market interest rate." This definition is typically one of Present Value (PV) rather than of NPV. A more accurate estimate of NPV would use opportunity cost of capital rather than market interest rate, which is usually higher than the former. Thus, the current estimates are of higher magnitudes than realistic ones. The method being used by the IMF and the World Bank has the following implications (for more details see Cosio-Pascal, 1997, p. 17):

If the debt reduction is applied to the PV amount rather than to the stock of outstanding debt, the creditors are implicitly transferring the opportunity cost of the original concessional loan to the debtor. The debt relief applies then to the amount that would have been lent in the absence of concessional terms. This amounts to asking the debtor pay upfront an amount equivalent to the grant or concession of the loan for rescheduling. Also, in the context of poverty alleviation, it is important to note that the current practice of using NPV for debt reduction is independent of its direct relationship with desired quantum of poverty reduction in a target country (Rao, 2003).

What is sustainable external debt for a country? This has been defined (Boote and Thugge, 1997, p. 10) as a situation when a country is "expected to be able to meet is current and future external debt obligations in full, without recourse to debt relief, rescheduling of debts, or the accumulation of arrears and without unduly compromising growth." This definition is built on several explicit and implicit assumptions, some of them relate to export finances, credit terms and economic stability in the presence of unknown external and internal shocks to the economic and other systems.

Currently, a sovereign debtor state cannot be helped by a qualified majority of its creditors for debt restructuring since they cannot bind a solution on the minority of creditors. The IMF launched during 2002 a set of measures that are engaging attention for reform in debt restructuring. There are cumbersome problems for assisting the debtor (except through debt waiver itself). The two main elements of this reform proposal are:

a) an amendment of the IMF Articles of Agreement that could create a legal framework within which creditors and debtors coordinate and cooperate for debt restructuring of any debtor country; and

b) provision of contractual clauses, including 'Collective Action Clauses' can facilitate debt restructuring with less complexity and time.

Some of the suggested new provisions include the following:

- representation clauses that authorize a trustee of bondholder syndicate to coordinate between the debtor and the bondholders at early stages of debt rescheduling or restructuring,

- temporary legal protection to insolvent or potentially crisis-ridden debtors, and

- aggregation of creditor claims and possible adoption of majority stakeholders' decisions for effecting relevant changes in the debt restructuring.

New Reforms

In a recent proposal, Krueger (2002) of the IMF suggested that the role of contract mechanism for sovereign debt restructuring might be of limited use for the reasons:

a) the design of a perfect contract may be impractical,

b) even if a contractual basis can be devised, such a framework may not provide a "comprehensive and durable solution to collective action problems." (Ibid, p. 31), and

c) "a statutory regime is….likely to provide a more stable background than contractual provisions…" (Ibid, p. 33).

Krueger favored a statutory international treaty to bring an effect to some of the reform proposals for addressing sovereign debt restructuring.

Additional legal reforms relevant for sovereign debt reorganization and long-term debt management in relation to some of the US legal provisions are explained in Box 6.3.

When a debtor claims insolvency (treated on par with the declaration of bankruptcy by creditors), there may be two remedial measures for possible adoption in relation to the US laws; these are summarized below.

1. If section 109 of Chapter 11 of the US Bankruptcy Code were modified to allow a sovereign state to utilize the provisions of the Bankruptcy Code, a voluntary petition could be filled under section 301. The debtor must file (in accordance with section 521 of Chapter 11) various statements and schedules of information including details of assets and liabilities, and a comprehensive listing of creditors. This requirement enables information revelation by debtors. The provisions of Chapter 11 set a strong basis for resolving sovereign bankruptcy problem. An important function of the bankruptcy court in Chapter 11 reorganization is detailed scrutiny of the debtor's actions, possibly leading to liquidation of the debtor's assets. In sovereign bankruptcy, this may not be entirely feasible.

2. A suitable framework for resolving sovereign insolvency (bankruptcy) could be a revised global Chapter 9 (GC9) of reorganization; the debtor would retain the ability to borrow money even after the insolvency has been filed. Under the US law, an entity seeking Chapter 9 proceedings must have Section 109 (c), 11, USCA): "either obtained the agreement of the majority of each class of creditors affected, or have attempted to work out a plan without success, be unable to negotiate with creditors because this is impracticable, or reasonably believe that a creditor may attempt to gain preference." Eligible petition allows an automatic granting of stay of enforcement of claims against the debtor.

Box 6.3: Sovereign Debt Reorganization and Global Chapter 9

Insolvency and Global Bankruptcy Code

Because creditors are usually not equipped with legal remedies for breach of contract in a debtor's political jurisdiction, mutually advantageous contracts common to the domestic corporate bond-finance in the developed world are unenforceable in the international credit market. A parallel does not exist in the international credit markets to the provision of Bankruptcy Codes such as Chapters 9 (of primary use in the local government or municipalities) and 11 (of primary use in the corporate sector) of the US system. Such a provision, when devised and operative, tends to offer efficiency gains by limiting possible individual actions of creditors that could force a firm into liquidation. Sovereignty of borrowers limits these possibilities, but a global version of Chapter 9 (let us call this GC9) of the US Bankruptcy Code may be relevant. Raffer (1990) called for a fair sharing of risks in light of advise and conditionality imposed by the IMF and the World Bank in the case of 'structural adjustment', and for the application of a GC9: "Combining a uniform framework with the flexibility needed in particular cases, an international Chapter 9 would bring debt service obligations again in line with the capacity to pay". (Ibid, p. 310).

Role of GC9

Chapter 9 of the US Bankruptcy Code allows affected institutions to voice their arguments, in contrast "with the lot of those who are affected by structural adjustment." Credits granted during the Chapter 9 proceeding to keep the country afloat should not be affected by it. One of the disincentives for availing provisions of Chapter 9 by debtors includes 'loss of face' as a result of filing insolvency (Miller, 1991).

Chapter 9 does not involve any subsidies by the taxpayers, not even increased risk via a public international debt authority. Lenders face their own risk, although regulation relief could accompany the first application of any international Chapter 9; the procedure instead sticks to restoring economic viability. The international scope of lending to a debtor country via multiple bilateral and multilateral creditor institutions could diminish the possibility of filing sovereign bankruptcy in the US court system. However, Chapter 9 of the US Bankruptcy Code could form the logical basis for international adjudication, possibly with adjudication under the aegis of the Bank of International Settlements (BIS) or a new independent institution that may be formed. An appropriate type of bankruptcy proceedings for a foreign nation would be a Chapter 9 version of the US Bankruptcy Code (Miller, 1991). The judicial institution in administering Chapter 9 proceedings will have no control over expenditures of the affected entity unlike in the Chapter 11 proceedings. It was pointed that an important aspect of Chapter 9 is that the court will not interfere with governmental powers or functions and the affected entity's ability to retain access to credit remains in tact.

With the provision of a meaningful GC9 at the international level, the debtors can retain their ability to borrow funds even after the insolvency process has been initiated. The loans of multilateral and other creditor institutions may be brought under the process of GC9 proceedings rather than holding the borrower country to hostage whenever insolvency problems arise. Let us recall that liquidity and solvency problems could visit almost any state at some time. Historically even the British and French Governments defaulted in the 1930s when they placed the needs of their citizens more important than the legal obligations for repayments.

Is there a significant cost for a country to seek GC9 proceedings for resurrecting its access to international credit markets? Among other costs, the loss of 'face value' itself should act as a disincentive and the application of GC9 should remain an action of last resort rather than an easy escape route from financial responsibility of a borrower state.

6.8 Concluding Observations

Attempts to minimize informational asymmetries between international creditors and sovereign borrowers are likely to be fruitful if:

a) there is a greater role for provision of incentives (for example, concessional interest rates) in debt contracts that encourage compliance with agreed terms;

b) regular renegotiation occurs with a rolling plan approach; and

c) the focus on provision of default penalties is shifted to that on optimal incentives for compliance with contract terms.

Short-term contracts can generally be more attractive to the lenders who could discount future rather significantly; some of these discounts could also be due to the 'tragedy of the commons', where each participant creditor tends to ignore the combined effect of similar behavior of other participant in the lending markets. The role of institutional reform in enhancing the effectiveness of aid and debt is important.

It is useful to recognize that a good loan portfolio is one that balances welfare gains from each activity with the costs generated by that activity's contribution to default risk and to potential loss of economic resilience. An important objective of the state in debtor countries needs to focus on managing financial institutions and policies to avoid potential financial crisis.

Credit lending can be self-eliminating unless the lenders' policies (including conditionalities) and borrowers' credit use efficiency are meaningful. In the past debt forgiveness has not been used to reward countries with good governance and this might not have sent the right signals or incentives for improved institutional and economic governance (see also Neumayer, 2002). Major donor countries and the international financial institutions they control must afford due recognition for the institutional quality in recipient countries and seek a gradual reform on a sustainable basis to restore better governance in the borrower countries. If this does not materialize, externalities of the latter's mismanagement tend to be incurred by the former without devising a corrective mechanism to reduce repetition of the phenomena.

Debt contracts, by design, should be contingency contracts. This is not to state that the contingency applies to the total quantity of repayable loans but to scheduling of repayments in relation to unforeseen and random shocks to the economic systems of the borrowers. World Bank (2003, p.1-2) noted, without mentioning any corresponding policy measures, that the 'fixed commitments' of debt service are "not well suited to the swings in nominal income experienced by many developing countries, especially those dependent on primary commodities."

A parameterized and indexed (to export prices and earnings) debt contract eliminates (or at least reduces) the stigma of borrower defaults, and reduces consequent costs to creditors and borrowers. Besides, this could possibly form one of several measures required as per the 2002 Monterrey Consensus (see chapter 4 for more details) stated (at the Resolution paragraph 47): "… Debtors and creditors must share the responsibility for preventing and resolving unsustainable debt situations."

In the context of the design and enforcement of sovereign debt contracts, the scope for improvement lies in the following directions:

1. Since the enforcement of debt penalty clauses is often neither interests of the creditors nor debtors, greater role of incentives is required for the purposes:

    a) debtor compliance with the terms of the contract;

    b) effecting a screening method for the degree of commitment of borrowers; and

    c) rewarding commitment and compliance.

    The incentive could be in terms of differential interest rates, as part of the contract agreement, in relation to the type and degree of compliance with the agreed terms. This approach can be useful only when there is prior agreement on such schedules of rewards as well.

2. A Global Chapter 9 version of the US Bankruptcy Code for effecting debt restructuring under insolvency / bankruptcy of sovereign states needs to be formulated with the involvement of different categories of stakeholders.

Review Exercises

1. If the price of credit in bank lending to international entities is enhanced to reflect potential risks in debt repayment, examine the credit market efficiency implication in terms of the roles of asymmetric information, costs of contract enforcement, moral hazard, adverse selection and credit risk management.

2. Examine the validity of the following claim in an ideal world (Bulow and Rogoff, 1989): "if loans are perfectly indexed to all possible shocks then one need never observe rescheduling negotiations".

3. The role of political factors is at least as important as economic factors in country-specific debt management, especially debt forgiveness. Explain the role of incentives and information at donor and recipient levels in reducing debt burden.

4. It has been observed in some studies that aid has a positive impact on growth in countries with an institutionalized check on governmental power. Is it feasible that this conclusion, if valid, readily extends to debt also as in the case of aid? Explain the reasoning for the answer.

5. What are the main elements of the HIPC and where might be its potential contribution to the alleviation of debt problems in some of the countries?

References

Aiginger, K. (1987): Production and Decision Theory under Uncertainty, Basil Blackwell, New York.

Aizenman, J. (1989): Country Risk and Contingencies, International Economic Journal, 3, 81-102.

Bolton, P. (1990): Renegotiation and the Dynamics of Contract Design, European Economic Review, 34, 303-310.

Boote, A. and Thugge, K. (1997): Debt relief for low-income countries and the HIPC Initiative, Washington, DC: IMF Pamphlet #51.

Buiter, W. (1981): The Superiority of Contingent Rules over Fixed Rules in Models with Rational Expectations, Economic Journal, 91, 647-70.

Bulow, J. and Rogoff, K. (1989): A Constant Recontracting Model of Sovereign Debt, Journal of Political Economy, 97, 155-178.

Calvo, G. (1989): A Delicate Equilibrium: Debt Relief and Debt Penalties in an International Context, Washington, DC: IMF Working Paper #10.

Cohen, D. (1991): Private Lending to Sovereign States, Cambridge, MA: MIT Press.

Cosio-Pascal, E. (1997): Debt Sustainability and Social and Human Development, UNCTAD Discussion Paper #128, Geneva: UNCTAD.

Devlin, R. (1989): Debt and Crisis in Latin America – The Supply Side of the Story, Princeton: Princeton University Press.

Dooley, M. (2000): Debt management and crisis in developing countries, Journal of Development Economics, 63, 45-58.

Dooley, M. and Svensson, L. (1990): Policy, Inconsistency and External Debt Service, IMF Working Paper #35.

Eaton, J. (1992): Sovereign Debt – A Primer, Working Paper WPS 855, Washington DC: World Bank.

Eaton, J. (1990): Debt Relief and the International Enforcement of Loan Contracts, Journal of Economic Perspectives, 4.1, 43-56.

Eaton, J. and Gersovitz, M. (1981): Debt with potential repudiation – Theoretical and empirical analysis, Review of Economic Studies, 48, 289-309.

Froot, K., et al. (1988): Forgiveness, Indexation, and Investment Incentives, NBER Working Paper #2541.

Fudenberg, D., Holmstrom, B. and Milgrom, P. (1990): Short-Term Contracts and Long-Term Relationships, Journal of Economic Theory, 51.1, 1-31.

Grossman, H. and van Huyck, J. (1988): Sovereign debt as a contingent claim – Excusable default, repudiation, and reputation, American Economic Review, 78, 1088-97.

Guth, W. and Kalkofen, B. (1989): Unique Solutions for Strategic Games – Equilibrium Selection Based on Resistance Avoidance, Springer-Verlag, NY.

Harsanyi, J and Stelton, R. (1988): A General Theory of Equlibrium Selection in Games, MIT Press, Cambridge.

IMF (2002): Debt Relief under the Heavily Indebted Poor Countries (HIPC) Initiative – A Fact Sheet, Washington, DC: IMF.

IMF and IDA (2002): The Enhanced HIPC Initiative and the Achievement of Long-Term External Debt Sustainability, Washington DC: IMF.

IMF and World Bank (2002): Joint Ministerial Committee (Development Committee) of the Board of Governors on the Transfer of Real Resources to Developing Countries, Washington DC: IMF / World Bank.

Kaletsky, A. (1985): The Costs of Default, New York: Twentieth Century Fund.

Krueger, A. (2002): A New Approach to Sovereign Debt Restructuring, Washington, DC: IMF.

Laffont, J. and Tirole, J. (1988): Comparative Statics of the Optimal Dynamic Incentive Contract, European Economic Review, 31, 901-926.

Lindert, P. and Morton, P. (1989): How Sovereign Debt Has Worked, pp. 39-106, in J. Sachs (Ed.), Developing Country Debt and Economic Performance, Chicago: University of Chicago Press.

Marin, D. and Schnitzer, M. (2002): The Economic Institution of International Barter, Economic Journal, 112, 293-316.

Miller, B. H. (1991): Sovereign Bankruptcy – Examining the US bankruptcy system as a forum for sovereign debtors, Law and Policy in International Business, 22, 107-131.

Neumayer, E. (2002): Is good governance rewarded? A cross-national analysis of debt forgiveness, World Development, 30, 913-930.

Pattillo, C., Poirson, H. and Ricci, L. (2002): External Debt and Growth, Finance and Development, 39, 32-35.

Pearce, D. and Stacchetti, E. (1988): The Interaction of Implicit and Explicit Contracts in Repeated Agency, Cowles Foundation Discussion Paper #892.

Raffer, K. (1990): Applying Chapter 9 Insolvency to International Debts: An Economically Efficient Solution with a Human Face, World Development, 18, 301-311.

Rao, P. K. (2003): Donor Aid Policies Report- Select Aspects (Sponsored Study, processed), New York: UNDP.

Rey, P. and Salanie B. (1990): Long-Term, Short-Term, and Renegotiation – On the Value of Commitment in Contracting, Econometrica, 58.3, 597-619.

Rubinstein, A. and Wolinsky, A. (1982): Renegotiation-proof Implementation and Time Preferences, American Economic Review, 82, 600-614.

Sachs, J. (1984): Theoretical Issues in International Borrowing, Princeton: Princeton Studies in International Finance #54, Princeton University.

Stiglitz, J. and Weiss, A. (1983): Incentive effects of terminations – Applications to the credit and labor markets, American Economic Review, 73, 912-927.

Stiglitz, J., and Weiss, A. (1981): Credit Rationing in Markets with Imperfect Information, American Economic Review, 71, 393-410.

UN Commission on Human Rights (2001): Effects of Structural Adjustment Policies and Foreign Debt on the Full Enjoyment of all Human Rights, Particularly Economic, Social and Cultural Rights, Resolution 2001/27, adopted 20th April, 2001.

UN Conference on Trade and Development (UNCTAD) (2001): Trade and Development Report 2001, Geneva: UNCTAD Secretariat.

UN Secretary General's Report (2001): We the Children – Meeting the Promises of the World Summit for Children, New York: United Nations.

Varian, H. (1990): Monitoring Agents with Other Agents, Journal of Institutional and Theoretical Economics, 146.1, 153-174.

Webb, D. C. (1991): Long-term financial contracts can mitigate the adverse selection problem in project financing, International Economic Review, 32, 305-320.

World Bank (2003): Global Development Finance 2003, Washington, DC: World Bank.

Zou, L. (1992): Threat-based Incentive Mechanisms under Moral Hazard and Adverse Selection, Journal of Comparative Economics, 16, 47-74.

CHAPTER 7:

Project Appraisal – Improved Methods

7.1 Introduction

Development projects need to stay focused on the achievement of economic development objectives, and need to use monetary valuations of project performance only in a meaningful context. This chapter provides a brief overview of current methods of project appraisal, role of costs and benefits, role of information and transaction costs, and incommensurability of some of the objectives of project appraisal. The focus here is to address some of the important issues that are relevant in the context of development finance. For a full account of details of project appraisal methodology, see for example, Layard and Gleister (1994). Project appraisal, using methods of cost-benefit analysis (CBA) involves essentially a comparative analysis of costs and benefits 'with' the project and 'without' the project, rather than 'before' and 'after' (since the latter approach fails to account for changes in production/consumption that would occur without the project). An important aspect of project appraisal in development projects is to comprehend multiple criteria of development effectiveness, in addition to the conventional monetary assessment of costs and benefits over a relevant time horizon.

Since not all the indicators of development can be lumped into a single index to rank projects, and since there are problems of uncertainty and incomplete information for assessing futures scenarios with any project, a comprehensive assessment of projects and their potential effectiveness requires a careful scrutiny of multiple criteria. This remains the focus for the following section. Later sections deal with an outline of standard methods of project appraisal, the logic of discounting future values of costs as well as benefits, the need to incorporate the role of changing preferences over time, and a framework for improved methods of appraisal. Among the important aspects for the comprehensive assessment of costs and benefits in project appraisal, discussed in this chapter, are: accounting for various transaction costs and uncertainties, examination of the role of 'missing markets' for economic factors, recognition of the role of dynamic discount factors in long-term projects, and due consideration of income distribution and poverty reduction in assessing the social benefits of investments.

7.2 Objectives and Commensurability

Much of the application of CBA presumes some type of 'commensurability'. This makes sense in a context with profit maximization or monetary value as the only underlying objective and driving force, but not in general. Two concepts of commensurability are relevant here:

- Strong commensurability
- Weak commensurability

Strong commensurability assumes the existence of a common numeraire that enables assigning numerical values to each factor and function involved in the decision-making context, models, and policies. The preferences are usually based on the magnitudes of the numerical values assessed. The numbers also assist in arriving at tradeoffs, wherever necessary, in compromising otherwise conflicting objectives. This approach could directly contrast some of the requirements of economic development, unless this is used only in relatively well-defined monetized sections of the system, with additional criteria serving as the binding constraints.

A weak commensurability approach relies only on ordinal ranking of preferences among alternatives and does not require assigning numerical values to all the parameters involved. None of the approaches can make sense devoid of the institutional implications, constraints and effectiveness. The constellations of market and the state institutions provide the relevant background.

Economic development and applicability of multiple values and objectives suggest the potential limitations of using a common numeraire and converting all economic goods and services into these common unitary scale units. Some of the dangers of forcing such a unitary scale approach are relevant in the evaluation of development projects. A broadened approach than being commonly practiced in the conventional CBA would incorporate indicators covering impacts on non-monetized aspects of the physical, social, cultural and human environment in the configurations of interest. Some of the basic definitions are given in Box 7.1.

Box 7.1: Main Definitions

> *Certainty equivalent*: The comparative certainty value C of an uncertain quantity X given in terms of a probability distribution, i.e. if the expected value $E(X) = C$, then C is the certainty equivalent of X.
>
> *Consumer surplus*: The enhanced utility that might be available to a consumer or economic entity because of a change in price or non-price factor relative to the scenario without such a change.

Foreign Exchange Premium: The quantum of local currency value that exceeds fixed rate conversion of a specific foreign exchange into local currency. Market distortions influence the magnitude of this premium.

Risk-averse behavior: The decision making approach in which the certainty equivalent value must be augmented by an additional quantity G to offset the uncertainty, i.e,

$$E(X) + G = C$$

Risk taking behavior is the converse of the above: $E(X) - G = C$

Social rate of time preference (SRTP): The preference for a given time interval (such as the current year) over its successive time interval (such as next year), applicable to both benefits and costs of a project or entity that has implications on costs and/or benefits. Usually this is less than individual time preference rate because society as a whole considers a longer time horizon and lower discounting of future. More details are given in section 7.3.

7.3 Standard Methods of Cost-Benefit Analysis

The foundations of methods of cost-benefit analysis (CBA) arose from the classic contributions of Hicks (1939) and Kaldor (1939). The criterion of 'efficiency maximization' was named after both of them. This criterion requires that a project merits its desirability when the total benefits exceed total costs. This criterion merely requires that those who gain from an activity be able to compensate losers and still remain better off. It does not ensure that losers are in fact compensated or that there is any fair arrangement for redistribution of gains of efficiency improvement. A fundamental and simplistic economic assumption in this process is that the marginal utility of income is constant and remains the same among all people (including gainers and losers in any activity).

Several foundations and applications continue to remain rather shaky. The standard financial methods of benefit – cost calculations draw upon the calculation of the discounted stream of cash flows, both the sequences of costs Ct and of benefits Bt, for the period of concern T for a project or component of economic activity. The discounted lumped sum is called the net present value (NPV) and depends on the choice of the discount rate r. NPV is given by the expression:

$$\int_0^T e^{-rt}[B(t) - C(t)]\,dt$$

If the inflation needs to be taken into account, r is replaced by $r\text{-}i$, where i is the rate of annual inflation. The new measure $r\text{-}i$ corresponds to the real rate of interest wherever the formulation is carried out only in financial terms.

This description holds for cash flow based CBA. In general, true worth of resources is hardly reflected in the above estimates of benefits and costs. At the minimum, one needs to assess the shadow prices for each of the inputs and outputs involved in the flows of benefits and costs. This exercise then converts financial assessment into economic assessment of relevant costs and benefits.

When we move beyond monetary values, a standard form of Social Cost Benefit Analysis (SCBA) starts with the formulation of the main objective or frame of reference for the analysis: that of maximizing social welfare or an equivalent social objective. It is not always possible to construct and solve complex optimizing models to generate these shadow prices. Instead, approximations are often made to assess these 'true values' of resources with an intuitive approach. This requires an assessment of opportunity costs and benefits of each of the inputs involved in the SCBA.

The SRTP, as determined by the consumption rate of interest, is the social discount rate (SDR) (Lind, 1982), explained below. In the context of long-term projects, resource allocations must be based on considerations involving intergenerational equity. A proxy for these was suggested as the government's long term borrowing rate (Lind, 1990). Standard methods for assessing costs and benefits or project appraisal require the following: find the relevant 'shadow price on capital' and translate all capital investment effects into 'consumption equivalents', and discount consumption at the SRTP for consumption.

7. 4 Changing Preferences and Discounting

Historically, Fisher (1930) was among the first who argued that the pure rate of time preference need not be constant and that it should not be independent of the size and shape of the consumption profile. However, in the conventional intertemporal utility maximization approach, the independence arises from the strong separability property of the utility function: marginal rate of substitution for consumption at any two-time instants is independent of the rest of the consumption profile. A constant time discounting does imply that the discount factor at any instant is independent of the underlying consumption path. This may not be a realistic description of the real life features.

Much of the conventional methods of project appraisal and CBA have been founded on two concepts toward discount rates. These are consumption rate of interest (also called the pure time preference), and the opportunity cost of capital that is based on the marginal productivity of capital.

What constitutes a discount rate? This may be defined as the rate of decline in the value of the numeraire against which goods are valued each time interval, in each year, for example. The numeraire and the discount rate need to be considered together. A rigorous analysis of the theoretical issues in this framework can be seen in Dreze and Stern (1987). The shadow discount factor in their analysis is the valuation of the discount factor in accordance with the formulation of the underlying objective function. It can be seen as the marginal social value of a unit of numeraire accruing in year t. The shadow own rate of return on the numeraire is generally known as the SDR.

The social value of a project or activity is a discounted stream of social benefits expressed in terms of a common numeraire. The shadow discount rate is a number defined as the rate of decline of the discount factor D, which is an implicit function of time, given by the expression:

$$r = -(d/dt) \log D (...)$$

This represents the rate of decline in the marginal social value of the numeraire. The shadow discount rate is defined as the rate of decline in the discount factor

$$r_t \equiv \frac{a_t - a_{t+1}}{a_{t+1}}$$

From this it follows that if $a_0 = 1$,

$$a_{t+1} = (1 + r_t)(1 + r_{t-1}) \ ......(1 + r_0)$$

It can be seen that when the shadow discount rate remains a constant, the discounting formulation reduces to the conventional inversion of the compounding formula for n periods, like in $(1 + r)^{-n}$.

In general, the shadow discount rate in the private sector does not equal the social rate of return. If private producers are unconstrained and relative producer prices are equal or proportional to relative shadow prices, the marginal rates of the shadow discount rate is the same as the private rate of return, i.e. the rate of return in terms of market prices.

The application of SDR requires that all relevant effects of an activity or project be transformed into their equivalents in a common numeraire, usually in terms of consumption equivalents. SDR are to be viewed as percentage rates of change of inter-temporal relative shadow prices of the consumption bundle. Some of the proxies for SDR are the following:

a) social rate of time preference (explained below);

b) comparable market rate of return (even though these are, typically, unsustainable);

c) risk-free interest adjusted for inflation; and

d) variable endogenous discount functions that reflect changing preferences and consumption levels, and possibly additional factors.

Among these, (b) and (c) are not usually equated with SDR because of the nature of pure capital appraisal in perfectly competitive markets should form the relevant arena for its application, and not socioeconomic and environmental concerns of long term.

In the conventional approach, SRTP can be estimated using a utility-based discount rate. In this framework, the SRTP (observed from the consumption rate of interest) and the opportunity cost of private capital (observed from the marginal rate of return on private investment) are the same and equal the market rate of interest in a perfectly competitive ideal non-distortionary economy. This follows from Solow (1970) derivation, explained below.

The optimality criterion is to maximize the discounted social value of all future utility streams of consumption,

$$W = \int_0^\infty \exp[-(r-n)t] U[c(t)] dt$$

where W is the social value of consumption stream, r the pure time preference factor, n the rate of growth of population, and c is per capita consumption.

The first-order necessary condition for optimality yields the expression

$$\frac{\frac{d}{dt}[U']}{U'} = -[r*(t) - r]$$

which upon differentiation leads to the following

$$\frac{U''(c^*) \cdot \frac{d}{dt}(c^*)}{U'(c^*)} = -[r^* - r]$$

This is summarized as

$$r(t) = \alpha g + r$$

where α is the absolute value of the elasticity of the social marginal utility of per capita consumption, and g the growth rate of consumption.

The above expression clarifies that the discount function $r(t)$ is a composite effect of three ingredients:

i) the pure time preference or time-impatience,

ii) the consumption-impatience represented through the elasticity parameter, and the growth effect.

Thus, r is not simply a time-discounting factor but is also a measure of discounting of goods. This r is relevant for SCBA. If one suggests that the welfare of future generations should not be discounted heavily, the suggestion is simply that r the pure time-impatience factor should be low, and not that r should be low for that reason.

Solow (1996) emphasized that along any optimal path, the appropriate discount rate to apply to goods has two components:

a) the pure rate of time preference; and

b) the factor that depends on the marginal product of capital, thus allowing transformation of goods into greater quantities of goods over time.

The second component usually dominates the first, except in very inefficient economies. These features provide a fundamental explanation to the suggested phenomenon in Becker (1998): preferences and rates of economic growth are correlated partly because tastes, such as a lower rate of preference for present utilities, are more conducive to rapid economic growth.

From the above expression for r(t), it is clear that even when the utility rate of discount is set equal to zero, the SRTP will be positive as long as consumption grows with time. The consumption rate of discount need not equal the utility rate of discount. Thus, discounting benefits and costs at a positive rate does not necessarily entail lesser weightage to the welfare (as measured by utility) of the future generations or future itself. However, this may not be valid in economies where future prospects of higher consumption levels are bleak. The growth component g in the expression for the discount rate allows several alternative decompositions and interpretations. This has implications for the choice of discount rates in relation to the underlying factors affecting growth. Such an assessment also clarifies the need for a variable rather than fixed discount rate.

In general, time preferences comprise of at least two effects:

a) relative value attached to present consumption (in relation to the level of consumption) and its comparative valuation of a future specified level of consumption at a specified time point; and

b) impatience as defined by pure time preference (for a given level of consumption, held constant, but occurring at two different time instants).

Discount Factors and Discount Rates

Conventional constant rate of discounting brings down the valuation very rapidly to insignificant levels even with rather modest rates of discount, after a period of about 50 years. A class of functions, called hyperbolic discount functions, is found to have some merits in getting over conventional constant discounting methods. These functions are explained in Box 7.2. The use of these functions is to allow valuation of resources over time at a distant future as well.

It is important to note that a constant rate of time discounting does imply the independence of the discount factor at any time point of the underlying consumption path (and hence of the corresponding changes in other related factors).

Box 7.2: Hyperbolic Discount Functions

Hyperbolic discount functions imply discount rates that decline as the discounted event is moved further away in time (Lowenstein and Prelec, 1992). Prelec (1989) suggested a hyperbolic form of discounting function

$$D(t) = (1 + at)^{-\frac{b}{a}} \qquad a, b > 0$$

These are characterized by a relatively high discount rate over shorter horizons and lower discount rates over longer horizons.

Within the class of hyperbolic functions, Laibson (1997) suggested the discount rate function that falls with increasing time t

$$D(t) = \frac{b}{1 + at}$$

A number of alternative formulations of non-constant discounting functions can be seen in Harvey (1995), including 'slow discount functions'. These functions have a main characteristic of changing preferences, and these preferences are classified into different categories. These functions possess desirable properties like declining over time and not exponentially declining to zero at fast speed (as in regular exponential discounting functions). These are useful for projects with long time horizons (thirty or more years). However, the financial decision making models based on these formulations may not always possess behaviorally consistent optimal solutions.

Measuring time by equal proportional increments rather than equal absolute values is sometimes referred to as 'logarithmic discounting'. The following discounting function attaches greater weight to time and valuation of resources at distant time points unlike in the case of conventional exponential discounting. The discount functions of the type given below constitute special cases of the above hyperbolic class. These were suggested in the class of proportional discounting and depict inverse proportionality with the distance of time element from the present time:

$$a(t) = \left[\frac{b}{b + t}\right]^{\eta} \qquad t \geq 0, \quad b > 0, \quad -\infty < \eta < \infty$$

The scope and technical aspects of the issue of non-constant discounting of future have been examined analytically by Harvey (1994, 95), Laibson (1997), and Rao (2000).

A Framework for Improved Methods

The critical ingredients requiring clarification are in terms of the analytical or logical decision model or structure that clarify the objectives, constraints, factors and institutions, in addition to the choice of appropriate discount rate. Both efficiency and equity issues must be taken into account together.

Efforts are needed to deal with the distant future even with several unknowns and uncertainties and to grapple with limited information basis so that the direction of progress may be at least approximately right.

CBA methodology has been playing an important role in various public and private investment decisions. This methodology requires further strengthening to reflect the following features:

a) the economic time horizons involved are usually longer than the administrative time horizons often used in CBA;

b) there is no unitary decision making mechanism;

c) most factors to be considered are largely outside market parameters – as they are not necessarily affecting the market signals at the present time instant; and

d) many arbitrary assumptions could be used in the specification of numerical values to bring the multiple factors to a common numeraire and a common scale.

The ranking of alternative projects based on a common scale of measurement or numeraire presumes the existence of a 'complete ordering' of alternatives (i.e. ranking of all alternatives, assuming their comparability on the same scale). However, such an ordering need not exist in the presence of uncertainties and unforeseen contingencies. This situation calls for the use of 'partial orderings' only; all the alternatives cannot be completely ranked, there remain indeterminate cases. Besides, there exist severe problems of using 'consumer surplus' argument-based CBA for dealing with uncertain economy-environment interactions when the implications of alternative activities or policies differ in their relative risk attributes. The use of expected consumer surplus methods do not approximate to welfare of consumers (or other groups of society) in the presence of risk-averse behavior of such societies (Stennek, 1999).

Transient Costs and Equilibrium Costs

Any assessment of costs and benefits is based on a pattern of equilibrium that enables such assessment. However, in a relatively medium/long term (10 or more years) framework, it is important to recognize that the equilibrium is not expected to remain invariant to the continued disturbances to the systems involved and the significant possibilities of mechanisms of adaptation. Costs of adaptation and of transition are important in project appraisal, but it is far from a common practice to account for these costs.

Missing Markets, Uncertainty and SCBA

Can we rely on markets and related institutions to lead to intergenerational efficiency? The most significant bottlenecks in this regard are the absence of informational and institutional settings, especially missing markets. Markets are missing in the sense that there is no interaction and exchange for mutual gain that is taking place between present and future generations, or in considering the value of some of the intangibles such as the richness of biodiversity for which markets may not readily exist.

Missing markets, like other missing institutions, make it hard to realize long term and intergenerational efficiency. The well-known problems of market failures in terms of their inability to correct for externalities are additional problems to be taken into account. Problems of excessive discounting of the future may also be viewed in terms of the failure of intergenerational product and markets. The roles of uncertainty and risk in project appraisal methodologies remain significant. Box 7.3 provides some of the relevant analytical approaches.

Box 7.3: Uncertainty and Discount Rates

It is a well-known result in the economics under uncertainty and risk that the expected value of marginal utility is greater than the marginal utility of expected income. Under uncertainty, the simplistic view of treating costs as negative benefits does not hold any more. If there is risk-averse attitude, estimated benefits should be discounted more than in the certainty case or the certainty-equivalent case. For a risk-averse decision maker, the expected utility of initial wealth plus the random increment is less than the utility of the expected value of the initial wealth plus the random increment. This follows from the well-known inequalities applicable when the utility function U possesses the properties of a strictly concave function:

$$E[U(W_t + W_{t+1})] < U[E(W_t + W_{t+1})]$$
$$= U[W_t + E(W_{t+1})]$$

The above inequality (see Thompson, 1997) shows that the certainty equivalent of the random wealth Wt is less than the expected value of W_t. Enhancement in the certainty-equivalent is possible with increased discount rate. Similarly, in risk-averse decision making, if the costs are ranked under uncertainty, the converse holds: lower the discount rate for valuing costs over time.

7.5 Concluding Observations

A broadened approach than being commonly practiced in the conventional CBA would incorporate indicators covering impacts on non-monetized aspects of the physical, social, cultural and human environment in the configurations of interest.

The economic time horizons involved are usually longer than the administrative time horizons often used in CBA. Besides, most factors to be considered are largely outside market parameters – as they are not necessarily affecting the market signals at the present time instant. These features have implications for development finance when these affect the design of projects and policies for the alleviation of poverty and contribution to sustainable development (further details given in chapter 8).

Much of standard methodology used in project appraisal remains somewhat simplistic because of the following limitations:

1. The role of transaction costs and their multiple effects are ignored, thus constituting an underestimation of total costs and also projecting lopsided scenarios of interactions of various elements of costs and benefits;

2. In projects involving long time horizons, using a constant rate of time discounting (often exogenously prescribed) for valuing future costs and benefits is unrealistic since changes in preferences (including the role of endogenous preferences) and their effects on the valuation of costs and benefits are ignored.

3. Although there is awareness of the role of various obvious elements such as direct subsidies in the accounting of costs/benefits, there is little recognition of several other subsidies such as those of non-market ecosystem services, labor of children and volunteers or others.

These deficiency need to be rectified in commonly used methods of project appraisal. Besides, the costs of adaptation and of transition are important elements in project appraisal. However, it is far from a common practice to account for these costs. These aspects are significant in evaluating projects involving development finance and require modifications in current practices.

Hyperbolic discount factors allow declining discount rates over time so that longer term inputs and outputs are also accounted, rather than reduced to zero levels rapidly over time. It is desirable to explore further the theory and applications of these and similar classes of discount functions.

Review Exercises

1. What are the two basic differences in commensurability of objectives, and what roles do these play in CBA?

2. Explain the rationale behind each of the following:

    a) hyperbolic discounting;

    b) discounting with endogenous preference changes; and

    c) constant exponential discounting.

3. Examine the role of transaction costs in the CBA of a credit lending scheme catered to:

    a) exclusively for the poor; and

    b) for all eligible borrowers based on credit worthiness.

4. What is the role of missing markets when SCBA is applied to project appraisal involving reduction of poverty?

5. How is project appraisal methodology for development-oriented projects different from that of other investment appraisal?

References

Becker, G. (1998): Accounting for Tastes, Cambridge, MA: Harvard University Press.

Dreze, J. and Stern, N. (1987): The Theory of Cost-Benefit Analysis, pp. 909-989, in A. Auerbach and M. Feldstein (ed), Handbook of Public Economics, Vol. II, New York: North Holland.

Fisher, I. (1930): The Theory of Interest, New York: Macmillan.

Harvey, C. M. (1995): Proportional Discounting of Future Costs and Benefits, Mathematics of Operations Research, 20, 381-99.

Hicks, J. R (1939): The Foundations of Welfare Economics, Economic Journal, 49, 696.

Kaldor, R. N. (1939): Welfare Propositions of Economics and Intertemporal Comparisons of Utility, Economic Journal, 49, 549-

Laibson, D. (1997): Golden Eggs and Hyperbolic Discounting, Quarterly Journal of Economics, 62, 443-477.

Layard, R. and Glaister, S. (Ed.) (1994): Cost-Benefit Analysis, New York: Cambridge University Press.

Lind, R. C. (1982): A primer on the major issues relating to the discount rate for evaluating national energy options, in Lind et al (Ed): Discounting for Time and Risk in Energy Policy, Baltimore: Johns Hopkins University Press.

Lind, R. C. (1990): Reassessing the government's discount rate policy in light of new theory and data in a world economy with a high degree of capital mobility, Journal of Environmental Economics and Management, 18, s8-s28.

Lowebstein, G. and Prelec, D. (1992): Anomalies in intertemporal choice – evidence and an interpretation, Quarterly Journal of Economics, 57, 573-98.

Prelec, D. (1989): Decreasing impatience- definition and consequences, New York: Russell Sage Foundation Working Paper.

Rao, P. K. (2000): Sustainable Development: Economics and Policy, Oxford: Blackwell.

Solow, R. M. (1970): Growth Theory – an Exposition, New York: Oxford University Press.

Solow, R. M. (1996): Comments on net national product, communication to the author.

Stennek, J. (1999): The expected consumer's surplus as a welfare measure, Journal of Public Economics, 73, 265-88.

Thompson, P. B. (1997): Evaluating energy efficiency investments – accounting for risk in the discounting process, Energy Policy, 25, 989-96.

CHAPTER 8:
Finance and Sustainable Development

8.1 Introduction

Sustainable development (SD) requires a balance in the use and exploitation of environmental resources for economic development in order to protect the interests of the future generations. The role of development finance needs to be carefully integrated with the principles of SD, and this involves due recognition in the design of policies and their implementation. Global financial institutions and their counterparts at the national levels need to address relevant issues more systematically than has been done in the past. Integration of financial and environmental dimensions of development remains an important task.

This chapter examines the role of global finance in mitigating environmental problems and the contributions (mainly in the form of its negative environmental externalities) of different types of lending operations and other investments in developing countries. Relevant reforms for integrating financial, economic and environmental issues are discussed in different sections of this chapter. Among the specific issues examined are: the use of green taxes for curbing environmental damage and also using the tax revenue potential for effecting desirable income redistribution policies, debt relief and the role of environmental protection, reform of international financial institutions and their policies for the protection of the environment, the roles of lender liability and extended producer liabilities, and financial aspects of meeting environmental and development goals (including those set by the UN Millennium Declaration).

A detailed examination of the integral definition of SD, the role of protection of the interests of the future generations, and of reduction of poverty are some of the areas of attention in the following section.

8.2 Sustainable Development

We first begin with an explanation of the functional role of the environment, later explain the concept of SD, and summarize some of the global attempts in translating relevant development goals into operational targets.

Classification of Environmental Dimensions

Functional classification of environmental resources deserves to be elucidated here. An important clarification on the environmental dimensions of economic development may be broadly specified in terms of three groups of environmental resources/factors (Rao, 2002):

1. Environmental amenities: these include fresh water for human consumption, clean air for survival, and physical facilities such as proper housing and sanitation.
2. Primary environmental assets and resources: these lead to the first, and these include ecosystems, ozone layer, marine fisheries and marine resources, biodiversity, tropical forests and other habitats for biodiversity, and biogeochemicals that offer a wide variety of environmental resources from planet Earth's multiple sources and sinks. The sinks provide absorption and renewal capacities.
3. Environmental bads: these are in contrast to environmental goods in the first two groups. The disamenities in this group include such items as toxic chemicals, greenhouse gases, acid rain, air pollution, and land/water contamination.

The general objective of an environmental governance policy is to maximize the potential for the first two while minimizing the risks of the third, on a sustainable basis (that is, seeking environmental sustainability). The main issue of concern in this chapter is to integrate financial governance at national and international levels with environmental governance.

Categories of Capital

It is important to recognize different components of capital in the general economic production system, resultant economic welfare and sustainability. Broadly, four types of capital may be classified:

a) Person-made capital (based on manufacturing or related economic activities);
b) Natural capital (consisting of non-renewable and renewable resources including the atmosphere, sources and sinks of the planet, and several other ecological resources);

c) Human capital (knowledge, technical know-how, health); and

d) Social capital (culture, peoples' institutions, efficacy and quality of various institutions, cooperative behavior, trust, social norms, and peoples' participation in decision-making).

These forms of capital components are partly complementary, and are not always mutually exclusive. The comprehensive valuation and assessment of these features could form a beginning in the interpretation of sustainability. Although a formal comprehension of all forms of capital and their relative sustainability is not contemplated below, the following important concept seeks to capture some of the most important aspects of economic development with due care for the environment.

Sustainable Development

The World Commission on Environment and Development (WCED, also known as the Brundtland Commission) Report (1987, pp.332-333) has been the most influential document regarding the SD concept. The report defined:

> "Sustainable development is development that meets the needs of the present without compromising the ability of future generations to meet their own needs. It contains within it two key concepts – the concept of 'needs', in particular the essential needs of the world's poor, to which overriding priority should be given; and the idea of limitations imposed by the state of technology and social organization on the environment's ability to meet present and future needs".

Most of the literature on SD addresses only the first part of the above definition and ignores the urgency of meeting the genuine needs of the poor. An integrated approach should recognize the concept in its entirety and devise policies accordingly. Development finance fits precisely into such an effort. Some of the important elements of environmental governance can be integrated with those of financial governance. This is done, for example, in the use of green taxes for curbing environmental damage and using the tax revenue potential for effecting desirable income redistribution policies. These aspects are detailed later in section 8.3.

The focus on the environment and protecting environmental assets for future generations has been maintained at the global level for at least three decades. Box 8.1 highlights, as an illustrative list, some of the multilateral declarations and treaties that explicitly stipulate duties and responsibilities of states.

Box 8.1: Protecting the Environment for Future Generations

1. The Stockholm Declaration, 1972

   "...man ...bears a solemn responsibility to protect and improve the environment for present and future generations." (Principle 1)

2. UN Charter of Economic Rights and Duties of States, adopted by the UN General Assembly Resolution 3281, 1974

   "The protection, preservation and enhancement of the environment for the present and future generations is the responsibility of all States. ..." (Article 30).

3. Convention on the Conservation of Migratory Species of Wild Animals, 1980

   ".....each generation of man holds the resources of the earth for future generations and has an obligation to ensure that this legacy is conserved and, where utilized, is used wisely." (Preamble, p.1)

4. UN Convention on Biological Diversity, 1992

   "Sustainable use means the use of components of biological diversity in a way and at a rate that does not lead to the long-term decline of biological diversity, thereby maintaining its potential to meet the needs and aspirations of present and future generations." (Definition)

5. Statement of Principles for a Global Consensus on the Management, Conservation and Sustainable Development of all Types of Forests, UN Conference of 1992:

   "Forest resources and forest lands should be sustainably managed to meet the social, economic, ecological, cultural and spiritual human needs of present and future generations." (Principles)

6. The Rio Declaration on Environment and Development, 1992

   "The right to development must be fulfilled so as to equitably meet developmental and environmental needs of present and future generations." (Principle 3).

7. Aarhus Convention on Access to Information, Public Participation in Decision-making and Access to Justice in Environmental Matters, 1998 (in the region of the United Nations Economic Commission for Europe (ECE); it was signed by 35 states and the EC).

   The Preamble states, *inter alia,* "every person has the right to live in an environment adequate to his or her health and well-being, and the duty, both individually and in association with others, to protect and improve the environment for the benefit of present and future generations".

The Convention Article 1 (Objective) states:

> "In order to contribute to the protection of the right of every person of present and future generations to live in an environment adequate to his or her health and well-being, each Party shall guarantee the rights of access to information, public participation in decision-making, and access to justice in environmental matters in accordance with the provisions of this Convention."

Millennium Development Goals (MDG)

At the global level, all 189-member countries of the UN adopted the Millennium Declaration of the UN General Assembly in September 2000. This Declaration stated a set of goals of national and international development that approximate to some degree the imperatives of SD. Box 8.2 summarizes some of the important elements of these goals.

Box 8.2: Millennium Development Goals

By the year 2015, the following goals or measures are proposed to be achieved on global basis; these are in addition to important goals for health and AIDS, gender equality, school literacy and related aspects:

1. Eradicate extreme poverty and hunger: Reduce by half the number of people earning less than US$ one per day, and reduce hungry people by the same magnitude;

2. Reduce infant and maternal mortality: Reduce by two-thirds the mortality rate of children under five, and by three-fourths the rate of maternal mortality;

3. Environmental sustainability: "integrate principles of sustainable development into country policies and programmes; reverse loss of environmental resources"; reduce by half the number of people without access to safe drinking water; and improve the living standards of 100 million slum dwellers by 2020.

4. Develop a global partnership for development: "develop further an open trading and financial system that is rule based, predictable and non-discriminatory; …commitment to good governance, development and poverty reduction, nationally and internationally"; debts of developing countries to remain at sustainable levels in the long term.

Regarding the least developed countries, the following policy measures have been suggested for implementation: enhanced debt relief for the heavily indebted; cancellation of official bilateral debt, and greater official development assistance to countries committed to poverty reduction.

> The MDG have been partly translated into 18 targets and 48 indictors to enable quantified assessment and evaluation of progress in various countries. All the major UN organizations are involved in devising some of the policies and their monitoring. Specific to the goal of ensuring environmental sustainability, the following five indicators have been identified by the UN, in addition to the indicators for slum reduction and access to safe drinking water: Proportion of land area covered by forests; Ratio of area protected for the purpose of maintaining biodiversity relative to the total surface area; Energy use per $1 Gross Domestic Product; Per capita carbon dioxide emissions and consumption of ozone-depleting substances; and, Proportion of population using solid fuels.
>
> Source: http://millenniumindicators.un.org/

Financial Aspects

Vast majority of developing countries (140 out of 166) receive less than 5 percent of the total capital flows to developing countries; only about a dozen countries account for nearly 80 percent of the total flows in 1997; for details see Gunter (1997). Besides, recent trends in capital flows are depictive of reverses, with the developing world turning a net exporter of capital. These features are indicative of the serious financial constraints that limit the fulfillment of the MDG.

One of the estimates of the World Bank indicate that the additional financial resources needed to attain the MDG are of the order of $40 billion to $60 billion per year for the next dozen or more years. These estimates are based on the assumptions of rather minimal improvements in the policies and institutions of developing countries that require assistance. A recent report (World Bank, 2002) suggests that: a) an 'effective institutional mechanism' to deliver desired development outcomes is needed at individual country levels and international levels; and b) the World Bank, as a major player in the MDG process, needs to provide 'tangible improvements' in the implementation aspects.

The effectiveness of external aid is a result of mapping of demand and supply factors in a cost-effective manner, where the costs include all direct and indirect costs, leakages and transaction costs (Rao, 2002). Stakeholder participation and accountability are among the prerequisites for the efficacy of the programs. The greater the degree of inequality within and across countries, the greater is the cost of reform and achievement of desired development goals. The role of market institutions and the private industry must be fully explored in this context. Cost effective measures need to be fully explored in terms of plausible institutional alignments and policies.

Among various environmental amenities, provision of safe drinking water remains the most important environmental and economic problem of the developing world. Diseases such as diarrhea (and associated dehydration and mortality in some cases), malaria, and malabsorption of nutrition are directly related to access to clean water. More than 118 million life years are estimated to have been lost per year during the 1990s because of these health impediments (for details see chapter 3 of the report World Resources 1998-99 by WRI, 1999). The economic loss on this account alone may amount to about $118 billion per year, if an average life year is valued at $1000 (in relation to the annual per capita income in developing countries). The extent of economic and environmental damage due to the severe constraints on the safe drinking water dimension remains substantial, and it exceeds by twice the amount of all the official development assistance (ODA) that is currently provided by the capital-rich countries to the developing world (Rao, 2002). As a relevant policy, the developed countries can possibly provide interest-free loans for mitigating this problem, and involve the private sector for implementing effective water resource programs. Often, these programs can be meaningfully combined with irrigation water supply schemes and can utilize conjunctive use of ground and surface waters. This combination of schemes can effect cost savings and lead to financial viability within a few years.

8.3 Environmental Taxes

Among important fiscal instruments for the regulation of the environment are a set of environment-influencing taxes, broadly called green taxes. The terms green taxes, environmental taxes, and pollution taxes are often interchangeably used, although they do not precisely mean the same. Although the above categories include carbon taxes, the converse does not hold. These taxes are usually not aimed at financing and provision of environmental amenities themselves.

Pigou (1932) was among the economists who advocated pollution taxes. A Pigouvian tax is tax applied on each unit of pollution output. This tax amount equals the marginal damage the pollution causes to the economic system at an efficient level of production system or output level. This taxation method may be feasible if the source of pollution, and its relative contribution and damage are known. Much of the literature on Pigouvian taxes did not address the issue of revenue mobilization or the consequent decisions of levying pollution taxes. Pollution taxes promise the potential to offer a better tax structure for any given economy and also enhance environmental quality, if the tax instruments are properly formulated and implemented, thus constituting to a case of (potential) double dividend, where accruing transaction costs (TC) must also be accounted for.

In recent years, industrial countries instituted some form or the other of green taxes to achieve reduction of pollution emissions and to use the revenues to effect personal tax at lower income levels. An element of revenue-neutrality has been a common feature in these tax shifts where imposition of green taxes is simultaneously carried out with a reduction in personal income tax. Some of the recent examples include landfill tax in the UK, carbon taxes in Finland, the Netherlands, and Sweden. The revenues from the use of the new tax instruments were proposed to offset relatively heavy income taxes with a reduction in personal tax rates. Table 8.1 provides a summary of green tax imposition as well as relief in other taxes.

The phenomena of 'dividends' of various types were also touted in support of various types of environmental tax measures, stated below.

1. Single Dividend: Environmental taxation increases the total welfare of the society by reducing or eliminating negative environmental externalities, assuming these taxes do not dampen economic productivity.

2. Double Dividend: Shifting tax burden from personal taxation to environmental resource use reduces the relative cost of labor and augments employment.

3. Triple Dividend: Reduces tax distortions and increases economic output toward more efficient paths – economically and environmentally.

Most of the economic analyses and policies for effecting environmental concerns ignored the interactions of new taxes with the existing tax system. This approach, including the classic Pigouvian tax method overestimates the required tax for achieving the environmental goals. It is relevant to recognize that the overall effect of the tax consists of the following:

1. the Pigouvian effect in the partial equilibrium sense;

2. the tax interaction effect; and

3. the revenue recycling, or more generally, the fiscal effect.

The basic partial equilibrium analysis of optimal environmental tax invokes the Pigouvian method, where the optimal tax rate equals the marginal external costs or marginal environmental damages (MED). This implies the gross marginal cost or marginal abatement cost associated with an environmental tax equals the tax rate. The role of preexisting taxes needs to be taken into account whenever green taxes are considered for their imposition (Bovenberg and Goulder, 1996). The optimal environmental tax works out to about 70 percent of the Pigouvian tax (or of the MED) (Parry, 1997). In the presence of existing tax distortions, imposition of new green taxes can sometimes outweigh the efficiency gains from revenue recycling; in such cases, there may not be a significant double dividend (Goulder, 1995).

The difficulty of establishing the strong double dividend does not contradict that an environmental tax can promote higher national income when tax revenues are earmarked for capital formation. The main findings of recent significant contributions in environmental taxation are the following (Rao, 2000):

a) they are useful instruments if devised and implemented efficiently;

b) because of the tax interaction effect with the prevailing taxes in the economy, the magnitudes of optimal environmental taxes tend to be about 10 to 30 percent less than those indicated by traditional (partial equilibrium) analyses; and

c) depending on the revenue recycling or other patterns of utilization of these tax revenues, the net effect of the tax levies can be progressive, neutral, or regressive for various economic classes.

Table 8.1: Environmental Double Dividend Packages

Country	Start Year	Taxes Raised	Tax Cut	Magnitude as % of TTR
Sweden	1990	CO_2, SO_2, Other	a, d, e	2.4
Denmark	1994	CO_2, SO_2, Other	a, b, CI	6
Netherlands	1996	CO_2	a, b, CT	0.5
UK	1996	Landfill	b	0.1
Norway	1999	CO_2, SO_2, Diesel	a	0.2
Germany	1999	Petroleum Products	b	1
Italy	1999	Petroleum Products	b	0.1

Sources: Rao (2002), OECD (2001b), Table 2; Bosquet (2000); Notation: a -personal income tax, b -social security contributions, CI -Capital Income, CT -Corporate Tax, d - energy taxes on agriculture, e -continuing education, and TTR – total tax revenue.

Environmental Taxes and Double Dividend

Beginning in the 1990s, taxes have been raised for carbon dioxide emissions, sulfur dioxide and petroleum products in some of the industrial countries: Sweden, Denmark, The Netherlands, UK, Norway, Germany, and Italy. These tax impositions were followed by tax cuts in personal income tax, social security tax, and corporate tax in some of these countries. The magnitudes of tax cuts ranged from 0.1 percent (Italy) to about 6 percent (Denmark).

As an illustration of the effect of $100 carbon tax on production costs in select countries, the following estimates may be indicative of the magnitude of differences involved (OECD, 2001b) (increases in percentages given in brackets):

Table 8.2: Carbon Tax – Select Countries

Country	Carbon Tax
USA	2.8
Canada	4.1
Japan	1.2
Australia	5.2
France	1.4
Germany	1.6
UK	1.6
Italy	1.4
Belgium	2.3

The implications of green taxes on the cost of production and on potential competitiveness deserve attention at the national and international levels. It is desirable to form a Green Tax Commission at the international level to examine these issues and their practical usefulness, and differentiate the tax regimes in varying economic and institutional settings across the world.

The significance of green tax must be fully explored for each country. There is a need for an independent International Green Tax Commission for this purpose; this entity should come up with practical plans for various member countries of the UN. Among the other specific policy actions required are the following (Rao, 2002):

1. The role of efficiency-improving, loss minimizing operational aspects of every sector of the economic and environmental activity must be critically examined, remedied for curbing inefficiencies, and the marginal costs for this assessment should be weighed in relation to marginal benefits of such improvements; both costs and benefits should be assessed based on relevant assessments of ecosystem-wide factors.

2. Environmentally sound/efficient technologies should be made available to developing countries for the above refinements along with new projects that offer local and global environmental benefits.

3. The role and application of economy-wide yet sector-specific and activity-specific green taxes must be assessed for each country, with due consideration to costs of administering such a system (including the entire set of transaction costs involved, scope for leakages and corruption), transparency and accountability of new systems.

The World Bank and IMF Role

The approaches of the IMF and the World Bank utilize standardized Structural Adjustment Lending (SAL) methods of credit lending. These approaches assume that a 'one size fits all' approach makes sense even in the development context of diverse socioeconomic systems and are inefficient both for lenders and for borrowers. Unforeseen disturbances could arise from a variety of economic, environmental, social and political changes. Therefore, there is a need for a built -in mechanism for adjustments that do not entail sacrificing human capital, environment, and economic stability of a borrower country system. In a case study relating to the African and Latin American regions, Stewart (1995) found that per capita expenditure on the social sectors fell significantly by about 30 percent among the 'adjusting countries' and about 17 percent in Latin America. It was also observed that cuts in food subsidies were part of the programs of adjustment; any replacements with target subsidies were inadequate as they rarely maintained the purchasing power and a larger proportion of people were left out. Several additional studies documented significance of drop in education and public health services for the poor in most countries in Africa and the correlation of this feature with increases in debt servicing to international lender institutions, including the multilateral official institutions. This phenomenon is hardly consistent with the objectives and methods of a meaningful development finance mechanism.

There is little evidence that many of the IMF policies recognized the problems of poverty and environment (and their synergistic interactions). Stewart (1995) argued that the strongest verifiable criticism against the World Bank and the IMF is that adverse effects on poverty and environment occurred when the borrower countries undertook adjustment policies at the instance and insistence of these global institutions, and many of the problems were foreseeable and avoidable; yet these institutions did not share any responsibility for these adverse consequences. This is a form of exercise of lender power, and a manifestation of implications of lack of lender liability clauses in the debt contract agreements (Rao, 2002).

The economic stipulations of the lender often result in a sharp fall in real purchasing ability to purchase food and other essential items. The environmental repercussions are at times indirect and lagged (such as long-term environmental degradation), unpredictable in direction and depend on the duration of the programs (Rao, 2002). The problem of inadequate financing in the face of external shocks forces is such that developing countries make adjustments that are counter to the requirements of SD Some of the consequences include accelerated exports for debt repayment (often in conjunction with an exchange rate deflation, implying more volume of exports required to earn the same fixed level of foreign exchange) with substantial environmental and social costs. Thus, inefficient lending is a problem both to the lenders and to the borrowers, both in financial terms as well as in adverse development implications.

Reforms of the multilateral financial institutions need to ensure that their policies and operations are governed by the following:

a) a new charter of articles that include explicitly the role of 'environmental protection';

b) accept lender liability for wrong advice in economic, environmental or other matters to borrower countries; and,

c) forgive and/or write off loans that were ill designed by the lenders.

Debt Relief

Debt relief for the severely indebted, and debt rescheduling on concessional terms for other developing countries could enhance environmental and economic sustainability provided the beneficiary countries agree to accord due importance to these issues. This could lead to a win-win solution of debt and environmental management for both the creditor and borrowers. An unhealthy borrower economy cannot be more useful than a healthy one for the creditors.

Mounting real debt and debt-service payments exacerbate the risk premium and cost of capital, thus worsening the potential for real economic development. Ever increasing or very high real debt levels lead to higher discount rates in the valuation of the future, and thus compromise the long run sustainability of many ingredients of development, especially those of environmental resources that are not directly marketable (Rao, 2000).

New Deal for Debt-For-Nature Swaps?

Debt-for-nature swaps (DNS) have been used for some years to convert external liabilities into funding for environmental initiatives. They are voluntary transactions in which a portion of a developing country's hard-currency debt is cancelled or reduced by a creditor in return for an agreement by the debtor to allocate a certain amount of local currency to environmental programs or projects. In practice, DNS can be highly complicated. The creditor can be relieved of a (non-performing) asset that might not be repaid in full, and the debtor can reduce its external debt burden without drawing down scarce foreign reserves.

In their early phase of development, Conservation International brokered the first DNS in 1987 in Bolivia in which $650,000 in debt was cancelled in return for certain conservation measures carried out in the country. Others such swaps followed in the same year in Costa Rica and Ecuador. Since 1987, over $1 billion in funding has been generated by DNS in nearly 30 countries. In the early years, most of the DNS were "private" swaps in which international environmental NGOs raised the funds and initiated the swap process. In recent years, the most common form of DNS has been bilateral, i.e., where both the creditor and debtor are governments. Such arrangements are often executed in the context of a "debt swap clause" in an agreement of the Paris Club (developed countries financing developing countries). Bilateral swaps allow developing country governments to reduce their debt obligations either partially through debt buy-backs at discounted prices or completely through debt forgiveness. The converted debt is usually deposited in the form of local currency denominated government bonds in a so-called conservation trust fund that becomes responsible for dispersing the funds for agreed conservation purposes.

A few donor countries – Canada, Finland, Germany, Netherlands, Switzerland and the US, have made use of bilateral DNS. The most important program of these bilateral DNS has been associated with the US government-sponsored "Enterprise for the Americas Initiative." It provides for a reduction in debt owed to the US government and allows interest payments in local currency to be applied to local environmental programs and projects. This initiative has been active in seven countries in the Latin America and the Caribbean region, including Argentina, Bolivia, Chile, Colombia, El Salvador, Jamaica, and Uruguay. It has provided $876 million for debt relief and $154 million in local donations (GEF, 2001). The US government has budgeted $225 million for this program over the 2002-2004 period.

The level of external debt of the developing countries reached approximately $2 trillion in 2000. Debt servicing has become a major constraint to environmental initiatives. The international donor community devised a rather comprehensive Heavily Indebted Poor Countries (HIPC) Initiative proposed by the World Bank and the IMF in 1996 (details provided in chapter 6). As a stipulation of the HIPC Initiative, countries receiving debt relief are obliged to allocate greater amounts to social spending in the context of their respective poverty alleviation efforts. Consideration should also be given to making environment sector conditions a part of the HIPC Initiative. This could also involve using debt relief as a means of encouraging increased government spending on environmental programs such as reforestation and soil conservation that address poverty alleviation aspects as well.

The issue of designing sovereign debt contracts to include cross-sectoral clauses linking potential debt defaults (in allowable limits) to a barter system to offset the repayment obligations deserves attention. Experience with schemes such as DNS suggests several limitations. Among the main limitations are that the so-called new projects 'created' in lieu of debt obligation were substitutes rather than net supplements to environmental activity of the sovereign borrower state (for more details see Rao, 2000). However, if these lessons of experience are useful for future guidance, it makes sense to include environmental asset preservation as a net new project to offset eventual debt repayment problems of a sovereign country.

Can we link debt default and environmental protection? Mohr and Thomas (1998) formulated an analytical model that considers joint decisions at the sovereign debtor level where the choices include a selection of strategies for default with varying costs, following a probability distribution of cost functions. They argued that the cross-default clause could create an incentive for Pareto-welfare improving DNS to be undertaken, and that such cross-contract linkages across financial and environmental agreements can enhance the incentives for the sovereign state to enter into environmental as well as financial agreements.

Until 1990s, most financial institutions had little interest in the environmental concerns of their business partners, or their provision of financial products and services. The risks for banks rose substantially in the 1980s due to a number of lawsuits (direct liability). US banks therefore began paying attention to environmental aspects before their European counterparts did. The foundation of the Dow Jones Environmental Sustainability Index at the end of 1998 marks a beginning for sustainable investment in the market and sensitivity of the financial industry to the environmental governance issues.

The World Bank's Prototype Carbon Fund (PCF) has been launched in 1999. The PCF is being regarded as a vehicle that will enable the participating parties to gain knowledge and experience so that economic solutions can be generated to fight the problem of climate change. Some banks perceive the importance and opportunities of sustainability (whether implicitly or otherwise) and have signed declarations, such as those by the International Chamber of Commerce (ICC) and the United Nations Environment Programme (UNEP), in which they endorse common and individual responsibility for bringing about sustainable development.

It is possible to use venture capital to help finance a commercial enterprise's switch to production methods using fuels that produce less CO_2, like gas instead of oil. Such financing can partly be made possible by trading the emission rights or credits this yields. In this way, the financing of sustainable energy can be given an impulse while retaining commercial viability of the economic activities and projects (Jeucken, 2001).

8.4 Finance and the Global Environment

Financial constraints are among the common barriers to environmentally sound technologies (EST) in many developing countries. OECD (2001a) suggested that the globalization of financial markets allows firms to improved access to capital and relax such limitations. However, this is a rather oversimplified suggestion since it is not only the access to initial capital resources but sustained profitability of such adopted technologies that remains to be an area of concern for investment decisions. Exclusive resource provisions and concessional terms of transfer of EST are important, and to some extent, this is independent of the patterns of change in the financial markets integration.

Zedillo Commission Report

The UN Commission on Financing for Development (known as the Zedillo Commission) that submitted its report in June 2001 suggested (Zedillo Commission Report, 2001) that the international community should consider whether the common interest and common benefits would be promoted by providing stable and contractual resources for these purposes. Politically, taxing for the solution of global problems will be much more difficult than taxing for purely domestic purposes. A currency transactions tax (also known as the Tobin tax) has often been proposed as a new source of finance. The report suggested that further rigorous technical study is needed before any definitive conclusion is reached on the convenience and feasibility of the Tobin tax. There is likely to be more promise in a carbon tax —a tax on the consumption of fossil fuels, at rates that reflect the contribution of these fuels to CO_2 emissions. Some of the proposals for augmenting global financial resources for promoting the environment and development are briefly stated in Box 8.3.

Box 8.3: Innovative Sources of Development Finance?

The UN Preparatory Committee for the Monterrey International Conference on Financing for Development (UN, 2001) suggested a few 'new' or 'innovative' sources of finance for further consideration. These proposals included the following – currency transaction tax, carbon tax, international air transport tax, and arms export tax.

The first two elements possess substantial revenue potential as elucidated below.

Currency transaction tax (CTT)

Total annual global transactions have been estimated around $360 trillion in 1998. The corresponding amount was $264 trillion in 2000. A tax rate of 0.01 percent on this could yield revenue of $26.4 billion, assuming there is an entity that could collect this cost-effectively and mobilize it to a designated common fund.

Carbon tax

Consumption of commercial hydrocarbon fuels is about 1 ton of carbon per person in a year. A uniform carbon tax of $2 per barrel (i.e., 4.8 cents per gallon) implies $17 per ton of automobile gasoline at carbon content of 0.81. This corresponds to $21 per ton of carbon and yields revenue of about $125 billion per year.

FDI, Environmental Standards and Global Finance

In theory, there may be scope for a 'race to the bottom' (RTB) when countries compete to relax environmental standards and regulations in order to attract FDI. In practice, however, this feature is largely unimportant, as documented in a number of studies (see, for example, UNEP, 2000). The costs of adhering to environmental standards has been generally in the range of 2 to 3 percent of total production costs, and these costs are relatively very small compared to other transaction costs and risk factors of managing a business. Business entities do not seem to rate lax environmental regulations as an important factor in their decisions regarding FDI. RTB remains an oversold concept, and perhaps its perception (rather than its practice by the investors) that it is relevant still daunts some of the potential FDI recipient entities. For a more detailed description, see Rao (2000).

Global environmental protection is currently being carried out by a number of organizations. Perhaps the most important one directly responsible for funding through various grants and promoting environmentally sound technologies within the areas of specific areas of focus is the Global Environmental Facility (GEF). Some of the details of its functions are given in Box 8.4.

In the absence of well-developed financial markets and instruments such as bonds for financing infrastructure development, developing countries can hardly finance these amenities from domestic resources alone. This situation could improve whenever relatively less capital-intensive projects (such as watersheds and drinking water supply) can be formed as quasi-public entities with the use of domestic and external resources including concessional capital.

Regarding the need for a global institution, the Zedillo Commission Report (2001) suggested the formation of a new global entity World Environment Organization (WEO), and the use of special taxes for financing global public goods including the environment. For a detailed statement on a relevant proposal, including possible role and functions of a WEO see Rao (2002).

Box 8.4: Global Environmental Facility

The GEF was formally established in 1994, following its pilot phase of operation starting in 1991 with an initial donor fund commitment of $1 billion. With a current membership of 174 countries, the GEF provides funds in the form of grants to eligible programs in developing countries to protect the global environment. The four focal areas for support are climate change, biological diversity, international waters, and ozone layer protection. In addition, incremental costs of some of the activities covered under Agenda 21, the action plan of the 1992 UN Conference on Environment and Development, are also funded by the GEF in eligible countries.

The donor countries provided fund replenishments in 1994 for $2 billion and later added a further amount of $2.6 billion in 1998. Since 1991, the GEF allocated $4.5 billion in grants and leveraged an additional $12 billion in co-financing from other institutional sources of finance for about 1000 projects in 140 developing counties. These amounts are significant, although small when compared to the magnitude of financial need to address problems that deserve attention in the global environmental arena. Currently these financial resources are rather thinly spread, and the administrative costs for managing the GEF are rather high (exceeding about $20 million per annum). This is in addition to accruing costs at the Implementing Agency (IA) levels, as the GEF does not directly implement its operations; The IA organizations are The World Bank, UNDP, and the IFC. Besides, the GEF's focus on specific projects (which may be called sub-projects) does not allow an element of sustainability because of their susceptibility to changes and disturbances (physical, environmental, and institutional) in their interdependent systems of these form only small components.

The possibility of project of integration into a larger and coherent system of environmental and institutional governance has not yet been fully addressed by the GEF approaches. Such an integration could yield net additional benefits in a cost-effective manner and ensures sustainability. The GEF plays a catalytic role in the promotion of the governance of the global environment, but a decade of experience seems to indicate only a limited success in addressing the problems.

8. 5 Environment and Lender Liability

Many of the major banks in the developed world have recognized the role of the environment in their business activities, both from raising their own range of financial products and services for profitably, and for minimizing potential liability costs. At least half of the major banks have specific environmental loans in their portfolio of services.

Export Credit Agencies

The role of Export Credit Agencies (ECA) in financing exports and implications for environmental protection deserve special attention, especially since the ECA are mainly for capital-rich countries and are not usually signatories to any environmental treaties. These are key entities for promoting globalization and global economic integration, governing financial resource mobilization. Their resource flows exceed in magnitude the aid and loan activities of all bilateral and multilateral institutions. Their increased activities coincided with an era of decline of foreign aid from developed countries to the developing world. In some cases the ECA seem to work at cross-purposes relative to some of the international development institutions such as the United Nations Development Programme (UNDP) and create distortions in the efficient governance of environmental assets in some of the countries. The irony is that the host countries of the ECA are often signatories to various international environmental treaties seeking to protect environmental resources, but these do not constrain the conduct of operations of the ECA. Clear recognition of their potential contribution to the environment was accorded at the July 2000 summit of the G8 countries. Their communiqué sought to devise common guidelines for the ECA activities in order to ensure their sensitivity to environmental issues.

The Ex-Im Bank of the US is an exception among ECA in that it is mandated by law to carry out environmental assessments in projects with environmental influences. There is a substantial lack of transparency of operations and relevant contract clause of most ECA projects. This feature implies that adverse environmental impacts may be known only after such occurrences, and thus would be too late to rectify the situation at any reasonable cost. Some of the ECA have formed their own guidelines for environmental assessment but these guidelines remain largely arbitrary and minimally comprehensive, and their application in practice is even less rigorous. During the past few years the ECA and their corporate clients formed a partnership that has resulted in the globalization of subsidized trade and lacked attention to environmental issues (Rich, 2000).

The World Bank

The World Bank's contributions to environmental protection have been very controversial. Several cases of failure in integrating economic and environmental issues emerged over the years; for a detailed narration see, for example, Rich (1994). It has been suggested (Ibid, p.186) that "a clear contradiction emerged between the Bank's efforts to deal with the macroeconomic crises of debt and adjustment and its purported goals of poverty alleviation..."

In 1987, the President of the World Bank admitted that the institution has been a part of the problem rather than contributing to the solution when it came to environmental governance. Ten years later, the Quality Assurance Group (QAG) of the World Bank stated (World Bank, 1997, p.15): "The lessons from past experience are well known yet they are generally ignored in the design of new operations."

For many years, the Bank (and its former President Conable) maintained that the lessons of experience in its policy design and operation enhances the Bank's capability for 'learning-by-doing'. To quote Rich (1994, p.171): "The Bank would always be 'learning-by-doing' as Conable and other officials put it, since it seemed to be incapable of remembering." The critical issue here is in the absence of best efforts and due diligence in some cases, who pays for the costs of such originating inefficiency? Usually the borrower state has been incurring the costs of all inefficiencies originating at both creditor and borrower levels.

During the two decades preceding the mid-90s, the World Bank financed activities involving colonization of rain forests in parts of Brazil and Indonesia, excessive grazing operations in Latin America and Africa and encouragement of exports of products that have been environmentally subsidized and unsustainable. Tobacco production was also encouraged as a cash crop. An Evaluation Study of the Bank reviewed 335 projects funded in the pre-1990s in agriculture and forestry sectors found that severe environmental consequences accrued with a time lag when the projects neared completion or after their completion. The experience in Nepal is a classic example: the Nepal Settlement Project sought to convert about 43,000 acres of tropical forest in Terai region in 1974, followed by another loan transaction to launch Terai Forestry Project in 1983. Considering several incomplete assessments that led to avoidable adverse consequences in the borrower countries, it appears important that a provision of lender liability in the debt contracts with the World Bank and the IMF should exist. These organizations do not have the word 'environment' in their articles of formation but influence economic and environmental patterns in the developing world. There are a few recent signs of concern for environmental protection, however.

Extended Lender Liability (ELL)

If lenders provide funds for predictable environmentally damaging activities, lender liability for damages may deserve merit. ELL is similar to the concept of Extended Producer Responsibility (EPR), which is defined as an approach where producers accept responsibility for consequences of the treatment and disposal of products. Internalizing externalities remains the guiding principle. The EPR Guidance Manual for Governments was published by the OECD in 2001 (OECD, 2001b). This applies to the production sector. A similar handbook is required for the financial sector. One of the direct implications of imposing liabilities may be to enhance the costs of provision of capital for lending or other products and services. It is not essential that a mandatory legal penalty be levied, but an environmental rating and signaling information could motivate the financial institution to accord due priority to environmental issues in relation to their activities.

8. 6 Concluding Observations

The operational use of the popular concept of SD needs to bear relationship with the original definition and maintain integrity of the components of the original definition. This involves an incessant attention to the issue of poverty eradication as an important element of SD process. A balance must be achieved in promoting productivity of financial and other resources and in the protection of the environmental assets. At the minimum, multilateral financial institutions must ensure that they do not function at cross-purposes or counteract SD efforts of other institutions.

The goals set forth by the UN Millennium Declaration deserve careful attention, perhaps to revise upwards in some cases and to integrate with several ongoing international economic and environmental strategies.

Among important policy instruments that raise financial resources and minimize environmental damages are green taxes. If instituted in a cost effective sense, these can reap their potential in yielding the double dividend.

Cross-contract linkages across financial and environmental agreements can enhance the incentives for the sovereign state to enter into environmental as well as financial agreements; further studies are required in terms of legal, economic and institutional implications of such linkages. Debt relief, when tied as a package to some of the environmental protection aspects, can possibly prevent some of the adverse consequences of debt default and country credit rating assessments.

The roles of the IMF and the World Bank have been far less than perfect in protecting the environment. Reforms of the multilateral financial institutions need to ensure that their policies and operations are governed by a new revised charter of articles that include explicitly the role of 'environmental protection'.

Export credit agencies need to follow a set of guidelines (to be devised and monitored perhaps by the UN) to ensure that their lending activities do not contribute to the damage of the environment and of the long-term productive capacity of a system.

Review Exercises

1. What is the role of SD concept in protecting the environment and reduction of poverty in the short-run and in the long run?

2. What policy measures are relevant in fully addressing the issues of SD in terms of the provision of resources for development finance?

3. Examine the role and limitations of DNS. Suggest potential refinements in order to revitalize and improve the effectiveness of DNS.

4. What guidelines are necessary for the activities of the ECA in order to fulfill the objective of SD?

5. Examine the scope and limitations of environmental taxes in a developing country setting.

6. Examine the relationship between each category (of the three major classifications) of environmental resources and reduction of poverty.

References

Bosquet, B. (2000): Environmental Tax Reform: Does it Work? A Survey of the Empirical Evidence, Journal of Ecological Economics, 34, 19-31.

Bovenberg, A. L. and Goulder, L. H. (1996): Optimal environmental taxation in the presence of other taxes: general equilibrium analyses, American Economic Review, 86, 985-1000.

Goulder, L. H. (1995): Environmental Taxation and the Double Dividend – A Reader's Guide, International Tax and Public Finance, 2, 157 – 183.

Global Environmental Facility (GEF) (2001): Financing for Environment and Sustainable Development in Developing Countries, Washington, DC: GEF Secretariat.

Gunter, T. (1997): Institutional Mechanisms shaping the Environmental Impact of Transboundary Capital Flows, Washington, DC: World Resources Institute.

Jeucken, M. (2001): Sustainable Finance and Banking, London: Earthscan Publications.

Mohr, E. and Thomas, J. P. (1998): Pooling Sovereign Risks- The Case of Environmental Treaties and International Development, Journal of Development Economics, 55, 173-190.

Organization for Economic Cooperation and Development (OECD) (2001a): Foreign Direct Investment and Sustainable Development, Paper for Conference at Mexico City on "New Horizons and Policy Changes for Foreign Direct Investment in the 21st Century", November 2001.

OECD (2001b): Environmentally Related Taxes in OECD Countries: Issues and Strategies, Paris: OECD.

OECD (2001c): Extended Producer Responsibility, Paris: OECD Secretariat.

Parry, I. (1997): Environmental Taxes and Quotas in the presence of distortionary factor markets, Resource and Energy Economics, 19, 203 – 220.

Pigou, A. C. (1932): The Economics of Welfare, London: Macmillan.

Rao, P. K. (2002): Environment and Development: A Policy Framework, Lawrenceville, NJ: Pinninti Publishers.

Rao, P. K. (2000): Sustainable Development: Economics and Policy, Oxford: Blackwell.

Rich, B. (2000): Exporting Destruction, The Environmental Forum, 17, 33-41.

Rich, B. (1994): Mortgaging the Earth- The World Bank, Environmental Impoverishment, and the Crisis of Development, Boston: Beacon Press.

Stewart, F. (1995): Adjustment and Poverty – Options and Choices, New York: Routledge.

United Nations (UN) (2001): Existing Proposals for Innovative Sources of Finance, Technical Note #3, Preparatory Committee for the International Conference on Financing for Development, UN General Assembly Document A/AC.257/xx, New York: UN.

United Nations Environment Programme (UNEP) (2000): Environment and Trade: A Handbook, Nairobi: UNEP.

World Bank (2002): Achieving Development Outcomes – The Millennium Challenge, Operations Evaluation Department Report #25159, Washington, DC: World Bank.

World Bank (1997): Portfolio Improvement Program: Draft Review of Sector Portfolio and Lending Instruments- A Synthesis, Washington, DC: World Bank.

World Commission on Environment and Development (WCED) (1987): Our Common Future, New York: Oxford University Press.

World Resources Institute (WRI) (1999): World Resources 1998-99, New York: Oxford University Press.

Zedillo Commission Report (2001): The UN Commission on Financing for Development, New York: United Nations. Details may also be seen at www.un.org/reports/financing/index.html

CHAPTER 9:

Perspectives

9.1 Broad Approaches

The major issue of relative roles of market institutions, state control and regulatory institutions remains unresolved even after many years of experience in various countries. This is because there are only a few common prescriptions that fit every economy and institutional configuration; differentiated policies are necessary for diverse settings. A classic observation on a proposal by some stakeholders for almost complete reliance on market forces and corresponding market institutions, with limited (if any) nonmarket institutional interventions may be quoted here. Decades ago, Karl Polanyi (1944, p. 57) stated:

> "Ultimately....the control of an economic system by the market is of overwhelming consequence to the whole organization of society: it means no less than the running of society as an adjunct to the market. Instead of economy being embedded in social relations, social relations are embedded in the economic system."

This observation remains a relevant pointer to the limitations of contemporary global attempts toward globalization through marketization. Development finance, expressed by its objectives and means, requires non-market interventions in addition to the use of market-based instruments.

Market imperfections and the role of nonmarket factors affecting the efficiency of markets suggest that markets need to be defined in relation to various specifications regarding interdependent institutions as well. Stated differently, the interdependencies of institutions must be recognized in the governance of market-related functions and institutions; market is not to be deemed a separate institution capable of yielding socially optimal results, just as the institution of the government or regulation cannot deliver proclaimed results in the absence of other checks and balances for efficient governance of the systems.

A socioeconomic system that pays attention to the dire needs of the relatively deprived population by creating productive capacities for the full enjoyment of life of its citizenry achieves in return, not only potential for enhanced economic productivity but also a path for egalitarian and harmonious economic development on a sustainable basis. Eradication of abject poverty, reduction of other forms of poverty, and provision of infrastructural capacities to sustain economic development are some of the objectives of development finance. None of these objectives is purely economic or value-free, but these recognize that economic formulations are meaningless without their sensitization in human welfare terms.

Even after an agreement on the objectives, the means of achieving these differ depending on one or more of the following:

a) the current characteristics as well as historical background features of socioeconomic, political and legal institutions for each system and country;

b) the costs of adjustment, including transaction costs, related alternate forms of governance;

c) sociological and anthropological traits of the population; and

d) the role of external or international factors.

Reverting to the primary objectives, means and ends of 'development finance', it is important to recognize the following features.

Technical economic analysis should focus more on the economics of adjustment than on the economics of stable economic equilibria. Although the latter are useful for long-term policy guidance, lack of attention to the governance of transition (the most import aspect of economic adjustment and development in all developing economies) leads to the result that the stable equilibria may not arise at all. Methods of transaction cost economics should play a major role in all economic analyses and policy prescriptions of multilateral development institutions.

Since the demand for and supply of development finance are not cleared by the markets, institutional interventions are essential for the fulfillment of development aspirations of different societies. The key issue is to design and implement relevant policies in a cost effective manner. The functional role of development finance may be reiterated here: minimization of poverty and enhancement of economic development, both on a sustainable basis. These objectives need to be achieved by maximizing productivity gains of financial resources and institutions. The methods for attaining these objectives should recognize the concurrent roles of potential risks such as banking and financial risks. These risks as well as other potential risks (briefly stated in various chapters of this book) constitute the economic environment within which stated objectives need to be realized. An important aspect of risk management relates to financial stability, discussed below.

Maintaining Financial Stability

The Financial Stability Forum (FSF) Working Group on Capital Flows in its report of 2001 (details given at the FSF website wwww.fsforum.org) offered a number of recommendations dealing with financial risk management and identified several data gaps, information requirements and organizational capacity building aspects, summarized below.

- Abrupt portfolio adjustments can involve sudden cessation or reversals of flows and sharp changes in asset prices.

- National authorities, as well as international bodies should assess the possible adverse consequences of their policies in terms of creating biases toward short-term capital flows or otherwise encouraging a build-up of unwarranted external exposures, and should take prompt corrective measures.

- The development of a domestic bond market can help a government to avoid concentrating its borrowing in short maturities or in foreign currencies, instead creating a diversified portfolio strategy with more dispersed maturities.

The need for the development of domestic bond markets has been highlighted by recent financial crises. The risky debt structure of the sovereign and corporate sectors, characterized by heavy concentration in short-term and foreign currency debts because of the lack of developed domestic bond markets, has often been blamed as the cause of many crises. In the absence of developed domestic financial markets, even countries without a net external financing requirement can incur external or foreign currency mismatches.

The FSF Working Group recommended that the provision for official reserves should increase:

a) when a country is operating a fixed exchange rate regime;

b) the lower its standing in and routine access to international capital markets; and

c) the shorter the maturity of the public sector's external or foreign currency liabilities.

Two definitions are useful here:

Liquidity risk: This refers to liabilities being shorter maturity than assets, so that the borrower is subject to rollover or refinancing risk.

Foreign currency risk: This refers to liabilities and assets being denominated in different currencies, so that net worth is sensitive to changes in the relevant exchange rate.

Despite a declining share of bank lending in total private capital flows to developing countries, short-term claims (debt claims due within a year) on developing countries held by banks reporting to the Bank of International Settlements (BIS) more than doubled from end-1990 to end-1996.

National authorities should aim at obtaining sufficient information not only to assess the risk exposure and concentrations to foreign currency funding of individual banks, but also to monitor, as part of macro prudential assessments, the overall exposure of the banking system to the risks of foreign currency funding through analysis of aggregated information.

Infrastructural Improvements

Institutional infrastructure remains a critical factor for the effective provision of development finance. Often, this infrastructure acts not only as a promoter of the sectoral or regional development but also offers spillover benefits across the economic system.

The World Bank (2002) in its annual report noted that developing countries lost over $1 trillion during the 1980s and 1990s because of banking (and financial) crises. A sizeable segment of the losses may be traceable to the role of external or international financial and economic shocks. However, the role of institutions and their resilience (as opposed to their fragility) remains very important. The role of domestic or internal institutional infrastructure, in addition to the fundamental structures of the economic systems themselves, remains very important in minimizing the adverse consequences and incidence of costs of crises. Resilience of a financial and economic system is not merely a function of resources such as capital and labor, but is also heavily influenced by the institutional infrastructure that enables efficient transformation of resources into relevant outputs on a sustainable and predictable basis.

The Multilateral Investment Guarantee Agency (MIGA), an affiliate of the World Bank, provides risk coverage for eligible investments in its member countries. During 2001, this list included 24 countries and 33 projects and covered $1.4 billion in developing countries. Evidently, the magnitude of operations remains rather small and the scope for expansion is significant. The geopolitical risks and other related investment uncertainties are some of the risk factors that seem to have added the demand for MIGA services during 2002, and the trend continues. It is desirable that capital-rich countries support the operations of MIGA and other related organizations in the interests of providing requisite insurance services and promoting expanded credit facilities.

Important elements of requisite institutional infrastructure include the following:

a) transparent and effective laws and regulations governing financial institutions and protecting creditor rights;

b) cost effective mechanisms for dispute resolution, including efficient judiciary and Alternate Dispute Resolution (ADR) systems;

c) systems of governance that take into account the totality of costs, including transaction costs, and seek to minimize these costs;

d) corporate governance, including corporate laws, accounting standards and information disclosure requirements as well their effective enforcement; and

e) coherence of micro and macro institutional arrangements and stability of organizations.

9.2 Country Risk Analyses and Credit Ratings

Sovereign credit rating plays an important influence on the working of capital flows and access to capital markets, and consequentially on the incidence of debt burden in a specific time interval, on smoothing of financial shocks and consumption smoothing (or lack of it). This section is primarily concerned with development implications of sovereign credit ratings and their potential effects. Since credit ratings have been influenced largely by sovereign debt and related aspects, we focus on the underlying issues as well. Let us first examine the important motives for external borrowings and sovereign debt contracts, since these have a bearing on the patterns of borrowing and repayment by state parties and thus affect assessments of their credit ratings.

Motives for Borrowing and Assessment of Risk

In order to understand the broader underlying framework for external borrowings, it is relevant to note that the motives for borrowing include mainly the following categories:

a) consumption motives: these are to ensure and enhance consumption in various sectors and segments of the society so as to sustain the interests of the stakeholders controlling the state and its entities;

b) production and investment motives: these are to augment domestic production with external resources and investments, and reap gains of comparative economic advantage whenever the domestic marginal productivity of capital is higher than the cost of external capital borrowings; and

c) adjustment and private motives: these are to enable consumption smoothing for the population as a whole in light of shocks and shortfalls in domestic output and resources, and to gain special or private benefits (including a variety of spending and resource cornering privileges) for some of the influential stakeholders of the state or its ruling regime.

If we consider the motives of external borrowings, and the potential for economic shocks (both domestic and international), it is no surprise that there are different types of risks associated with debt repayments. The sovereign debt management problem involves a careful assessment of contractual, legal and other institutional factors that contribute to the provision of external credit and subsequent recovery as well as adjustments as may be necessary.

Given the role of sovereign debt in meetings possibly multiple objectives, it is important to examine the operationally relevant policies that govern both the design and implementation of sovereign debt contracts. Also of importance here are potential directions for an improvement in relevant strategies.

Sovereign Debt

Among analytical policy studies that suggest a few reforms in sovereign debt policies are the following. Some of these are based on some of the analytical findings of Aizenman (1989).

a) Contingency plans that make the debt default costs of sovereign borrowers dependent upon the intensity of default level are inferior (in the sense of potential welfare maximization) relative to contingency plans that make the interest rate dependent upon observable variables that are correlated with the default penalty.

b) Provision of optimal contingencies could be beneficial in terms their effects of raising the credit ceiling levels and of expected income, in addition to stabilization of risk shocks.

c) There is a trade-off between the usefulness of policies and the optimal use of contingencies; an important requirement for the feasibilities is that the realization of the default penalty should be public information. For some of the borrower states that rely mainly on exports for their foreign exchange earnings this statement has the implication that a contingency plan could index interest rates and/or debt repayment schedules to the realization of the price of export items, and this reduces the effective magnitude of country risk and smoothens debt rating shocks or their consequences.

The unenforceability of sovereign debt contracts implies that credit may be rationed, and that lending activity is likely to be lower than the corresponding level of fully enforceable contracts (Eaton et al, 1986). On the other hand, asymmetric information features do not allow lenders to observe fully some of the relevant economic and other factors, and these lead to greater credit operations than in the corresponding case with full information (Kletzer, 1984). The issues of the design and implementation of 'efficient debt contracts' remain invariably linked to the issues of financial performance and contractual compliance at the borrower levels. The question of credit rating needs to be evaluated in this perspective, so should the development effectiveness of external resources.

Sovereign Risk

Government policies, legal structures and enforcement policies constitute major elements of what is often called 'sovereign risk'. This risk arises from the likelihood of the sovereign state's exercise of the sovereign powers whenever need and opportunity arises in the context of international financial transactions. Some of the elements of country risk are exogenous and some are endogenous. To a large extent, sovereign risk constitutes an exogenous risk for the international financial entity. Strategic behavior of the host country in relation to the design of contracts and financial transactions (including conditionalities for transfer of resources) constitute factors behind endogenous risk. Let us clarify two definitions relevant here.

Credit Risk

Credit risk is normally defined in terms of the probability that a loan will not be repaid according to the terms of the contract. This can be estimated ex post if there is a long history, and can be assessed ex ante based on various future parameters. Generally, this concept refers to a forward-looking assessment for credit operations. The credit risk of newly extended loan is usually higher than that applicable on an average for borrowers. At the margin, the risk thus is an increasing function of the number of loan transactions and their volume.

The design of regulatory mechanisms should aim at encouraging investors themselves to differentiate credit risks. To facilitate this task, the FSF Working Group on Capital Flows in its report of 2000 emphasized the importance of disclosure of information by borrowers. Improved disclosure of information by borrowers to the market in terms of both quality and timeliness would help create an environment in which investors can do better credit analysis. Improving disclosure standards not only reduces investors' dependence on rating agencies but also allows them to judge better whether rating agencies are making proper credit assessments.

Country Risk

Capital resource flows with a specific country destination are largely affected by a set of risk factors that apply as a common factor for that country, even when contractual specifications of various investments and loans differ significantly. Definitions of country risk vary considerably. Some of these originate in the motives for assessing country risk. Some authors defined this as the inability of a country to generate sufficient foreign exchange resources to pay for its external debt obligations. This is a rather narrow specification and its focus excludes several important features relevant for a broader understanding of country risk.

A distinction should be made as to whether economic shocks, if they were to occur, would give rise to a liquidity problem or to a solvency problem, or both.

The national authorities should employ cause-effect relationships and relevant indicators that help them to measure and analyze these different risks. It would be desirable for the emerging market economies to deploy a more sophisticated approach to their management of their financial risks. Applied risk management techniques as 'value at risk' (VAR) (see chapter 1) are relevant for adoption. Promoting the right kind of risk sharing among creditors and debtors through financial contracting should also be a medium-term policy goal.

Box 9.1 provides a preliminary formulation of solvency assessment; further improvements are needed, however. The main task is to identify a set of interrelated parameters in the context of solvency and country risk assessment.

Box 9.1: Solvency Assessment

> The ability of a sovereign borrower to repay debt according a predetermined schedule is often a critical issue, rather than assessing her ability to repay debt as a lump sum over a fixed time horizon. Most of the literature has been directing its attention to the latter issue, which has less operational or policy relevance.
>
> The following identities are modified versions of their counterparts given earlier by Eaton et al (1986).
>
> If D is total outstanding debt of a country, R its repayment and r, a weighted sum of applicable interest rates for different loan components (weights being the magnitudes of loans involved) for different loans, the balance of trade B in any time period follows the identity
>
> $$B = rD + R$$
>
> Besides, R obeys the following identity, assuming there is also a foreign aid component and that aid is fungible:
>
> $$R = (S - I) + (T + A - G)$$
>
> where S is private savings, A foreign aid, I domestic investment, T total tax revenue (not adjusted for costs of collection and other transaction costs) and G government spending.
>
> The ability of a borrower state to repay debt arises a net result of S, A, I, T, G, assuming r and B are exogenously determined. However, B and r are also endogenous in terms of various factors such as the role of foreign direct investment, country credit rating and foreign exchange policies.

Box 9.2 summarizes some of the important elements of country risk assessment.

Country Risk Analyses and Credit Ratings   193

Box 9.2: Country Risk Analysis and Managing Risk

The structure of the stock of a country's external financial liabilities (both claims and obligations) results from the past capital gross inflows and outflows, and from the nature of any contingent contracts with the external sector, in addition to the role current flows that contribute to future stocks. In terms of its risk and liquidity exposures of a country, relevant features of the external balance sheet (that are typically thought to be off-balance sheet exposures) are the maturity structure and currency composition of loans to and from the external sector, inward and outward equity investment, and the contractual specifications of any contingent contracts.

Debt maturity structures and foreign currency mismatches are important to macro prudential assessments as well as to the regulation of enterprise financial activities. In addition, there are interactions between the composition of a borrowing country's financial balance sheet and the structure of its economy and in particular its sources of income for servicing external debt. Thus, the net worth and credit standing of a country heavily dependent on income from commodity exports (foreign currency) might be affected by changes in commodity prices. These features in turn affect the exchange rate, and have further effects on country credit ratings, especially if the country has substantial amounts of foreign currency-denominated or foreign currency-indexed debts. These ratings affect economic prospects, especially when the financial information and governance of the system is not transparent.

Source: www.fsforum.org

A government should identify the main economic risks to which it is directly exposed and to which it is indirectly exposed via the economy as a whole. This can be viewed as conducting a risk audit. A list of possible risks includes (more details may be seen at www.fsforum.org):

- Global business cycle shocks and interest rate shocks;
- Shifts in market sentiment towards regions or particular groups of countries;
- Fluctuations in the prices of key goods and services (e.g., commodities) produced or consumed;
- Risks originating from government guarantee/insurance arrangements for public sector companies and/or private sector financial institutions; and
- Risks arising out of any exchange-rate commitments.

Sovereign Credit Ratings and Limitations

The role of sovereign credit ratings in the context of development finance is significant and perhaps not yet fully recognized in academic studies and policy applications. These ratings carried out by a diverse group of private agencies, whose objectives of reference include providing market guidance to potential and existing investors, are not expected to take into consideration various economic development perspectives. Yet their functions and information outputs in the form of credit ratings from time to time play major role in the flows of capital and precipitate policies that directly affect vulnerable sections of the society.

The ratings phenomena have asymmetric effects on poor and non-poor. The effects are also asymmetric when it comes to upgrading versus lowering of rating scores and grades for a country. These indicators accentuate boom and bust cycles, and make greater impact on less than transparent economies and on fragile economic systems. If they err on the negative side in terms of lowering of credit rating for a less than robust economy, it spells a self-fulfilling prophecy; the *ex ante* assertion becomes an *ex post* phenomenon at least for some short-term or medium-term, or until a reversal occurs in the rating level. There is thus an externality problem of using credit rating indicators as market signals. Given these serious implications, it is important that the rating exercises be carried out rigorously, objectively and in accordance with a set of internationally devised guidelines. At the same time, national economies need to offer credible and transparent information so that a mechanism of balancing and verification emerges from multiple sources of information. These tasks are awaiting further attention at national and international levels.

In one of the augmented roles of credit rating indicators, the Basel Committee on Banking Supervision (BIS, 1999) suggested due consideration of sovereign credit ratings derived by private credit rating agencies in order to determine the risk exposures to different borrowers. However, in the absence of complete enforcement of legal claims in various countries, subjective judgments about countries' willingness to repay loans may be challenged as arbitrary rating exercises that are based on partial information.

There is a basic problem in devising sovereign credit ratings. The common practice of the credit rating agencies is to assess a sovereign's 'default risk level' in relation to outstanding debts and liabilities, and the ability or willingness of the government to adhere to agreed payment arrangements. This assessment is distinctly different from a basic and more comprehensive assessment of the economic resilience of the sovereign's economy, whether there are economic and institutional fundamentals that enable the country to maintain creditworthiness in the short-term and in longer time horizons.

Regarding some of the limitations of the practices of most rating agencies, the World Bank (2000, p.48-49) observed: "because credit ratings have tended to react to changes in creditworthiness rather than accurately predict them, their use in determining capital requirements could accentuate the procyclical nature of capital flows to emerging markets.... ratings are primarily based on publicly available information; the conventional belief that they are based on advance knowledge or superior information is questionable." It has also been observed that most of the credit rating agencies neither conduct rigorous studies nor deploy sophisticated methods for predicting the borrower default potential or probabilities.

Sovereign credit ratings are often closely correlated with per capita gross national product (GNP) of specific countries. They are more reactive than predictive or preventive, and they lag rather than lead financial markets (Reisen and von Maltzan, 1998). Credit rating agencies seem to do better in predicting (and thus rating debt) of potential default risks of sovereign debtors than in predicting currency crises. The latter may often arise from the former, in conjunction with lowering of ratings by these agencies, however. Reinhart (2002) offers a detailed analysis of some of the relevant interrelationships; substantial additional investigations are needed for analyzing these issues. It has also been observed in an empirical study by Kaminsky and Schmukler (2002) that credit ratings agencies, by their current methods of processing and relaying rating information, contribute to the financial instability in emerging market economies. Besides, the authors noted that the effects of such ratings seems stronger (in terms of changes in economic outlook) in economies that are less transparent in their financial activities.

It has been observed that the incentive for rating agencies to indulge in 'herd behavior' is due to the cost savings that result from following other agencies' leads (World Bank, 2000, p. 49). The issue is who is to 'bell the cat', and at whose initial cost will others follow? The larger agencies such as the Standard and Poor can possibly take the lead and the smaller ones may follow. Is this a Stackelberg game (follow the leader and play a game of business survival) or a fair and equitable one? The role of national and international supervisory agencies such as the BIS is important here. The BIS and the international community need to set forth guidelines that are more detailed and rate the credit rating agencies themselves.

9.3 Main Conclusions

Let us summarize, firstly, some of the basic phenomena:

1. Financial Resources and Financial Institutions lead to Financial Development and Economic Growth.
1. Economic Growth and Development Finance leads to Economic Development.
2. Economic Development and Environmental Development leads to Sustainable Development.

Secondly, among the important policies and principles of significance in development finance are the following:

1. Financial liberalization combined with effective market supervision;

2. Promotion of innovation and entrepreneurship with efficient incentive mechanisms at different levels of financial and economic governance;

3. Adoption of macro prudential norms of financial management;

4. Government borrowings and loan portfolios to seek a balance between welfare maximization and minimization of potential risks of insolvency or other debt hangovers; and

5. Promotion of efficient microfinance institutions and operational activities conducive for the minimization of incidence / prevalence of poverty.

The role of development finance in fulfilling its objectives of reduction of poverty, and promotion of economic development leading to sustainable development must be perceived in the context of economic globalization (its role and limitations), global financial architecture (and its reforms), financial governance (supervision and regulation at national and international levels). Relevant institutional reforms, both at national and international levels, should precede policy reform, if both reforms cannot be undertaken simultaneously.

Developing countries possess potential to obtain greater returns (relative to their developed countries) to their efforts and investments in institutional infrastructure in general and financial institutional development in particular. These institutions and institutional arrangements at the macro level include: legal infrastructure and the role of rule of law, cost effective methods of enforcement of property rights and contracts, transparent and comprehensive systems of information and financial governance (including corporate governance at enterprise levels), pragmatic but effective regulation and supervision of code of conduct of various financial and non-financial operations of public and private enterprises. The role of microfinance and efficient governance of economic entities remains an important element of sustaining macro financial resilience and stability.

The processes of economic growth and economic development follow the process of financial development, as long as relevant infrastructural improvements supplement financial development. These infrastructural improvements should include legal, administrative, and other institutional reforms such that financial goods and services are provided to the society in a cost effective and sustainable manner. Various aspects of institutional infrastructural improvements (including data improvements), and reforms in country risk assessments and sovereign debt policies (among other policy recommendations given in this chapter), are expected to enhance the effectiveness of development finance.

The Monterrey Consensus, the Zedillo Commission Report and the UN Millennium Declaration should be three major pillars of policy based on which further advancement of reforms of policies and institutions at national and international levels should follow.

The role of formal approaches and methods of analysis to assist policy formulations and their effective implementation remains to be strengthened further. Among the important areas for further study are:

1. exploring the role of the economics of transaction costs in the design and implementation of:
   a. financial policies at the national level,
   b. sovereign debt contracts, and
   c. loan conditionalities;
2. development of analytical methods, in the framework of comprehensive systems studies and optimizing framework (with reference to objective criteria), for sovereign credit ratings;
3. the design of optimal debt models with efficient features of:
   a. contracting,
   b. renegotiation and rescheduling, and
   c. contingency planning;
4. the design of incentives for:
   a. efficient governance of financial institutions,
   b. microcredit management, and
   c. compliance with terms of contract; and
5. the structure and design of optimal external aid policies and conditionalities that contribute to sustainable finance and sustainable development.

In addition to the above themes, previous chapters have identified several specific issues and gaps in current knowledge. These elements could form an agenda for further research and development of the subject of development finance in theory and practice. Additional studies on these lines could enrich the analytical foundations, lead to the design of improved financial and institutional mechanisms, and to the implementation of effective policies at local, national, international levels.

Review Exercises

1. If the ratio of imports to GNP constitutes the average propensity to import, what explains:

   a) decline in this ratio for developed countries; and

   b) stationary levels of this ratio for some countries.

2. a) What are the policy assumptions and implications of utilizing the income elasticity of demand for imports (IED) as a measure of economic progress (as suggested, for example, in Simpson, 2002)?

   b) If developed countries are those with less levels of country risk, elucidate how IED and country risk are correlated.

3. What are the implications of exogenous economic shock-indexed debt repayment in sovereign debts, and in the assessment of country risks?

4. Suggest relevant indicators for assessing the quality of credit rating agencies involved in country risk analysis.

5. State the objectives and means of development finance, and identify constraints in terms of: a) resources; b) organizations and institutions at national and international levels; and c) non-economic factors.

References

Aizenman, J. (1989): Country Risk and Contingencies, International Economic Journal, 3, 81-102.

Bank of International Settlement (BIS) (1999): Supervisory Lessons to be drawn from the Asian Crisis, Working Paper, Basel: Basel Committee on Banking Supervision.

Eaton, J., Gersovitz, M. and J. Stiglitz, J. (1986): The pure theory of country risk, European Economic Review, 30, 481-513.

Kaminsky, G. and Schmukler, S. (2002): Emerging market instability: Do sovereign ratings affect country risk and stock returns? World Bank Economic Review, 16, 171-195.

Kletzer, K. M. (1984): Asymmetries of information and LDC borrowing with sovereign risk, Economic Journal, 94, 287-307.

Polanyi, K. (1944): The Great Transformation, New York: Rinehart.

Reinhart, C. M. (2002): Default, currency crises and sovereign credit ratings, World Bank Economic Review, 16, 151-170.

Reisen, H. and von Maltzan, J. (1998): Sovereign Credit Ratings, Emerging Risk and Financial Market Volatility, Intereconomics, March-April Issue, 43-85.

Simpson, J. (2002): An Empirical Economic Development Based Model of International Banking Risk and Risk Scoring, Review of Development Economics, 6, 91-102.

World Bank (2002): World Bank Annual Report 2002, Washington DC: World Bank. This report can also be viewed at the following website: www.worldbank.org/annualreport/2002/chap0405.htm

World Bank (2000): Global Development Finance 2000, Washington DC: World Bank.

Select Website Addresses

African Development Bank – www.afdb.org

Asian Development Bank – www.adb.org

Bank of International Settlements – www.bis.org

Basel Committee on Banking Supervision – www.bis.org/bcbs

European Bank for Reconstruction and Development – www.ebrd.com

Financial Stability Forum – www.fsforum.org

Inter-American Development Bank – www.iadb.org

International Monetary Fund – www.imf.org

Organization for Economic Cooperation and Development (OECD) – www.oecd.org

United Nations – www.un.org

US Federal Reserve Board – www.federalreserve.gov

World Bank – www.worldbank.org

Index

A

adverse selection 11, 15, 44, 65, 76, 135, 145, 146, 148, 157, 160
agency cost 3, 9, 11, 36, 43
AI 2, 3, 7, 8, 9, 10, 11, 12, 16, 17, 18, 19, 26, 44, 64, 70, 74
aid effectiveness 9, 100, 109, 116, 119, 123
AS 10, 11, 12, 16, 17, 19
asymmetric information 2, 15, 44, 64, 76, 122, 138, 148, 157, 210

B

Bank of International Settlements 82, 220
banking crisis 22
bankruptcy 38, 129, 153, 156, 159
bargaining cost 2
barter 140, 192
biodiversity 179
BIS 82, 85, 92, 93, 153, 207, 214, 215, 219

C

capital 179, 184, 187, 189, 190, 195
capital adequacy 83, 85, 90
capital inflows 22, 34, 35, 36, 37, 48, 52, 54, 115
capital market VIII, 5, 14, 21, 25, 30, 33, 34, 38, 42, 52, 53, 91, 108, 121, 206
capital outflows 28, 34, 108
capital utilization 17, 26, 34
CAPM 21
carbon tax 185, 188, 194

CBA 162, 163, 164, 165, 171, 173, 174
certainty equivalent 10, 11, 164, 172
commensurability 163, 174
comparative advantage 48, 62
complete contract 7, 26
compliance 19, 51, 61, 64, 65, 69, 73, 75, 77, 90, 136, 137, 138, 140, 144, 145, 146, 147, 148, 149, 154, 156, 210
concessional 109, 113, 115, 141, 151, 154, 190, 193, 195
concessional lending 195
conditionality 95, 96, 103, 116, 140, 147, 153
consumer surplus 171
consumption 179
contract design 7, 60, 64, 135, 148
cooperative game 139
cooperatives 62, 69, 73
corruption 25, 50, 51, 110, 114, 189
cost effective 70, 199, 205, 208, 216
cost of capital 66, 84, 150, 166, 190
Cost-Benefit Analysis 164, 175
country risk analysis 218
credit institutions 24, 63, 66, 67, 74, 76
credit rating 22, 82, 84, 85, 86, 101, 210, 213, 214, 215, 218, 219
credit rating agencies 84, 87, 101, 214, 215, 218
credit rationing 13, 14, 15, 16, 17, 18, 26, 28, 65, 67, 73, 132

credit risk 19, 20, 85, 87, 157, 210, 211
credit worthiness 146, 174
crisis management 81, 98
currency crisis 22

D

debt VIII, 3, 4, 9, 12, 15, 25, 34, 36, 40, 44, 48, 50, 53, 68, 69, 81, 83, 84, 85, 87, 91, 92, 93, 94, 96, 97, 100, 101, 115, 117, 119, 120, 129, 130, 131, 132, 133, 134, 135, 136, 137, 138, 140, 141, 142, 143, 144, 145, 146, 147, 148, 149, 150, 151, 152, 153, 154, 155, 156, 157, 159, 178, 183, 189, 190, 191, 192, 197, 198, 206, 207, 209, 210, 211, 212, 215, 216, 218
debt crisis 81, 98, 117, 131, 134, 149, 150
debt reduction 134, 140, 142, 143, 149, 151
debt relief 100, 129, 133, 143, 145, 151, 178, 183, 191, 192
debt renegotiations 98, 130, 136
debt reorganization 129, 148, 152
debt repayment 190
debt valuation 133
default 11, 65, 67, 68, 72, 73, 84, 85, 130, 131, 135, 138, 140, 144, 145, 146, 147, 148, 150, 154, 155, 159, 192, 209, 210, 214, 215
developed countries 19, 41, 63, 94, 100, 119, 183, 184, 191, 196, 218
developing countries 16, 22, 23, 24, 28, 30, 35, 41, 46, 49, 63, 64, 66, 71, 73, 75, 76, 81, 82, 83, 88, 90, 91, 96, 97, 98, 99, 108, 109, 111, 112, 113, 115, 118, 120, 129, 130, 133, 140, 141, 150, 158, 178, 183, 184, 189, 190, 191, 192, 193, 195, 207
development effectiveness 96, 99, 117, 162, 210

discount factor 8, 162, 166, 169, 173
discount rate 132, 137, 138, 165, 166, 167, 168, 169, 170, 172, 173, 175, 190
discounting 8, 76, 162, 164, 166, 168, 169, 170, 172, 173, 174, 176
disincentives 64, 77, 130, 140, 143, 144, 145, 147, 148, 150, 153
DNS 191, 192, 200
double dividend 185, 186, 187, 199
drinking water 184, 195

E

ECA 196, 197, 200
economic development VII, VIII, 1, 14, 24, 32, 33, 34, 37, 38, 39, 45, 47, 48, 49, 52, 54, 55, 56, 57, 60, 81, 82, 86, 88, 91, 95, 101, 107, 111, 112, 114, 124, 162, 163, 178, 179, 180, 190, 205, 216
economic efficiency 5, 8, 26, 45, 46, 47, 70, 75, 91, 120
economic growth VII, 1, 3, 6, 8, 14, 23, 24, 32, 33, 34, 35, 36, 37, 38, 39, 40, 41, 42, 43, 44, 45, 46, 47, 48, 49, 50, 51, 52, 53, 54, 55, 57, 58, 81, 89, 90, 95, 96, 99, 108, 111, 112, 113, 114, 115, 118, 119, 122, 124, 131, 132, 133, 140, 143, 168, 216
economic inequality 32
economic performance 56, 115, 116, 140
economic reforms 89, 95, 96, 149
economic sustainability 190
economics of information 10
ecosystems 179
emissions 185
endogenous growth 47, 53, 55
enforcement 2, 3, 6, 7, 8, 9, 11, 14, 15, 16, 19, 24, 39, 45, 49, 50, 51, 53, 54, 56, 60, 61, 62, 63, 64, 65, 68, 74, 76, 118, 129, 136, 145,

146, 147, 148, 153, 155, 157, 208, 210, 214
entrepreneurship 40, 47, 48, 54, 109
environment 5, 49, 50, 51, 70, 87, 114, 116, 149, 163, 171, 173, 178, 179, 180, 181, 182, 185, 189, 192, 195, 196, 197, 198, 199, 200, 205, 211
environmental 1, 32, 98, 100, 149, 167, 178, 179, 180, 181, 182, 183, 184, 185, 186, 187, 188, 189, 190, 191, 192, 194, 195, 196, 197, 198, 199, 200, 201
environmental amenities 179, 185
environmental externalities 149, 178, 186
environmental sustainability 179
environmental tax 185, 186, 187, 200, 201
environmental taxes 185, 187
EPR 198
equilibrium 2, 10, 13, 14, 15, 16, 17, 18, 23, 26, 28, 107, 139, 171, 186, 187, 201
equilibrium credit rationing 2, 16, 17, 18, 26, 28
equitable 88, 99, 215
equity VIII, 3, 9, 34, 50, 53, 71, 77, 83, 85, 149, 165, 170, 212
EST 193
expectations 13, 22, 44, 69, 96, 133
external aid 9, 36, 107, 108, 109, 111, 112, 114, 115, 117, 118, 120, 121, 124, 184
External Debt 141
external finance VIII, 22, 46, 48, 50, 92, 108
externalities 186
externality 4, 25, 34, 55, 66, 67, 72

F

FD 33, 43, 44, 45, 46, 47, 48, 54, 55
FDI 4, 23, 24, 28, 48, 54, 194

FI 3, 4, 5, 11, 12, 19, 33, 37, 38, 39, 40, 41, 42, 43, 44, 45, 46, 49, 53, 55
financial crisis 22, 149, 150, 155
financial development VIII, 33, 42, 43, 45, 46, 47, 48, 49, 50, 55, 81, 83, 216
financial intermediaries 22, 24, 28, 33, 55, 60, 63, 75, 76
financial liberalization VII, 1, 36, 45, 52, 86, 88, 89, 90, 91, 96, 101, 103
Financial Soundness Indicators 83, 105
financial stability 36, 75, 82, 83, 85, 86, 206
Financial Stability Forum 36, 82, 206, 220
financing gap 111, 112, 113, 119, 125
foreign debt 107, 149
foreign direct investment VIII, 4, 23, 35, 48, 88, 96, 149
FSF 36, 82, 92, 93, 206, 211
FSI 83
future generations 168, 169, 172, 178, 180, 181, 182

G

game-theoretic 108, 121, 122, 139
GBB 61, 62, 63, 67, 69, 70, 71, 74, 75, 76, 78
GC9 153, 154
GEF 191, 195, 196, 201
Global Chapter 9 156
Global Environmental Facility 195, 201
globalization VII, 1, 14, 82, 86, 87, 88, 91, 94, 101, 107, 109, 193, 196, 197, 204, 216
governance VII, 1, 2, 3, 6, 7, 8, 19, 33, 34, 36, 48, 53, 54, 68, 70, 76, 77, 81, 82, 87, 89, 90, 91, 94, 99, 101, 109, 114, 115, 116, 117, 118,

126, 143, 149, 150, 155, 159, 179, 180, 183, 193, 196, 197, 204, 205, 208, 215, 216
Grameen Bank of Bangladesh 61, 74
green tax 178, 181, 185, 186, 188, 189, 199
green taxes 185, 186, 189
greenhouse gases 179
group-based lending 24, 60, 63, 69, 71, 73, 74, 78

H

Harrod-Domar 111, 112
HB 11, 12
Heavily Indebted Poor Countries 159, 192
herd behavior 11, 35, 53, 215
HIPC 134, 141, 142, 150, 157, 158, 159, 192
HIPC Initiative 134, 141, 142, 150, 158, 159, 192
hyperbolic discount functions 169

I

IMF VII, 6, 52, 56, 82, 83, 88, 90, 92, 94, 95, 96, 97, 98, 99, 100, 103, 104, 105, 109, 117, 126, 141, 142, 143, 150, 151, 153, 158, 159, 189, 192, 198, 199
incentive-compatible 123, 135
incentives 19, 23, 44, 64, 65, 73, 77, 87, 99, 101, 110, 116, 118, 127, 130, 131, 133, 134, 136, 137, 138, 140, 143, 144, 145, 146, 147, 148, 150, 154, 155, 157, 192, 199
incomplete contract 7
inequality 184
information cost 9, 17, 38, 39, 40, 53
information revelation 136, 137, 147, 148, 152

informational asymmetry 4, 5, 9, 12, 43, 65, 131, 134, 136, 139
infrastructure 1, 3, 6, 7, 23, 32, 34, 35, 43, 47, 50, 51, 54, 70, 91, 101, 195, 207, 208
innovation 38, 40, 43, 44, 48, 54, 215
insolvency 84, 149, 153, 154, 156, 216
interest rate 4, 5, 14, 15, 16, 17, 18, 19, 24, 26, 38, 61, 65, 66, 67, 68, 71, 75, 89, 122, 132, 136, 138, 142, 145, 147, 148, 150, 154, 156, 209, 210, 212, 213
intergenerational 165, 172
international financial architecture 81, 82, 94, 97, 99, 105
International Monetary Fund VII, 6, 82, 105, 220
international trade 42, 46, 48, 54, 56, 118
inverted banking 61, 63, 74
investment 4, 23, 24, 25, 34, 35, 36, 39, 40, 42, 51, 52, 57, 75, 76, 92, 95, 96, 100, 108, 111, 112, 113, 114, 121, 127, 140, 165, 167, 171, 193, 207, 209, 212

J

joint liability 71, 72, 73, 74, 78

L

law 6, 7, 9, 50, 51, 82, 152, 197
lender liability 178, 190, 198
lending 189, 190
Lewis Committee 117, 119
liability 73, 83, 95, 192, 196
liquidity risk 19, 92
loan 15, 16, 17, 18, 19, 24, 25, 26, 38, 51, 60, 61, 62, 63, 64, 65, 67, 68, 69, 70, 71, 72, 73, 74, 75, 76, 77, 78, 83, 88, 99, 100, 102, 132,

138, 150, 151, 155, 196, 198, 210, 212
loan contract 16, 19, 63, 64, 65, 71

M

market 184
market discipline 86, 87
market failure 64, 66, 79, 121, 172
MDG 182, 183
Meltzer Commission 98, 104
MH 10, 11, 12, 16, 17, 19
microcredit 60, 61, 62, 70, 74, 76, 77
microfinance 60, 61, 62, 74, 76, 77, 216
Millennium Development Goals 182, 184
missing markets 162, 172, 174
Monterrey Consensus 82, 89, 99, 100, 109
moral hazard 11, 65, 76, 86, 90, 124, 131, 148, 157
multilateral 189
multilateral financial institution 81, 91, 98, 100, 101, 113, 129, 142, 190, 199

N

non-compliance 69, 77, 138, 145, 146, 147
NPV 133, 142, 150, 165
nutrition 184

O

ODA 82, 100, 108, 109, 110, 119, 120, 122, 123, 184
Official Development Assistance 82, 108, 109
openness 36, 46, 52, 89
optimality 5, 120, 167

P

peer monitoring 61, 75
poverty VII, 2, 24, 32, 60, 61, 62, 63, 74, 75, 77, 91, 99, 101, 107, 110, 115, 116, 118, 148, 163, 174, 178, 183, 189, 192, 197, 198, 200, 205, 216
preferences 8, 12, 13, 115, 135, 162, 163, 167, 168, 169, 170, 173
principal-agent 2, 8, 134
private capital flows 35, 36, 50, 96, 103, 115, 207
procyclical 11, 84, 214
production 179, 185, 188, 198
productivity 24, 25, 35, 38, 39, 40, 41, 43, 44, 47, 51, 52, 54, 68, 89, 111, 112, 132, 166, 186, 198, 205, 209
productivity of capital 25, 35, 68, 112, 166, 209
project appraisal 162, 165, 166, 171, 173, 174
property rights 6, 39, 50, 51, 56, 76, 88, 118
prophecy 101

R

recontracting 135, 136, 137, 138, 139, 140
regulation 32, 34, 37, 66, 81, 89, 90, 97, 101, 153, 185, 204, 212, 216
renegotiation 19, 65, 130, 131, 134, 135, 136, 137, 139, 146, 148, 149, 154
renewable resources 180
repeat contract 73
repeat transactions 69
repudiation 130, 137, 138, 158, 159
reputation 8, 46, 144, 147, 159
Rio Declaration 182
risk exposure 19, 36, 52, 63, 207, 214

risk factors 20, 68, 194, 207, 211
risk management VIII, 2, 3, 19, 25, 36, 37, 39, 40, 44, 53, 63, 82, 206, 211
risk premium 21, 25, 66, 67, 190
risk-averse 146, 171, 172
rolling plan 138, 154
rule of law 1, 32, 39, 50, 51
rural credit 64, 66, 67, 68, 69, 74, 76, 77, 79

S

savings 5, 35, 37, 38, 39, 40, 41, 42, 43, 53, 62, 63, 75, 77, 89, 111, 112, 113, 115, 185, 212, 215
SCBA 165, 172
SDR 165, 166, 167
self-interest 110
shadow discount factor 166
sinks 179, 180
social collateral 24, 61, 62, 63
social discount rate 165
social rate of time preference 167
solvency 88, 137, 154, 211
sources 179, 180, 195
sovereign debt VIII, 93, 94, 129, 130, 132, 134, 136, 142, 143, 145, 146, 148, 149, 150, 151, 152, 155, 159, 192, 208, 209, 210, 215, 216, 218
sovereign risk 84, 130, 210, 219
SRTP 164, 165, 167, 168
stabilization 90, 95, 209
Stackelberg 122, 127, 215
strategic 12, 107, 108, 110, 121, 129, 136, 138
Structural Adjustment 189
subsidies 189
subsidy 75, 107, 145, 147
supervision 6, 34, 39, 82, 88, 91, 97, 101, 215, 216
sustainable VIII, 2, 32, 33, 36, 41, 52, 60, 72, 74, 76, 77, 90, 99, 100, 101, 107, 110, 115, 131, 132, 143, 148, 151, 155, 179, 183, 192, 193, 205, 207, 216
sustainable debt 100, 131
Sustainable Development 175, 179, 180, 181, 201

T

TC 2, 3, 5, 6, 7, 8, 9, 11, 14, 15, 16, 17, 18, 19, 22, 23, 24, 25, 26, 28, 33, 38, 39, 40, 43, 44, 45, 47, 53, 55, 60, 61, 62, 63, 64, 65, 66, 69, 70, 71, 76, 77, 78, 91, 185
technical progress 41, 42
technological change 41
TFP 41, 55, 132
threshold levels 34, 45
time horizon 8, 13, 18, 20, 35, 132, 137, 138, 139, 147, 162, 164, 170, 171, 173, 211, 214
time-consistent 120, 135
time-preference 136
total factor productivity 41
transaction costs 2, 33, 38, 60, 68, 72, 79, 81, 89, 97, 101, 112, 124, 137, 139, 147, 148, 162, 173, 174, 184, 185, 189, 194, 205, 208
transparency 12, 28, 49, 50, 86, 90, 92, 101, 189, 197
two-gap 111, 112, 113, 123, 124

U

uncertainty 2, 4, 11, 15, 122, 131, 138, 162, 164, 172

V

volatility 12, 23, 35, 36, 37

W

Washington Consensus 88, 103, 105
water 179, 184

welfare 5, 8, 12, 13, 26, 28, 53, 54, 63, 77, 110, 111, 120, 121, 131, 135, 137, 139, 148, 150, 155, 165, 168, 169, 171, 175, 180, 186, 192, 205, 209, 216

World Bank VII, 25, 29, 30, 34, 35, 36, 49, 52, 56, 57, 59, 79, 82, 88, 92, 94, 96, 97, 98, 99, 100, 103, 104, 105, 108, 109, 114, 115, 117, 125, 126, 127, 141, 142, 150, 153, 158, 159, 184, 189, 192, 193, 196, 197, 198, 199, 202, 207, 214, 215, 219, 220

Z

Zedillo Commission 109, 127, 193, 195, 202

Econometrics
and Formulas for Economists

B.H. Baltagi
Econometrics
This textbook teaches some of the basic econometric methods and the underlying assumptions behind them. Some of the strengths of this book lie in presenting difficult material in a simple, yet rigorous manner.

3rd ed. 2002. XVI, 401 pp. 48 figs., 41 tabs. Softcover * € **42,75**; sFr 68,50 ISBN 3-540-43501-8

B. Luderer, V. Nollau, K. Vetters
Mathematical Formulas for Economists
The present collection of formulas has been composed for students of economics or management science at universities, colleges and trade schools. It contains basic knowledge in mathematics, financial mathematics and statistics in a compact and clearly arranged form.
Table of Contents available:
http://www.springer.de/books/toc/3540426167-c.pdf

2002. X, 186 pp. 58 figs., 6 tabs. Softcover * € **19,21**; sFr 31,-
ISBN 3-540-42616-7

K. Sydsaeter, A. Strom, P. Berck
Economists' Mathematical Manual
This volume presents mathematical formulas and theorems common to economics. The volume is the first grouping of this material for a specifically economist audience. This third edition is extensively revised and contains more than 250 new formulas, as well as new figures.

3rd rev. and enlarged ed. 1999. Corr. 2nd printing 2000. XII, 206 pp. 63 figs. Hardcover * € **24,02**; sFr 38,50
ISBN 3-540-65447-X

*Suggested retail price

Please order from
Springer · Customer Service
Haberstr. 7
69126 Heidelberg, Germany
Tel.: +49 (0) 6221 - 345 - 217/8
Fax: +49 (0) 6221 - 345 - 229
e-mail: orders@springer.de
or through your bookseller

Visit our homepage:
www.springer.de/economics

Die €-Preise für Bücher sind gültig in Deutschland und enthalten 7% MwSt.
Die mit * gekennzeichneten Preise sind unverbindliche Preisempfehlungen
inkl. 7% MwSt. Preisänderungen und Irrtümer vorbehalten. d&p · BA 00359/2

Springer Finance

M. Ammann, University of St. Gallen, Switzerland

Credit Risk Valuation

Methods, Models, and Applications

Credit Risk Valuation offers an advanced introduction to the models of credit risk valuation. It concentrates on firm-value and reduced-form approaches and their applications in practice. Additionally, the book includes new models for valuing derivative securities with credit risk, focussing on options and forward contracts subject to counterparty default risk, but also treating options on credit-risky bonds and credit derivatives. The text provides detailed descriptions of the state-of-the-art martingale methods and advanced numerical implementations based on multi-variate trees used to price derivative credit risk. Numerical examples illustrate the effects of credit risk on the prices of financial derivatives.

2nd ed. 2001. Corr. 2nd printing 2002. X, 255, 17 figs., 23 tabs. Hardcover **€ 69.95**; sFr 116.50; £ 49 ISBN 3-540-67805-0

A. Ziegler, University of Lausanne, Switzerland

Incomplete Information and Heterogeneous Beliefs in Continuous-time Finance

This book considers the impact of incomplete information and heterogeneous beliefs on investor's optimal portfolio and consumption behavior and equilibrium asset prices. After a brief review of the existing incomplete information literature, the effect of incomplete information on investors' expected utility, risky asset prices, and interest rates is described. It is demonstrated that increasing the quality of investors' information need not increase their expected utility and the prices of risky assets. The impact of heterogeneous beliefs on investors' portfolio and consumption behavior and equilibrium asset prices is shown to be non-trivial.

XIII, 194 p. 51 illus. 2003. Hardcover **€ 64.95**; sFr 108; £ 45.50 ISBN 3-540-00344-4

Springer · Kundenservice
Haberstr. 7 · 69126 Heidelberg
Tel.: (0 62 21) 345 - 0 · Fax: (0 62 21) 345 - 4229
e-mail: orders@springer.de

Die €-Preise für Bücher sind gültig in Deutschland und enthalten 7% MwSt.
Preisänderungen und Irrtümer vorbehalten. d&p · BA 42333/2

Michael Carlberg, Federal University of Hamburg, Germany

Inflation in a Monetary Union

This book studies the causes and cures of inflation in a monetary union. It carefully discusses the effects of money growth and output growth on inflation. The focus is on producer inflation, currency depreciation and consumer inflation. Further topics are real depreciation, nominal and real interest rates, the growth of nominal wages, the growth of producer real wages, and the growth of consumer real wages. Another important issue is target inflation and required money growth. A special feature of this book is the numerical estimation of shock and policy multipliers.

2002. XVI, 305 pp. 2 figs., 26 tabs. Hard cover
€ 74.95; £ 52.50; sFr 124.50
ISBN 3-540-43359-7

Giancarlo Gandolfo, University of Rome „La Sapienza", Italy

International Finance and Open-Economy Macroeconomics

Study Edition

From the review:

„This book deals with the financial side of international economics and covers all aspects of international finance. Prof. Gandolfo has written what will be a classic in international finance. His erudition, expository and technical skills are combined to fulfill the needs of undergraduate and graduate students, researchers, and staff members in international economic organisations. (...) This is followed by a mathematical analysis, which uses the state of the art techniques. In this manner the reader can go from the intuition-literary argument to the formal derivations and proofs. There are many books and articles by exponents of alternative points of view. I know of no other book that provides the scope, balance, objectivity and rigor of the book."

Professor Jerome L. Stein, Brown University

1st ed. 2001. 2nd printing, 2002. XXIII, 613 p. 51 illus. Soft cover **€ 39.95**; £ 28; sFr 68.50 ISBN 3-540-43459-3

Michael Carlberg, Federal University of Hamburg, Germany

An Economic Analysis of Monetary Union

This book explores the new economics of monetary union. It carefully discusses the effects of shocks and policies on output and prices. Shocks and policies are country-specific or common. They occur on the demand or supply side. Countries can differ in behavioural functions. Wages can be fixed, flexible, or slow. In addition, fixed wages and flexible wages can coexist. A special feature of this book is the numerical estimation of shock and policy multipliers. Further topics are inflation and disinflation.

2001. XV, 255 pp. 21 figs., 22 tabs.
Hard cover **€ 64.95**; £ 45.50; sFr 108
ISBN 3-540-42045-2

Springer · Kundenservice
Haberstr. 7
69126 Heidelberg
Tel.: (0 62 21) 345 - 0
Fax: (0 62 21) 345 - 4229
e-mail: orders@springer.de

Die €-Preise für Bücher sind gültig in Deutschland und enthalten 7% MwSt.
Preisänderungen und Irrtümer vorbehalten. d&p · BA 42333/2